WORKS ISSUED BY

The Hakluyt Society.

———◆———

THE VOYAGE

OF

FRANÇOIS LEGUAT.

VOL. I.

No. LXXXII.

SKELETON of LEGUATS SOLITAIRE.
PEZOPHAPS. SOLITARIA, in the
Museum of Zoology Cambridge.

THE VOYAGE

OF

FRANÇOIS LEGUAT

OF BRESSE

TO

RODRIGUEZ, MAURITIUS, JAVA, AND THE
CAPE OF GOOD HOPE.

TRANSCRIBED FROM THE FIRST ENGLISH EDITION.

Edited and Annotated

BY

CAPTAIN PASFIELD OLIVER,

LATE ROYAL ARTILLERY.

"*Si forte necesse est*
Indiciis monstrare recentibus abdita rerum."

VOL. I.

LONDON:

PRINTED FOR THE HAKLUYT SOCIETY,

4, LINCOLN'S INN FIELDS, W.C.

———

M.DCCC.XCI.

COUNCIL

OF

THE HAKLUYT SOCIETY.

CONTENTS.

ENGLISH EDITION.

FIRST PART.

ILLUSTRATIONS AND MAPS.

[1] Reduced from Admiralty Charts.
[2] From lithograph in *The Dodo and its Kindred*, by Strickland and Melville.
[3] For description, see Appendix B, p. 387 *et seq.*

EDITOR'S PREFACE.

In the following story of the remarkable adventures and sufferings endured by François Leguat, events are narrated which belong to a period considerably later than that of any other travels or voyages treated of in former publications undertaken by the Hakluyt Society; nevertheless, the date of the personal record follows somewhat closely upon the time of the latter portion of William Hedges' diary,[1] to which, indeed, it forms a not altogether unfitting sequel, by affording information regarding the system of Dutch administration and colonisation in the East Indies, and at the Cape, towards the end of the seventeenth century, and by giving a graphic sketch of the circumstances of French Huguenot emigration from Europe to South Africa at that epoch. The chief modern scientific interest, however, in Leguat's description undoubtedly hinges upon the circumstantial delineation which he gives of the curious bird-fauna then extant in the Mascarene Islands, the subsequent destruction of which has rendered the personal observations of the philosophic Huguenot invaluable to naturalists, marked as they are by such evident simplicity and veracity.

[1] The last entry in Wm. Hedges' diary is dated 1688, and Leguat's narrative commences in 1689.

It is now the pleasurable duty of the Editor to acknowledge and place on record, in the commencement of this volume, the kindness and ready assistance which he has met with in every branch of his inquiries from numerous literary and scientific friends during its preparation. First and foremost, it is to M. James Jackson, the well-known librarian of the Société de Géographie, that the Editor owes his acquaintance with the early French editions of the Huguenot author. To the researches of M. J. Codine, of the same Society, are due the more exact knowledge, which geographers possess, as to the approximate date of discovery of the several Mascarene Islands, on which subject most erroneous views had previously been entertained. It is regrettable that want of space has compelled the abridgment of M. Codine's admirable reasoning on this subject.[1] M. Sauzier's discovery and reproduction of the rare Du Quesne *Mémoire*[2] have contributed largely to the better comprehension of several of Leguat's allusions, although there is yet reason to doubt whether the particular *Mémoire* from which the quotations were taken has been absolutely identified. Several of M. Eugène Muller's notes have been utilised by permission of the annotator, and the clues afforded by the Appendix of the small edition of Leguat's book, republished by the Librarian of the Arsenal at Paris, have been found most suggestive. Naturally, the contribu-

---

[1] *Vide* Appendix A, p. 308.
[2] *Vide* Introduction, *infra*.

tions of M. Alph. Milne-Edwards to the *Annales des Sciences Naturelles*[1] and other periodical scientific journals have been largely used for the elucidation of the natural history of Rodriguez; it would be impossible to illustrate any work on the Mascarene Islands without incurring a heavy debt to this celebrated naturalist. M. Gabriel Marcel, of the Bibliothèque Nationale, has taken an infinity of pains in answering, most minutely and categorically, numerous and somewhat pertinacious questions, which have been addressed to him by the Editor on various points, bibliographical and geographical, in connection with this publication, thereby aiding largely towards its correctness. M. A. Bouquet de la Grye, the French Hydrographer, most courteously enabled the Editor to obtain an accurate transcript of the Abbé Pingré's original manuscript journal at Rodriguez, hitherto unpublished, which has proved most useful in elucidating certain doubtful points. Mr. R. W. Shufeldt, of the Smithsonian Institution (Washington, U.S.), has readily permitted the reproduction of his clever restoration of the Giant bird of Mauritius, whose existence, however, is still problematical; and Mr. Van Kampen has been good enough to revise whatever passages have been translated from the Dutch of Valentyn by Mrs. Salmon. The thanks of the Hakluyt Society are due to all the above foreign contributors to their work, as well as the Editor's personal gratitude for their very sympathetic help and encouragement.

---

[1] *Vide* Appendix B, p. 320.

Having, as in duty bound, first of all made his too inadequate acknowledgments of what he owes to his friendly helpers across the seas, the Editor must now proceed to offer his no less sincere thanks to those of his own countrymen who have communicated so freely to him the results of their patient investigations of all branches of science treated of in the following notes.

Pre-eminent among zoologists and ornithologists, the Professor of Zoology at Cambridge (where Strickland and Melville's collection finds an honoured position), and his brother, Sir E. Newton (to whose indefatigable explorations the world owes the rehabilitation of Dodo, Solitaire, Aphanapteryx, and their congeners), have furnished far more material for notes and explanatory illustration of Leguat's text than the Editor has been able to treat properly or satisfactorily within the space at his command. Moreover, the learned Professor and his brother have taken much personal trouble to secure for the Editor, not only access to the rich store of osteological remains of the Mascarene birds in the museum (which, by the way, is constantly acquiring fresh *trouvailles* from the cave earths of Rodriguez and Mauritius), but also a photograph[1] of the skeleton of the bird which has conduced to render Leguat's name immortal. These scientists, so profoundly skilled in the subject of most enticing interest in Leguat's history, have also assisted the Editor by

[1] The photograph taken for Mr. Bidwell in November 1889, has been reproduced by Messrs. Morgan and Kidd, of Richmond.

their critical perusal of his proof-sheets, so far as they concern their special department.

Whilst the avi-fauna of the Mascarenes has received such close attention from Professor Alfred Newton and Sir Edward Newton, the flora of Rodriguez has been subjected to keen examination and classification by Professor Isaac Bayley Balfour, of Edinburgh; and in the report to the Royal Society, which resulted from his visit to the island in connection with the Transit Expedition of 1874, the Editor has been able to find all he could possibly desire in the task of identifying the plants mentioned with much *naïveté* by the Huguenot writer two hundred years ago. Mr. J. G. Baker, F.R.S., and Mr. Scott Elliot, of Kew, have also aided the Editor by suggestive advice in the difficult and unaccomplished problem of ascertaining the identity of a certain poison-tree of Mauritius, mentioned as causing disastrous effects on the old traveller. Professor Günther, likewise, has readily given all information asked of him with regard to the wonderful tortoises of the same islands; whilst Professors J. Legge, Sir Thomas Wade, and K. Douglas have courteously proffered helpful suggestions as to Leguat's rather confused ideas of the Chinese philosophers.

Dr. R. Rost, of the India Office, has rendered most important assistance to the Editor by permitting him to consult the various books of travel in the Library, which could not easily be elsewhere obtained. Indeed, his cordiality and kind advice have helped the Editor not a little. It may not be out of place also here to record the very great boon which the London Library has proved itself to be for any writer who resides out of town, and at a distance from the British Museum, when engaged on a work requiring constant references.

The secretary of the Hakluyt Society has obligingly revised, suppressed, altered, and added to many of the Editor's original notes throughout the first part. Whilst thanking him for his efforts to secure additional correctness by his revision, the Editor is reluctantly compelled to dissent from some of the conclusions arrived at and published by his coadjutor, especially in those notes on the Banyan, the Pandanus, and the Pepper, wherein Mr. Delmar Morgan differs from the opinion formed after personal observation by that expert botanist, Professor Bayley Balfour.[1] Finally, the revision of the second part by Mr. Clements R. Markham, and his timely correction of a very important mis-statement in the first part, deserves the hearty recognition and thanks of the Editor. Mr. Wm. Griggs, by his admirable *facsimile* reproductions of the original plates, has largely contributed to the complete illustration of the text.

S. PASFIELD OLIVER.

MORAY HOUSE, STOKES BAY, GOSPORT.
        16 *May* 1891.

----

[1] *Vide* pp. 65, 67, 103, 104, etc. The entire list of the numerous notes furnished by Mr. Delmar Morgan is given in the Index. The Supplementary Note on the Dugong is especially valuable.

BIBLIOGRAPHY.

ACOSTA, Joseph.—Histoire naturelle et morale des Indes, tant Orientalles qu'Occidentalles, etc. . . . traduite en françois par Robert Regnault Cauxois. Paris, 1598.

ALEMAN, Mateo.—The Life of Guzman d'Alfarache, done into English from the new French version. 1708.

AMYOT, J.—Plutarch's Lives ; see North.

ARISTOTELES.—Opera omnia. Edition of Du Val. 1599.

BENJAMIN, Rabbi, of Tudela.—Travels through Europe, Asia, and Africa. 1160-1173. Purchas, ii.

BÈZE, Théodore, et Clément Marot.—Pseaumes de David. 1580.

BOCHART, Samuel.—Hierozoicon. 1692.

BOSSUET, J. B., Evêque de Meaux.—Exposition de la foi Catholique. 1671.

BOULLAYE-LE-GOUZ, Sieur de la.—Voyages et Observations. 1657.

CADAMUSTO, Aloysio.—Navigationes Cadamusti, in the Novus Orbis of Grynæus. 1532.

CÆSAR, Julius.—Commentarii de Bello Gallico. 50 B.C.

CHAMBERLAIN, Dr. E.—Present State of England. 1687.

CHOISY, Abbé de.—Journal du Voyage de Siam. 1687.

CICERO, Marcus Tullius.—Epistolæ. 50 B.C.

COMTE, Père Louis de la.—Nouveaux Mémoires sur l'état présent de la Chine. 1701.

CONFUCIUS, Disciples of, B.C. 479.

CORNEILLE, Th.—Dictionnaire des Arts et des Sciences. 1640.

CORNEILLE, Pierre.—Le Cid. 1636.

DAVID, Pseaumes de.—Protestant version of, by Marot et Bèze. 1580.

DELON.—Relation de Voyage. 1685.

DIODORUS SICULUS.—Βιβλιοθήκη. (Time of Augustus, 50 B.C.)

DIOSCORIDES.—Fragmenta.

DU QUESNE, Marquis Henri.—Projet de République à l'île Eden. 1689.

FLACOURT, de.—Voyage à Madagascar. 1658.

FOURNIER, P. George.—Hydrographie. 1667.

GODEAU, M. de.—Poésie.

GRYNÆUS.—Novus Orbis Regionum et Insularum veteribus incog. 1532.

HERODOTUS.—Historia. B.C. 450.

HERVAGIUS.—Novus Orbis. 1537.

HOANGTI-XAO. (Time of Confucius, B.C. 480.)

HORATIUS FLACCUS, Q.—Carmina, "*Ad Virgilium*." B.C. 30.

JEREMIAS.—Lamentationes. B.C. 600.

LAMBARDE, William.—Perambulation of Kent. 1570.

MABILLON, J.—Musæum Italicum. 1687.

MAROT, Clément, et Théodore Bèze.—Pseaumes de David. 1580.

MATTHÆUS.—Evangelium Auctore Matthæi.

MELA, Pomponius.—Cosmographi Geographia. A.D. 600.

MOLIÈRE, J. B. P. de.—Œuvres. 1667.

MONTFAUCON, Dom. B. de.—Palæographia Græca. 1707.

MORGAN, Sylvanus.—Sphere of Gentry.

MOSES.—Libri Mosis.

NORTH, Sir Thomas.—Amyot's version of Plutarch's Lives translated into English. 1657. *Vide* Amyot.

OLEARIUS, Adam.—Voyages and Travels. 1662.

OVIDIUS NASO, P.—Opera. Cuippingii Ed. 1683.

PAULUS.—Episto¹æ.

PLINIUS, C., Secundus, or Major.—Encyclopædia. De¹phin Ed. 1685.

PLUTARCHUS.—Biographia. *See* North.

POINCY, L. de, et C. Rochefort.—*Vide* Rochefort.

POMPONIUS.—*Vide* Mela.

PROCOPIUS.—De Bello Vandalico.

QUINTUS CURTIUS, Rufus.—De rebus gestis Alexandri magni.

ROCHEFORT, César de (Poincy, L. de, et).—Histoire naturel'e et morale des iles Antilles. 1665, 1667.

RONDELET, Gal.—Libri de piscibus marinis. 1554.

SIMOND, Pierre.—Les Pseaumes de David. (1710 ?)

SOLINUS, C. J.—Plinianæ Polyhistoria Exercitationes.

SOLOMON.—Ecclesiasticus, et Proverbia.

TACHARD, Père Guy.—Voyage de Siam des Pères Jésuites. 1686.

TAVERNIER, Jean Baptista, Baron d'Aubonne. Les six Voyages. 1678.

URFE, Honoré d'.—Astrée.

VACCA.—MSS. *Vide* Montfaucon.

VARTOMANNUS PATRICIUS.--Navigatio: Novus Orbis. *See* Hervagius.

VIRGILIUS, Publius Maro.—Æneis. B.C. 21.

WILLUGHBY, Franciscus.—Ornithologiæ Libri. 1676.

N.B.—*Only works alluded to in original edition of Legnat's Voyage are included in above Bibliography.*

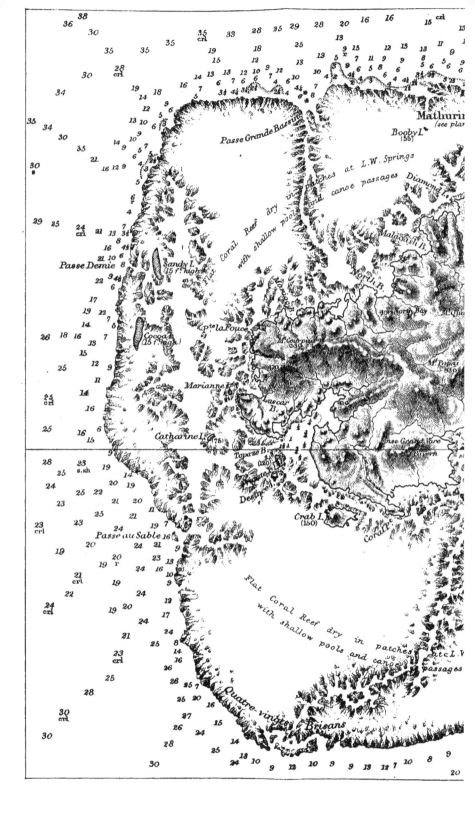

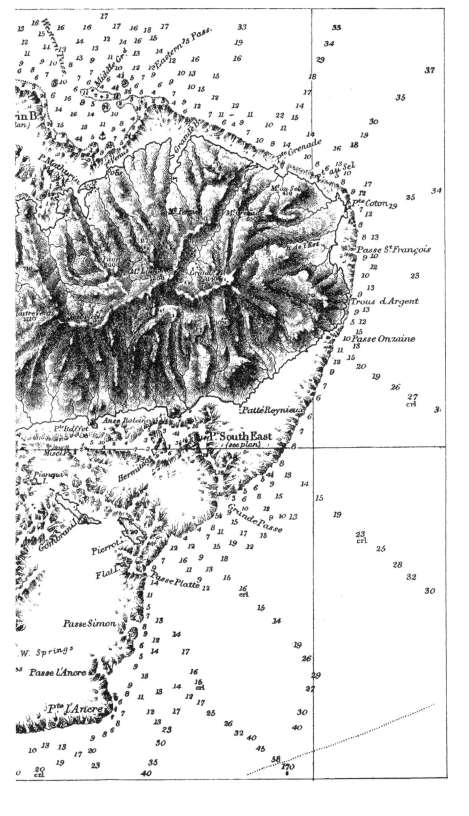

INTRODUCTION.

FIVE or six years before the deaths of Cardinal Richelieu and his sovereign, Louis XIII—that is, about the year 1637-38—François Leguat appears to have been born in Bresse, a small province (represented at the present day by the department of Ain, on the Savoyard frontier) between the confluent streams of the Rhône and Saône rivers. Our author's ancestor, Pierre le Guat, is mentioned as the Seigneur of la Fougère, in the *Histoire de Bresse et de Bugey*, by Samuel Guichenon.[1] Of his early days little is known ; but, according to his own account, when over fifty years of age, he was driven into exile, in consequence of the revocation of the Edict of Nantes (1685), and with many others took refuge in Holland in the year 1689. At this time the Marquis Henri du Quesne, son of the celebrated naval commander of that name, was projecting, under the sanction of the States-General and the directors of the Dutch East India Company,

[1] The arms of LE GUAT FOUGERE are given in the *Indice Armorial*, as : "d'azur à une fasce d'or, à un Lyon passant de mesme en chef, & 3 estoiles aussi d'or, en pointe." Guichenon writes : "Je n'ay point veu de plus ancien Seigneur de la Fougere que Pierre le Guat, Secretaire de Charles Duc de Savoye vivant en l'an 1511 & 1534, qui fit bastir la maison & en acquit le fief." (Vide *Histoire de Bresse et de Bugey*, par Samuel Guichenon, Seigneur de Painesuyt, Lyon, 1650, p. 54.)

b

the establishment of a colony of French Protestant refugees in the island of Mascaregne, now known as Ile de la Réunion. The Marquis had previously published[1] a glowing description of this island (which he proposed to name Eden), the largest of the group discovered by the Portuguese in the preceding century, but as yet imperfectly explored and vaguely marked as Las Mascarenhas in the old maps and portulans ; so that many refugees were desirous of becoming colonists in the new paradise of the southern hemisphere, and two ships were chartered for the purpose of taking possession of this hitherto supposed uninhabited island, to one of which Leguat was officially appointed as major.

On learning, however, later, that a French squadron[2] was under orders to sail for this island (which had, indeed, been re-annexed in 1674 by M. de la Haye, the French *Viceroi des Indes*, for the French East India Company), the Marquis du Quesne suspended the preparations for his abortive scheme, following the precise injunctions of his father, never to take up arms against the French Government, and, instead, contented himself with fitting out a small frigate, *La Hirondelle*, whose

---

[1] Vide *Un Projet de République à l'Ile d'Eden* (*l'île Bourbon*) *en* 1689, par Le Marquis Henri du Quesne. Réimpression d'un ouvrage disparu, par Th. Sauzier, Paris, 1887.

[2] A squadron of six ships, commanded by M. du Quesne-Guiton, left l'Orient de Port Louis, on the 24th February 1690, for the East Indies ; but not for Mascaregne. The Father Tachard, often quoted by Leguat, was a passenger for Siam in one of the ships.

commander was directed to reconnoitre the islands of the group, and to take possession of whatever island was found unoccupied and suitable for colonisation. This change of plan does not seem to have been communicated to the small band of adventurers who embarked as emigrants under the idea that they were to be landed on the Isle of Eden, the terrestrial paradise of their anticipations, and the small expedition finally left Texel on the 10th July 1691.

The commander of the *Hirondelle*, M. Valleau, whom Leguat charges with the basest treachery, having professedly discovered at the Cape that Mascaregne had been formally annexed by the French Compagnie des Indes Orientales (who had placed M. Vaubolon there as governor), passed by this delightful island, which, in truth, fully justified the praises and descriptions of the Marquis, tantalising the scurvy-stricken colonists by the enchanting prospect it exhibited to their eyes, and continuing his voyage to the eastward, anchored off the smaller island of Rodriguez[1]; and here, on the 1st May 1691, Leguat landed with eight of his fellow-adventurers, somewhat disappointed with the unexpected change in their programme, but sufficiently pleased with the place to decide that they would remain for two years and see how fortune might

[1] In the official colonial reports this island is now always styled Rodrigues, but in the Admiralty charts and sailing directions it preserves the name Rodriguez, and this latter nomenclature is adopted in the present work.

XX INTRODUCTION.

favour them. The *Hirondelle* shortly afterwards
sailed for Mauritius, having landed arms, utensils,
seeds, and provisions, in addition to the private
stock of supplies and necessaries which each colonist
had provided for himself.

It is the record of the careful personal and detailed
observations, made by Leguat on the then existent
fauna and flora of the island, during this period of
seclusion from the world, that has rendered the
simple story of the Huguenot exile so deeply interesting to naturalists of the present day ; and,
consequently, in the following notes and appendices
which accompany the text of the original translation, the confirmation of Leguat's remarks upon the
appearance and habits of the remarkable birds and
animals, now altogether extinct, by the late investigations of modern men of science, has been
especially dwelt upon ; for the veracity of the main
facts recorded in this charming narrative of adventure has been fully established in the most notable
particulars by eminent authorities in Europe.[1]

[1] " Telle est l'idée que Leguat nous donne du *Solitaire ;* il en
parle non seulement comme témoin oculaire, mais comme un obser-
vateur qui s'étoit attaché particulièrement et long-tems à étudier
les mœurs et les habitudes de cet oiseau ; et en effet, sa relation,
quoique gâtée en quelques endroits par des idées fabuleuses,*
contient néanmoins plus de détails historiques sur le *Solitaire* que

---

* " Par exemple, au sujet du premier accouplement des jeunes
solitaires, où son imagination prévenue lui a fait voir les formalités
d'une espèce de mariage ; au suject de la pierre de l'estomac, etc."
—As it happens, this so-called fabulous story of the stone has been
fully confirmed.

After a residence of two long years' duration in
Rodriguez, the settlers, wearied with discontent
and hopeless of assistance, constructed a boat, in
which they succeeded in reaching Mauritius after
a most hazardous voyage. Unfortunately, they
had only escaped from one evil to fall into
greater trouble, for the avarice of the governor
of the Dutch convict establishment caused them
to be treated with the utmost cruelty and
injustice. They were imprisoned on an exposed
rocky islet at a long distance from the shore, and in
attempting to escape, one of their number perished
miserably. At last the survivors, who had contrived
to send news of their sad plight to Europe, were
transmitted, still in confinement, to Batavia, where
they disembarked, in December 1696, only to be
again thrown into prison. After examination, however, before the Dutch Council their innocence was
established, but they were unable to obtain the
slightest redress for the pain and suffering they had
endured, or compensation for the losses they had
sustained. It was not until March 1698, after the
proclamation of the Peace of Ryswick, that Leguat
and two others, the sole survivors of the original
party, landed at Flushing.

At this period crowds of French refugees were

je n'en trouve dans un foule d'écrits sur des oiseaux plus générale-
ment et plus anciennement connus. On parle de l'autruche depuis
trente siècles, et l'on ignore aujourd'hui combien elle pond d'œufs,
et combien elle est de tems à les couver." (*Le Solitaire*. Art. par
M. de Guenau de Montbeillard, *Histoire Naturelle par Leclerc de
Buffon*, par C. S. Sonnini. An. IX.)

streaming over to Britain, and it is interesting to hear what a friend of Leguat, writing at this period (1697-1698), says on this subject. M. Henri de Valbourg Misson (not Maximilien Misson, whose connection with Leguat will afterwards be discussed) writes :

" The *French* Protestants that fled into *England* are so spread over the whole Country, that it is impossible to be certain or so much as guess at their Number. Besides the eleven Regiments which are wholly made up of them, there are some in all the other Troops. A vast many of both Sexes are gone into Service in various *English* Families ; so that there is scarce any considerable House, where you may not find some of our Nation. Many have set up Manufactures in the Country and Churches at the same time : Abundance went to *Scotland* and *Ireland,* to *Jersey* and *Garnsey.* At present there are Two and twenty *French* Churches in *London,* and about a Hundred Ministers, that are in the Pay of the State, without reckoning those that are arriv'd at other Means of subsisting." (M. Misson's *Memoirs and Observations in his Travels over England* (1697-98). Written originally in French, and translated by Mr. Ozell, 1719.)

Among others of his compatriots Leguat now migrated from Holland to England, where he seems to have settled for the remainder of his life. He was about sixty years old, but it was not until 1708, when he was a septuagenarian, that the manuscript of his *Relation* was printed and published in London, in French and English simultaneously, whilst a French edition was published in Amsterdam,[1] and

---

[1] Original French Title:—" Voyages et aventures de François Leguat et de ses compagnons en deux isles desertes des Indes Orientales. Avec la relation des choses les plus remarquables qu'ils ont observées dans l'isle Maurice, à Batavia, au Cap de

a Dutch version was printed at Utrecht *in quarto*.[1]
These original editions were soon followed by German translations printed at Frankfort and Leipsic in
1709, another French edition was produced in London in 1720, and an abridged edition appeared later
in 1792. [There was another abstract translation
published under the title of *The French Robinson*,[2]

Bon Espérance, dans l'isle de Sainte Hélène, et en d'autres
endroits de leur route. Le tout enrichi de cartes et de
figures." (Two vols., 12mo. London and Amsterdam, Mortier,
1708.)

[1] Original Dutch Title :—"De gevaarlyke en zeldzame Reyzen
van den Heere François Leguat. Met zyn byhebbend Gezelschap
Naar twee Onbewoonde Oostindische Eylanden. Gedaan zedert
den jare 1690, tot 1698 toe. Behelzende een nankeurig verhaal van
hunne scheepstocht; hun tweejaarig verblijf op het Eylandt
Rodrigue, en hoe wonderlyk zy daar af gekomen zijn. Als meede
De wreede mishandelingen door den Gouverneur van Mauritius ;
hun driejaarig bannissement op een Rots in Zee ; en hoe zy door
ordre der *Compagnie t'Amsterdam*, buyten verwagting, daar
afgehaald en naar *Batavia* gevoerd wierden. Uyt het Frans in't
Neerduyts overgebragt. En met noodige Landkaarten en
verdere Figuuren voorzien. *Te Utrecht.* By Willem Broedelet,
Boekverkoper op den Dam, 1708."

Translation :—"The perilous and wonderful voyages of Herr
Francois Leguat and his companions to two uninhabited East
Indian Islands, made between the years 1690 and 1698, containing
a minute account of their voyage, of their two years' stay on the
Island of Rodrigue, and of the wonderful escape from it. Likewise, of the cruel ill-treatment by the Governor of Mauritius, of their
banishment during three years on a rock in the sea, and how they
were unexpectedly fetched away by order of the Company at
Amsterdam and taken to Batavia. Translated from the French
into Dutch. With the necessary maps and other illustra-
tions."

[2] German abstract.—Der Französiche Robinson, oder F. L.'s
Reisen und Begebenheiten in Bibliothek der Robinsone, 1805.

and one[1] was prepared but never published in
1846.]

The book was well received, and reviewed favourably by the literary journals of the day, so that its
publication brought its author into notice, and
Leguat became acquainted with Baron Haller[2] and
other scientists of that day; among others who thus
came to know him was Dr. Sloane, the secretary of
the Royal Society. The adventurous traveller
remained in exile in England, and, from a contemporary notice in the *Bibliothèque Britannique*,[3] it
appears that he attained the great age of ninety-six
years before he died at or near London in September
1735.

According to M. Eyriès,[4] in the *Biographie
Universelle*, the narrative of Leguat's voyage was

[1] "One of these adventurers (Huguenots or refugee Protestants
of France), M. Leguat, has left a narrative of their sojourn on the
island, which, after relieving of its excessive prolixity, I purpose
publishing under a separate form." (*England's Colonial Empire*,
vol. i, by C. Pridham, 1846.)

[2] Baron Albert de Haller, a well-known anatomist, botanist,
and almost universal genius, was born at Berne, 1708, came to
England in 1727, so he could only have known Leguat when the
latter was in his extreme old age, nearly a nonagenarian.

[3] *Bibliothèque Britannique, ou Histoire des Ouvrages des savans
de la Grande Bretagne pour les mois de Juillet, Aout et Septembre*,
1735, tome v. Under heading "Nouvelles Litteraires":—'Mr.
Leguat est mort ici au commencement du mois de Septembre,
agé de nonante & six ans & aint conservé jusqu'à la fin une grande
liberté de corps d'esprit. C'est le même qui publia en 1706,
la Relation d'un Voyage, dont voici le titre. . . . ."

[4] M. Jean Baptiste Benoit Eyriès, author of the *Abrégé des
Voyages Modernes*. See *Biographie Universelle, Ancienne et
Moderne*, tome xiii. Paris, 1819.

generally supposed to have been published by a certain unfrocked Benedictine monk, named Frédéric Auguste Gabillon. This person was an ingenious literary adventurer, who, having completed his studies in Paris, joined the order of the Théatins, but soon, repenting the sacrifice of his liberty, escaped from his convent and fled to Holland, where he shortly after professed the reformed religion. Being without resources, he worked at compilations for booksellers, but getting into debt went over to England, where he took the name of Jean Leclerc (a noted journalist) and imposed on several persons of distinction.[1] It is certainly possible that this renegade may have imposed on the simple-minded

[1] "Mais à propos de Mr. *Le Clerc*, vous ne serez pas fâché, que je vous raconte une avanture où il a quelque part, sans qu'il le sache. Vous avez parlé autrefois dans vos *Nouvelles* du Sr. *Gabillon*, Theatin, venu de France en Hollande, au sujet d'un Livre, où il prétend expliquer les motifs de sa Conversion. Mais vous n'avez pas, je pense, jugé à propos de parler de celui qu'il fit l'année passée contre Mr. *Le Clerc*. Vous savez qu'il avoit taché de le dédier chez vous à diverses personnes, qui l'avoient refusé. Mais vous ne savez pas, qu'il a eu la hardiesse de le dédier ici (Londres) à Mr. le Duc. . . .* dont il a surpris l'honnêteté. Peu de temps après voyant que cela ne réussissoit pas à son gré, il a changé de batterie. Il est allé voir quelques Théologiens Anglois de cette Ville, qui ne connoissent Mr. *Le Clerc* que de réputation, & leur a dit qu'il étoit ce même Mr. *Le Clerc* sur quoi on lui a fait civilité. . . . On a, de plus, dit, qu'il avoit contracté des dettes, & attrapé un Libraire, chez qu'il a pris des Livres à crédit. . . . ." (*Nouvelles de la République des Lettres, op. cit.*)

* Possibly the Duke of Kent, to whom Leguat's English edition was dedicated.

Leguat; and, indeed, President Bouhier (as
evidenced by a note in his handwriting in his own
copy of Leguat's book) was of opinion that Leguat
owed to Gabillon *les faits altérés* and the digressions on the advantages and disadvantages of
marriage, which are so prominent in our author's
work. Baron Haller, who, as already mentioned,
knew him personally, always declared that Leguat
was a frank and sincere man; nevertheless, M.
Bruzen de la Martinière, also a contemporary, in
his *Geographical Dictionary*, does not scruple to
class Leguat's Voyage among "the fabulous travels
which have no more reality than the dreams of a
fevered brain". Ever since, this very inaccurate judgment has not seldom been held by many. On the
other hand, the observations of Leguat have been
amply confirmed by the evidence of his contemporaries
and of voyagers who followed in his footsteps; while
recent investigation has proved the general correctness of his observations in a remarkable degree.

M. Jacques Bernard (the successor of Pierre Bayle),
in his continuation of Bayle's *Nouvelles de la République des Lettres*, for December 1707, noticed Leguat's
volume when first published, and made the following
critical remarks on its authorship:

"The Preface of this Book is not by the Author of the
Work. He who has composed it maligns various persons
of merit, some of whom will perhaps scorn to notice his
insulting expressions, and others will not fail to retaliate on
the first opportunity. I (M. Jacques Bernard) have already
received from two separate sources a Memoir and a Letter

against this Preface. But as they concern personal quarrels
in which the Public has no interest, I have not thought fit
to insert them in my Review, especially the Memoir, in which
the attacks of the Author are warmly repulsed. I have already, elsewhere, advertised that, if I cared to utilise all
the writings which concern the personal disputes of Authors,
I should have room for nothing else. I repeat my notice
again, that unless the Memoirs sent to me contain something
useful to the Public, I cannot publish them.

" A person very well informed on all subjects of which the
narrative is given in this book of travels tells me that there
are some facts exaggerated, that some essential points have
been omitted, and that some others are inserted which are
absolutely false. In this last class may be placed a certain
argument of some length on the advantages and disadvantages of marriage, which is, to my taste, the most uninteresting
reading in the whole book ; the fictitious columns on which
were engraved the names of the voyagers, said to have been
left in the Island of *Rodrigue,* and the Epitaph on Sieur
Isaac Boyer, which may be said to be both ridiculous and
slightly fanatical. It is asserted that the author blames
without reason the design which the voyagers had in leaving
the spot where they were wasting their youth miserably in
idleness. It is said that he has had little consideration for a
distinguished family (Bénelle ?) in attributing to one of its
members frivolous schemes which he most assuredly never
advanced. In short we are told that the whole Book is a
tissue of rubbish (*fatras*), which so obscures the real adventures that it is necessary to recast it altogether in order to
correct it, which someone will, perhaps, be able to do some
day.

" It is astonishing that a stranger's hand should thus have
disfigured a Voyage which was perfectly capable of attracting
interest by the mere recital of the actual adventures, of which
it could have been composed. Those who have met with
some of the persons mentioned in it know that it was not
necessary to exaggerate these adventures to render them

interesting, as they were sufficiently so in themselves. We shall give a very short extract from it, in which we shall try to disentangle the truth from the false as much as we possibly can. . . .

"In spite of some additions, made in various places of this Voyage, which consist mostly of reflections, which it is easy to distinguish, the reading of it is most agreeable."

"In fact," writes M. Th. Sauzier[1] :—"Casimir Freschot (a laborious writer, translator and compiler, 1676-1716), the anonymous author of *Remarques Historiques et Critiques*, etc., whom Leguat, without naming, indicates and severely vilifies in his preface, tells us that this self-same preface[2] had been composed by one well-known Maximilien Misson, and that the work had been drawn up by Paul Bénelle of Metz." (*Vide, Nouvelle Relation de la Ville et République de Vénise.* Utrecht, 1709.) At the same time, M. Sauzier informs us, there appears under the name of Leguat, in the *Catalogue Général des Livres composant la Bibliothèque du Département de la Marine* (Paris, 1840), the following note: "The Preface is by Maximilien Misson ; the work has been written by Paul B... of Metz."

Nevertheless, Maximilien Misson apparently refers to this work on Venice in his preface to the fourth

[1] See *Un Projet de République*, p. 23.

[2] "Monsieur Misson, Autheur d'un Voyage d'Italie, ayant pris l'occasion d'un nouveau voyage de François Legaut, qui s'est imprimé pour y faire une préface s'y est terriblement déchaîné contre l'Autheur d'un autre voyage de même nature qui avoit oté remarquer quelques bevues qu'il avoit faites dans le sien. . . ." (pp. 221-95).

edition of his *New Voyage to Italy*, 1714, wherein he states :—

"Some Time ago, a friend of mine wrote me word from *Holland*, that a certain Priest of the Romish Sect[1] had published a *French* Translation of a little *Italian* Book, which is a small Abstract of the Lives of the Doges of Venice; and that this Man takes an Occasion to speak undecently of the worthy Mr. *Amelot* and of *Us*, because of certain Truths that we have both Written with some Freedom, concerning that Country. If that Book happens to come into *England*, and it should fall into our Hands, we may perhaps consider it a little, and say something more particular of it in some other Place. But since it seems to be condemn'd to the *Scombri* of *Horace* and *Martial*; and none of those that publish Journals of Litterature, having yet vouchsafed to mention it, I may very well say of the Censures of this Author, what the same Martial said of the despicable Verses of a certain *Diaulus*; without giving myself the Trouble of refuting him any other Way.

Versiculos in me narrant scripsisse Diaulum; at
Non scribit cujus Carmina nemo legit.

I will then content myself with adding a Word concerning the Book of Mr. Leguat (A good and honest Gentleman) in[2] which they assure me that the Priest speaks much otherwise than he ought to do. It seems, say they, that he grounds his unjust Liberty upon the Account he has seen of Mr. *Leguat's* Book, in the Journal that is intituled, *Nouvelles de la République des Lettres*; in which the Author of the said *Nouvelles* uses very ill, without any Reason, both Mr. *Leguat*, and the Relation he has published.

"These sort of *Journals* ought not to be turn'd into *Defamatory Libels*, no more than *Sermons*. The Journals of *Paris Amsterdam*, *Leipsick*, *Trevoux*, nor any of the Rest, have

---

[1] Casimir Freschot.
[2] This should probably read "*of which*", judging from the context.

nothing in 'em but what is civil; and the good *Republick of Letters*, is not at all pleas'd with Reading such slandering *News*. It would be a strange Thing indeed, that the most innocent and commendable Persons should be inevitably expos'd to the Mercy of malicious *Preachers* and *Journalists*, of the like Character, because their *Satyrs* generally go unpunish'd. Some Reasons which are not necessary for me to explain here, oblige me to say here in favour of Mr. *Leguat*, that the Relation he has published, is *faithful* and *true*; as reasonable Persons also agree that it contains many Circumstances which are very extraordinary and worth Relating; I am equally certain of both. The Objections that are made against an Epitaph, and two other small Particulars of that Nature, in his Book, are fit only to shew the Inconsideration of those that make 'em, as well as their great Unkindness. As it has often happen'd, that the Writer of the abovesaid *Nouvelles* has ridicul'd some Books of which he has made Extracts, so he took a Fancy (judging of others by himself) that Mr. *Leguat* was pleased to play upon the *Abbot de Choisy*, in quoting some Words out of one of his Books. But he ought not to give such a traducing Turn to Mr. *Leguat's* Conduct, which has been very innocent. I know upon his secret and sincere Protestation, that he never had the least Intention, in his mentioning the deserving Gentleman I just now nam'd, to say any Thing that cou'd be taken in a disadvantageous Sense, and might derogate from the great Esteem he has for him."

Now, it is noticeable that Maximilien Misson does not, in the above quoted extract, deny the authorship of Leguat's preface attributed to him; whereas in a few pages afterwards he takes the trouble to disclaim the authorship of another work fathered upon him, although he acknowledges to some share in its production :—

"The Authors of the Journal of *Trevoux*, have been misinform'd concerning another Fact, of which I shall take Notice here, since I have an Opportunity of doing it. I declare that the Book, which they mention, Page 323, of their Third Volume, and which is attributed to me, as they say, by the general Consent, is none of my Works. I had some Share in the Edition that was made of that Rhapsody. . . ."

M. Misson evidently thought that M. Bernard had a grudge against him, for he adds :—

"He of whom we have already spoken, who writes (or did write not long ago) *la suite des Nouvelles de la République des Lettres* (of which the Famous Mr. *Bayle* was the first contriver, and who always has sought after every Opportunity of disobliging, by a Miserable Return of Revenge, a Person who never gave him the least Offence whatsoever . . . . he affected to Advertise the Publick (or those that read his *Nouvelles*) that I was the Person whom Father *Montfaucon* attack'd and contradicted; for truly, this Father points at me without mentioning my Name."

Maximilien Misson, who was a Huguenot by birth, and a refugee in England subsequent to the revocation of the Edict of Nantes, was notable for his extreme fanaticism and Protestant zeal. He is best known by his *Nouveau Voyage d'Italie*, to which Addison added his remarks. The Benedictine monk, Père Freschot, in his *Remarques historiques* (Cologne, 1705), had exposed with vigour the rude jokes in which Misson had indulged against the Romish Church, and, writes M. Weiss, "Misson replied to him most bitterly in his preface to the *Voyage* of François Leguat, of which he was the real editor, and not Gabillon, as President Bouhier had supposed; and Freschot replied to him with sharp retorts in the *Nouvelle Relation de la ville de Venise.*" (Vide *l'Examen Critique des dictionnaires*, par M. Barbier, tom. 1er, p. 355, 1820.)

It indeed seems from the above, as well as from the internal evidence afforded by comparing many interpolations in the text of Leguat's narrative with parallel allusions in Misson's previous works, that either Misson must have been the compiler and collaborateur of Leguat's book, or Leguat must have repeatedly referred to Misson's publications. In the notes subjoined to the text several of these passages are brought to the attention of the reader; but, on the other hand, M. Th. Sauzier, whose careful examination of the subject entitles his opinion to be received with the greatest respect, seems to consider that the assertion, that Leguat was not the author of the whole work bearing his name, is without any foundation. M. Sauzier argues that the notice above quoted from the *Bibliothèque Britannique* establishes a perfectly clear and precise statement in an authoritative work,[1] published at the very

---

[1] *La Bibliothèque Britannique*, ou Histoire des Savants de la Grande Bretagne (La Haye, 1733-47), 25 vols., in 8vo. It is a continuation of the *Bibliothèque Anglaise* commenced in 1717 by Michel de la Roche. The writers in it were well-qualified authors, whose knowledge of English literature was considerable; their names are given in the *Historie d'un Voyage Littéraire, fait en* M.DCC.XXXIII, par Charles Etienne Jordan (La Haye, 1735), p. 159 :—" Il parut pendant mon Séjour à Londres, un nouveau Journal sous le Titre de *Bibliothèque Britannique.* Il y a toute

time of Leguat's death, that our centenarian, who
had preserved to the last his great freedom of mind
and body, was indeed the very author of the book
in question. " For besides," he writes, " what
credence can be placed in this Freschot, the very
same who is so abused in the preface of Leguat,
a nd who, without furnishin any proof, tells us that
neither the preface nor the work are written by that
traveller?" Had he not some interest in attributing this preface to Maximilien Misson, who,
in 1691, had published, like himself, a work
upon Italy: *Nouveau Voyage en Italie?* As
to the note inserted in the Catalogue of the
Marine Library, M. Sauzier is under the impres-
sion that it is merely a reproduction of what
Freschot said. " The son of a merchant of Metz,
Bénelle was one of the seven adventurers, the companions in misfortune of Leguat, the only one whom
he, from some motive of which we are not informed,
has designated by initials (see page 6). Bénelle
returned into Holland in 1698 with Leguat and
Jacques de la Caze. The last proceeded to settle in
America; Leguat proceeded to England, and
Bénelle lived at Amsterdam, where he died in 1746.
Jean Beckmann, in his *Histoire littéraire des
Voyages,* published at Göttingen in 1808-10,
writes :—·

apparance que ce Journal aura un heureux succès : les Auteurs
sont Gens de Mérite, & qui entendent tous parfaitement l'Anglois :
Messieurs Stahlin, Bernard, le Missy, le Mr. Duval, & le Savant
Mr. Darmigcaux, aussi M. Blanfort."

"'The truth of the Narrative of Leguat can be established by a valuable testimony: He names Paul B..., one of his two companions who returned with him, in 1698, to Flushing. A descendant of this B. is the wife of Councillor Von Martens, to whom I owe the following information :—Paul Bénelle was with his father, when they were obliged to quit France on account of their religion ; they betook themselves to Amsterdam, where, at the age of twenty years, Paul decided to make the voyage to Eden, which du Quesne had depicted in so charming a fashion. After eight years he came back to his father at Amsterdam. There he lived, after having contracted two marriages, until 1746 [that is, eleven years after Leguat's death], that is to say, until the age of 70 years. He has acknowledged the truth of Leguat's story, although, indeed, he was not precisely his friend. This Bénelle has also left a journal, which probably yet remains in the hands of the heirs of Pierre Bénelle, his grandson, deceased a short time ago at Amsterdam. Can this manuscript be published ? '

" Thus, Bénelle, who died eleven years after Leguat—Bénelle, the very same to whom has been attributed the authorship of Leguat's Adventures, who was not precisely the friend of Leguat, has formally acknowledged that Leguat was undoubtedly the author of that work.

" Any doubt is no longer possible ; the French Esquire, Leguat of la Fougère, the chief of the expedition of the *Hirondelle,* the exile of the desert islands Rodriguez and Marianne, is the self-same individual who has published *The Voyages and Adventures of François Leguat and of his Companions.*"

Nevertheless, M. Sauzier's arguments, forcible as they are, will not convince other critics who hold to their opinion that Leguat's MS. was largely manipulated by M. Misson, who not impossibly may have been assisted in the English translation by Ozell. An abstract of Leguat's narrative was published by M. Charles Grant, Viscount de Vaux, in his well-known *History of Mauritius*,[1] compiled from the papers of his father, Baron Grant. He writes:—

"N.B.—As the extract from Le Guat, on the Island of Rodriguez, may perhaps be found long, I think proper to explain my motives on the subject.

"The residence of Le Guat, and his companions in that island being the sole event which furnishes us a sort of historical description, it was necessary to mention it. By attachment to truth and justice, I could not do better than to let the author speak himself; knowing that this manner, which has been adopted by *Anacharsis*, &c., offers more interest to the reader. However, it has cost me more labour than if I had written the whole in my own way; because I have been obliged to correct the style, and to shorten it in every part, which seems to me tedious, prolix, and often of erroneous systems; besides he places Rodriguez at two hundred leagues from Mauritius, whereas, it is not half, as I make him say. . . . . I wish the knowledge I present of this island may be sufficiently convincing of the advantages which may be reaped from it, that it should no longer remain useless to humanity."

An abbreviated version of Leguat's adventures has lately been published with the annotations of M. Eugène Muller, the Librarian of the Arsenal at Paris, in the series of Voyages brought out by M.

---

[1] *The History of Mauritius, or the Isle of France, and the neighbouring Islands.* From their first discovery to the present time, composed principally from the papers and memoirs of Baron Grant, who resided twenty years in the island. By his son, Charles Grant, Viscount de Vaux. (London, 1801.)

Dreyfous.[1] M. Muller has kindly permitted the Editor of the following reprint to make full use of his notes, many of which have been thus utilised to the great advantage of the members of the Society.

By far the most valuable contribution, however, to the *literary* and bibliographical history of Leguat's work is the lately published *brochure*,[2] by M. Th. Sauzier of the Paris Geographical Society, including the reprint of what is perhaps an *abrégé* of Marquis du Quesne's remarkable pamphlet, till lately only known by the extracts quoted in Leguat's narrative. M. Sauzier's arguments, which are not indisputable, have already been quoted above as proving the authorship and veracity of the philosophic and pious refugee. A translation of du Quesne's original scheme for colonising Réunion was to have been included at the end of this present reprint, but want of space prevents its appearance.

The interest attaching to Leguat's narrative, as before observed, centres (apart from its simple and picturesque originality and charming style in which the touching story of adventure is told) in the important details of the natural history of Rodri-

[1] *Aventures de François Leguat et de ses compagnons en Deux Iles Désertes des Indes Orientales* (1650-1698). Publiées et annotées par Eugène Muller. Paris. Bibliothèque d'Aventures et de Voyages. (Maurice Dreyfous.)

[2] *Un Projet de République à l'Ile d'Eden (l'île Bourbon) en* 1689, par Le Marquis Henri du Quesne. Réimpression d'un ouvrage disparu, publié en 1689, intitulé Recueil de quelques mémoires servans d'instruction pour l'établissement de l'isle d'Eden. Précédé d'une notice par Th. Sauzier. (Paris, Librairie Ancienne et Moderne de E. Dufossé.)

guez which are contained therein. Before touching on this portion of the work, therefore, a few words on the island of Rodriguez may well find a place. The small island of Rodriguez, although but a poor dependency of the colony of Mauritius, has considerable interest, both for naturalists and geographers, yet it seldom receives much attention either at home or abroad, and it is only occasionally that the general public hears of its existence. Years ago, however, when the road round the Cape to the East Indies was first opened to navigators, this island was regarded as one of the ports of call, until the colonisation of Mauritius rendered the more important island a safer harbour of refuge, and a better haven for refit and refreshment.

Rodriguez, or Diego Rais, lies about 330 miles to the eastward of Mauritius, of which island it is a dependency, and is the third island of importance in the Mascarene archipelago. It is ten miles long, in an east-north-east and west-south-west direction, and four miles broad, with an area of about forty-three square miles.

An extensive coral reef encircles the island, varying much as to its distance from the shore. At the south-eastern point of the island it is only twenty yards from the shore; from the western end it extends four-and-a-half miles in a southerly, two-and-a-quarter miles in a westerly, and four miles in a northerly direction. The history of the discovery of this island will be found in the Appendix (p. 308), which deals with the earliest voyagers who touched at the Mascarene Islands. It may be mentioned here, however, that on the 25th of June 1638, the *St. Alexis* of Dieppe, commanded by Captain Alonso Goubert of Dieppe, came up with the island of Diego Ruiz, "lying in twenty degrees of south latitude, about forty leagues from Madagascar," as this was the first French ship that ever visited the Mascarene islands. "We landed," writes François Cauche of Rouen,[1] "and set up the arms of France on the trunk of a tree, our ship keeping out at sea, not being able to anchor by reason of the depth ; so that as soon as the King's Arms were fix'd, those who had done it, returned aboard in the boat, as they went."

After the departure of Leguat and his comrades in 1693, some English officers appeared to have stayed for a while and surveyed Port Mathurin in 1706 or 1707 ; as is stated in a report made by M. de Parat, Governor of Ile Bourbon in 1712 to the Minister of Marine in France, in answer to a request for information as to the capabilities of Rodriguez. Port Mathurin (now designated by this denomination for the first time) was described as being difficult to enter, but available for the anchorage of vessels of thirty guns ; and it was further stated that, apart from the quantity of tortoises found there, the island was of no use to the French East India Company.

---

[1] *A Voyage to Madagascar and the adjacent Islands and Coast of Africk*, by Francis Cauche. English translation of 1710, p. 4, by Capt. Stevens, after the *Relations véritables et curieuses de l'isle de Madagascar*, etc., par Le Sieur Morisot. (Paris, 1657.)

In 1725, says M. d'Avezac, the Government of Bourbon, under the President of Council, M. Desforges Boucher, decided to take possession of Rodriguez in the name of Louis XV, and a vessel was despatched thither, whose officers made a geodetic survey of the island, the original map of which is said still to exist in manuscript at the Dépôt of Charts, in the Marine Office at Paris.[1] The curious *Relation de l'Ile Rodrigue*,[2] found by M. Rouillard among the archives of the Ile de France at the Marine Office in Paris, dates from this period, as it follows the Proceedings of the Council, which ordained the project of settling the island of *Diego Ruys*, as Rodriguez was then named ; although, on this occasion, M. Th. Sauzier states that the name of Ile Marianne was given by the French visitors to the island.[3] A superintendent and guard were established on the island from this date, as it is mentioned that the guard-house of the French superintendent in the bay of the Ouen Valley was entrusted in the year 1740 to a negro family.

Thirteen years afterwards (1748), Admiral Boscawen, who so boldly led his squadron across the locality, supposed to be occupied by the reefs of Cargados Carayos (see Chart, p. 308), examined the capacity of the roadstead at Rodriguez for the

[1] *Vide* " Note sur l'Ile Rodrigue après le départ de Leguat," par Eugène Muller.

[2] *Vide* Appendix B.

[3] M. Sauzier adds : " *Coincidence bizarre*, this name of the Marianne is still applied to the rock on which Leguat was imprisoned after escaping from Rodriguez."

accommodation of shipping ; and it must have been previous to 1756 that a regular establishment was formed for the preservation of turtles to supply the Ile de France and Bourbon with such fresh provision.

" This fishery", wrote Mr. Charles F. Noble[1] (alluding to the sea-turtles), in that year, 1756, " is thought so useful at Mauritius, that they have always a sergeant's party on that little island of Rodriguez, who collect all the fish they can, for the boats that are sent to bring them at certain times, and the ships that generally touched there on their way to Mauritius. There is, also, a particular spot of ground inclosed here, for keeping and breeding land tortoises for the same purposes."

It was in the year 1671. that, on Thursday, 28th of May, the first scientific observer, Abbé Pingré, accompanied by his assistant, M. Thuillier—" un jeune homme tres versé dans la haute géométrie, et initié dans la théorie et dans la pratique de l'astronomie"—set foot on shore in the *isle desirée* of Rodriguez. The expedition had left L'Orient in January, on board the French East India Company's ship *Le Comte d'Argenson*, arriving at Mauritius on the 7th of May, where the news of the capture of Pondicherry had just reached. M. Le Gentil had embarked two months previously at Port Louis for the above-named Indian port, which

[1] *Vide* " Some Remarks made at the French Islands of Mauritius and Bourbon, 1755, by Charles F. Noble, to Governor Pigot at Madras." (Dalrymple's *Oriental Repository.*)

he was not destined to enter on this voyage. These
scientists had been dispatched by the French
Academy, under the auspices of the Cardinal de
Luynes and Mons. Le Monier, to observe the transit
of Venus on the 6th of June 1761. Pingré sailed
from Mauritius on the 9th of May, and was, therefore, three weeks in getting to Rodriguez from Port
Louis in the corvette *La Mignonne*, a dead beat to
windward, reaching as far south as 28° 30'. The
astronomical party remained at Rodriguez until the
8th of September, on which date the *Mignonne* took
them back to Mauritius. Pingré's journal has never
been published, for its interest was overshadowed by
the voluminous quartos of Le Gentil. The astronomical details duly appeared in the *Histoire de
l'Académie* (1761, p. 102) and *Mémoires* (1761, pp.
415, 985). Pingré planted his observatory on the
traditional site of Leguat's settlement, and it is
interesting to note his opinion of our adventurer
and the current judgment of contemporary opinion
at that period, presumably at Mauritius, as well as
in France. For doubtless Pingré, before starting,
would have taken an interest in ascertaining all
reliable information regarding the small islet where
he proposed to take his observations. He writes :

"I made my observations in the 'enfoncement nommé de
François Leguat', on the northern side of the island, at the
spot marked A on the plan, in 19° 40' 40" latitude, and 80° 51'
30" long. The name which this locality bears has been given to
it in memory of François Leguat, a Bourguignois gentleman
who, having left France for the sake of religion, in 1689

betook himself to Holland, where he embarked the following
year on the ship *Hirondelle.* He intended, in company with
several other French refugees, to found the nursery of a new
colony, either at Bourbon Island, which he believed had been
abandoned by the French, or at Rodriguez. In fact, they disembarked at Rodriguez, to the number of eight, on the 10th
of May 1691; they established their abode in the aforesaid
locality, and remained there until the 31st of May 1693,
when, tired of their solitude, they abandoned themselves to
the sea in a kind of boat which they had constructed for the
purpose. A stiff breeze occurred, and was taken by them
for a storm; they, nevertheless, arrived safe and sound at
Mauritius, on the eighth of the following month. *Les
Voyages et Aventures de François Leguat* have been printed
in two vols. in 12°, at Amsterdam, in 1708. This work *passe
pour un tissu de fables ; j'en ay trouvé beaucoup moins que je
ne m'y attendois.* We find in the narrative of Leguat a
plan of Rodriguez, which does not at all resemble that island.
[Compare maps, pp. xvii, 1.] That which I give here is
the result of a journey which we have made—M. Thuillier
and myself—around the island ; we have traversed many
times nearly all the northern coast line. As the sight of
M. Thuillier is far better than mine, I have let him take
nearly all the angles. The triangles which we have formed
round the island have been connected with a base which
we laid out in our *enfoncement de François Leguat*, and
which measures four hundred and eight toises (eight
hundred and three yards). . . . ."

The taking of Rodriguez by the English under
Captain Kempenfelt prevented the astronomers
completing their survey of the island.

We get a glimpse of the little colony from the
Abbé's journal. He says :—

" The island of Rodriguez is generally inhabited only by a
French officer, who commands a dozen or fifteen blacks,
whose principal occupation is to catch the tortoises in the

different parts of the island ; they collect these tortoises in a park, and send them to the Isle de France on the corvettes, which they dispatch from time to time for this cargo. These blacks, natives of Madagascar or from India, are, the most part, slaves of the Company ; there are, nevertheless, some free men. The work of these is paid for at the price agreed when they are hired. There was, besides, at Rodriguez, when I arrived there, a surgeon and a corporal of the island, both Europeans. The commandant can have with him his family and his slaves, if he has any. Such was the colony of Rodriguez in 1761. When the Governor of the Isle de France sends a corvette to load up with tortoises, he sends at the same time a provision of rice, sufficing for the main-tenance of the colony. For its defence, M. de Puvigné had erected on the sea-coast a battery of six pieces of ordnance, two prs.[1] Most of these cannons had belonged to French ships. As Rodriguez is only kept in order to obtain its tortoises one would think it unnecessary to place it in a state of defence. One would hardly imagine that it would enter into the minds of the English to form there a base from which they could attack the Isle of France to more advan-tage. . . . All those who live at Rodriguez make profession of being Christians ; but each one after his own fashion. This one may eat of everything, because the Capuchin priests who instructed him had represented that the distinction of victual customary in his country had resulted from superstition. Another would abstain from eating beef, because his conversion had been effected by the ministry of other missionaries, more accommodating to the opinions of the people. They called these *Paulist-Christians*, being baptised by those who belong to the Church of Saint Paul at Pondicherry. The others were named *Capuchin-Christians*. Public worship at Rodriguez was reduced to ringing the *Angelus* every day, which no one said. Besides, the Commandant insisted on his slaves attending prayers offered by a slave who had never

---

[1] *I.e.*, two-pounder guns.

been baptised. There was neither church nor chapel, and
there had never been anything of that kind there. François
Leguat and his companions served God, in their manner, with
greater exactitude than has been observed by the Catholics
ever since they have been established in this island. There is,
nevertheless, at Rodriguez a cemetery, consecrated by some
chaplain of a ship, who has wished to leave this monument of
the visit of a minister of the true Church to this neglected
island. At the same time, I am assured that this neglect
ought not to be imputed to the zealous missionaries, who till
the ground, otherwise almost uncultivated, of Bourbon, and
of the Isle of France. . . . ."

To commemorate the observations of the Transit
of Venus expedition under Pingré, Le Monnier proposed placing the *Solitaire* among the southern
constellation,[1] " but, being a better astronomer than
ornithologist, he, inadvertently," says Dr. Hamel,[2]

[1] This constellation, says Mr. Knobel, is a small one cribbed
from Libra and Virgo. The boundaries of it for the present epoch
lie between Right ascension 14 hours and 14 hours 40 minutes,
and within the parallels of 15° and 25° of South declination.
Devoid of bright stars.

" J'ai observé la plus grande partie de ces Etoiles à mes deux
quarts-de-cercles muraux, & la figure de la constellation du *Solitaire*
(oiseau des Indes & des Philippines) a été preservé en mémoire
du voyage en l'île Rodrigue, m'ayant été fourni par Mrs. Pingré
et Brisson ; voyez le tome ii de l'Ornithologie ; cette constellation
sera voisine du Corbeau & de l'Hydre sur nos planisphères &
globes célestes." (*Mémoire sur une Nouvelle Constellation*, par M. le
Monnier, lû 21 Août 1776 ; *Mém. de l'Académie Royale*, 1776,
p. 562, pl. xvii.)

[2] See Pamphlet by Dr. Hamel, entitled " Der Dodo, die Einsiedler
und der erdichtete Nazarvogel", *Bulletin Phys -math.-Acad.*, St.
Petersburg, vol. viii, Nos. 5, 6, 1846. Quoted by Strickland
and Melville in their postscript to their monograph on the Dodo,
p. 64.

" gave this honour not to the Didine bird of Rodriguez, but to the Solitary Thrush of the Philippines
(*Monticola eremita*), figured by Brisson, vol. ii, pl. 28,
f. 1, instead of copying Leguat's figure as he might
have done."

Kempenfelt surveyed Port Mathurin the same
year, by order of Admiral Cornish, who was then
cruising about the Mascarene Islands. A landing
was effected on the island,[1] but the mortality among
the crews of the ships was so excessive that they
very soon re-embarked.

In August 1764, the administration of the Mascarene Islands passed into the hands of the King,
Louis XV ; and in 1768, M. Dumas, the Governor
of the Islands, deported M. Rivalz de Saint-Antoine,
a member of Council of the Isle of France to Rodriguez, for having protested against the arbitrary
proceedings of the military administration. However, the exile of M. de St. Antoine did not exceed
a year, after which interval he was released on the
recall of M. Dumas to France. For forty years now
the little island enjoyed peace and tranquillity ; only

---

[1] " Upon the whole, if we consider the little trust that is
to be put in slaves, which forms the chief strength of the island,
their small force, besides the stony shoar which would render their
batteries scarce tenable, and, I may add, the terror of the English
arms, it may be presumed, that had our fleet under Admiral
Cornish, which cruised off Rodriguez in 1761, been ordered to
attack this island [Bourbon], it would have met with an easy
conquest, and a very important one, as it may justly be reckoned
a very healthy, pleasant, and profitable island." (Dalrymple's
Oriental Repository, loc. cit.)

the tortoises and turtles suffered deportation to the
hospitals of Bourbon and Mauritius; but Abbé
Pingré's surmise as to the improbability of the
English ever finding the advantage of holding
Rodriguez as an entrepôt, from which to organise an
attack on Mauritius, was destined to be put to proof
most decisively. As a preparatory measure to the
project of capturing the Ile de France and the Ile
Bonaparte (now Réunion), as the Ile de Bourbon
had been then lately renamed, Vice-Admiral Bertie,
commanding the Cape naval station, entrusted
Captain Rowley[1] with the strict blockade of the
Mascarene Islands in 1809 ; and early in that year a
small advanced force of 200 Indian troops, accompanied by 200 of the 56th Foot, under Lieut.-Col.
Keating, embarked from Bombay and occupied
Rodriguez, on the 4th of August, where a depot
was established for the supply of the cruisers
blockading the islands, and a small fort was erected.
From Rodriguez an expeditionary force of 368
officers and men, with 100 bluejackets and 136
marines from the squadron, proceeded in September
to the Ile Bourbon, and captured the insignificant
works at St. Paul's, where a landing was effected
and the shipping burnt; but the island was not
occupied, and Colonel Keating retreated his force
to Rodriguez, where preparations were continued
for the attack on Mauritius, and the force in the
British *place d'armes* at Rodriguez was augmented
by 1,700 Europeans and about 1,800 Sepoys. This

[1] Afterwards Admiral Sir J. Rowley.

expedition was detained on the island until the 3rd
of July 1810, when another attack was made in
force on Bourbon, which was now taken and properly occupied, whilst a closer blockade of Mauritius
was effected.

In November, Vice-Admiral Bertie having arrived
at Rodriguez, a division of troops from Madras
joined the convoy from Bengal, when the united
expedition sailed from Rod iguez, under General
Abercrombie, whose troops, being landed at Cape
Malheureux, accomplished the easy conquest of the
Ile de France by the 3rd of December, on which
date the capitulation was signed.

Subsequent to the capture of the Mascarene
Islands by the British, Rodriguez long remained
little heard of and unnoticed by the outside world.
The open-boat voyage of François Leguat, which by
many had been regarded as an improbable feat of
navigation, in spite of the sneer of the Abbé Pingré,
has, notwithstanding, been repeated more than once.
M. Th. Sauzier records the fact that, about 1825,
Captain Doret, who later became a Rear-Admiral
and Governor of Réunion, and later a member of
the French Senate, left Rodriguez in an open boat,
accompanied by a few sailors, and reached Mauritius,
where he succeeded in obtaining assistance and rescue
for the remainder of the crew of his ship which had
been wrecked on the reefs outside the island.

The interest in Rodriguez after the commencement of the present century was felt only by
scientific naturalists, who now began to appreciate

the loss sustained by the world through the total destruction and extinction of original fauna and flora in various countries throughout the world.

In Mauritius a Society of Natural History had been formed by Mr. Telfair, Dr. Lyall, and Professor Bojer, on the foundation of an older Société d'Emulation, when Sir Charles Colville was Governor in 1829. In the following year, the secretary of this Society, M. Desjardins, obtained certain bones encrusted with stalagmite, which had been found many years before (about 1789) in one of the caves of Rodriguez; and this find appears to have induced Mr. Telfair to urge Colonel Dawkins and M. Eudes, who were then at Rodriguez, to make further search for the bones of Didine birds. M. Eudes succeeded in digging up in the large cavern various bones, including some of a large kind of bird which no longer existed in the island. A bird of so large a size as that indicated by the bones had never been seen in the island by M. Gory, who had resided there for the last forty years, i.e., since 1790. It may be here remarked that Pingré had remarked with regard to the Solitaire, in 1761, that M. de Puvigné had assured him that these birds were not even then totally extinct, but that they had become extremely rare, and were only to be found in the most inaccessible parts of the island.[1] It would therefore be

---

[1] "Les solitaires étoient communes à Rodrigue du temps de François Leguat. M. de. Puvigné m'a assuré que la race n'en étoit pas encore détruite, mais ils se sont retirés dans les endroits de l'Isle les plus inaccessibles." (Pingré, *Journal*, MS., fol. 178.)

during the period between 1760-1790 that the final disappearance of the species may have taken place. The next excavations were made by Capt. Kelly, R.N., of H.M.S. *Conway*, at the request of Mr. Cunninghame, in 1845, but the search was unsuccessful. The bones procured by M. Telfair were exhibited by M. Cuvier in Paris, and subsequently compared by Messrs. Strickland and Melville with the remains of the Dodo in the Ashmolean Museum at Oxford. The reconstruction of the ideal skeleton from these fragments showed that the species to which they belonged was unquestionably allied to, though not identical with, the Dodo, and it was rightly assumed that they belonged to the species described and figured by Leguat as the Solitaire. It was also discovered by these eminent naturalists that the points of agreement between these two extinct birds are *"shared in common with the Pigeons, and exist in no other known species of bird"*. A triumph of ornithological diagnosis.

The coral reefs round Rodriguez have ever been a source of danger to seamen navigating those seas, especially on the homeward route. In 1843, two vessels were wrecked upon the *Quatre-vingt Brisans* at the S.W. extremity of the island, where the waves break at a great distance from the shore.[1] The

---

[1] "The *Queen Victoria*, 715 tons, which left Bombay on the 11th March 1843, bound for Liverpool, struck on the south-west reefs, off Rodrigues, during a gale of wind, on the morning of the 7th of April, and became a total wreck. The commander, Captain Black, most of the passengers, and several of the crew were

Queen Victoria and the *Oxford*, East Indiamen, were totally lost ; and Mr. Higgin, of Liverpool, who was a passenger by the former of these ships, during his enforced stay on the island for six weeks, was enabled to make some observations on the natural history of the island, which assisted Mr. Strickland, the President of the Ashmolean Society, and Dr. Melville, his coadjutor, in their magnificent monograph on the Dodo and its kindred, towards their investigation of the structure and habits of the Solitaire, which was named *Pezophaps solitarius;* a smaller species, *Pezophaps minor*, was determined in 1852. In 1859 the *Nassur Sultan*, another East Indian liner, was lost ; and it may be noted as a fact that in each case of wreck the vessel is reported to have struck at fifteen miles S.W., although, from subsequent examination, it has been

saved, but Mr. R. Plunkett, a passenger, and nine seamen were drowned in a hasty attempt to reach the shore. The survivors were hospitably entertained in the island of Rodrigues for thirty-six days, until they obtained a passage to Bourbon, the governor of which place forwarded them to Mauritius." (*Asiatic Journal,* vol. i, p. 662 ; 1843.)

" At 4, on the morning of 1st September 1843, the East-India packet ship, *Oxford*, Captain Marshall, on her passage from Calcutta to London, while under a press of sail, struck on a ledge of rocks off the island of Rodrigues, and shortly after became a total wreck. The crew and passengers having taken to the boats, were picked up by a Glasgow vessel and landed at Mauritius. The loss of this vessel and of the *Queen Victoria* is attributed to an error in the Admiralty Charts, in which this reef of rocks is laid down as extending only five miles, whereas it extends from fifteen to sixteen miles." (*Asiatic Journal,* vol. ii, p. 326 ; 1843-44.)

found that no reefs extend more than five or six miles from land.

It was not until 1864 that Mr. E. Newton, then Auditor-General in Mauritius, visited Rodriguez, and obtained some more bones; and in the two following years a large quantity of bones was obtained by Mr. Jenner, for Mr. Edward Newton, and forwarded to Cambridge, where Professor Alfred Newton, his brother, and himself succeeded in making an admirable, though not altogether perfect, restoration of the skeleton of the long lost Solitaire, the photograph of which appears in the frontispiece. The extraordinary fidelity of Leguat's account of the bird was confirmed in almost every point. The very singular knob on the wing, caused by injuries received in fighting, fully bore out the accuracy of Leguat as to the pugnacity of these most curious birds, which seem to have fought by buffeting with their pinions like pigeons.

When, in the year 1874, the British Government dispatched an expedition to observe the Transit of Venus at Rodriguez, by the request of the Royal Society some naturalists were sent to accompany the astronomers. Dr. Balfour as botanist and geologist, Mr. Gulliver, zoologist, and Mr. Slater, especially deputed to examine the remains of extinct animals in the caves.[1] The results of these investigations were

[1] The *Philosophical Transactions of the Royal Society*, vol. 168, 1879, reporting on the collections from Rodriguez, include *The Physical Features of Rodriguez* by Is. B. Balfour, Sc.D.; and

lii INTRODUCTION.

published in the *Philosophical Transactions* of the Royal Society. Professor Balfour succeeded in identifying the most characteristic of the plants described by Leguat, and his notes form the most interesting commentary possible on Leguat's faithful delineation of the productions of his island home.

One more ocean voyage of recent date in an open boat deserves recording; and it is to be hoped that it is the last of its kind, for surely the Government will insist on better provision being ensured for this most unfortunate poverty-stricken little colony.

At present the whole budget of the island barely exceeds some five hundred pounds *per annum*, from which the impecuniosity of the dependent islet can be judged.

On the 15th of April 1886, a very severe cyclone struck the island, which lies in the very track of the so-called Mauritius hurricanes, during which a colonial schooner was lost, adding the cost of maintenance of the shipwrecked captain and crew to the debt of the inhabitants. This cyclone, which occasioned the severest hurricane hitherto experienced by those longest in the colony, besides causing great damage to crops and property, was followed by an almost continual drought. The state of

reports of proceedings of the Naturalists, viz. : *Petrology*, by N. S. Maskelyne, F.R.S.; *Botany*, MM. Balfour, Mitten, Crombie, Berkeley, and Dickie; *Zoology, Extinct Fauna*, Bone Caves, by Mr. Slater ; *Birds*, by Dr. Günther and E. Newton ; *Osteology of the Solitaire*, by E. Newton and J. W. Clark ; *Reptiles*, by Dr. Günther; *Recent Fauna*, by Dr. Günther, MM. Sharpe, Smith, Miers, Butler, Waterhouse, Grube, Gulliver, Brüggemann, and others.

affairs began to assume a very alarming aspect towards the month of August, when it became evident that the crops would fail. Nor was it a vain surmise. The beans harvest was not one-third of what it had been on previous years; whilst, as regards the sweet potatoes, manioc, and maize, which, with rice, form the staple food of the creoles and Indians, hardly any could be raised. The stock of imported rice in the island being nearly exhausted at the beginning of September, and the ship expected with supplies being late, a meeting of the principal inhabitants was called together at the Town Hall, at which it was resolved that a boat should be sent to Mauritius, distant 330 miles, to ask for immediate relief. The Government pinnace *Victoria*, being then unfit for sea, another private boat, belonging to the Civil Commissioner, was fitted up. The Government pilot, Mr. Vandorous, consented to take charge of the expedition, assisted by Sergeant Aston, and two creoles, Genève and Prudence, all volunteers. The boat left on the 11th of September, and reached Mauritius after a three days' passage, during which they experienced some heavy seas and weather, which made the journey one of some little danger for an open boat. The Government of Mauritius, which was, surely, remiss in not having foreseen and anticipated the scarcity, despatched a tug with 350 bags of rice only for a population of 1,700 souls. This supply was soon exhausted, and it was not until the 21st December that a cargo of 1,000 bags of rice reached poor Rodriguez, to be *sold* (at what price, we may ask?) to the very patient and helpless islanders. "For this act of grace," naïvely adds the magistrate, "the Governor cannot be too much thanked." This adventure of an open boat proceeding 300 miles across the Indian Ocean, in the track of François Leguat's desperate voyage two hundred years before, led in fact to the present republication of his *Relation*, which may well be read again with profit by those who care for true tales of days gone by.

We can hardly conclude better than by quoting the testimony of a learned man of science who has carefully investigated Leguat's narrative, and compared his written description with the materials available after the lapse of two centuries.

"From Leguat's work we find," writes Professor Schlegel, "that he was a man of true refinement and much reading, that he possessed to a high degree the earnestness and piety which characterised the fervent Protestants of the time, and that, by his scientific disposition and imperturbable faith, as well as by his oppression and persecution of several kinds, together with his ripe age, he had obtained that unchangeable calmness of mind with which he felt so happy at Rodriguez that, had he not been compelled, he would have never left that resting-place."

"As to his love of truth, we find the contents of his work corroborated by what he says in his preface: 'La simple Vérité toute nue et la Singularité de nos Avantures sont le corps et l'âme de ma Relation.'"

The simple and pure faith in the Bible inculcated by the Huguenot religion is conspicuous in Leguat's pathetic story. We find the word "*Providence*" on

the first and last pages of his book, and it was this
reliance on divine support which upheld his equani-
mity during long years of trying exile. It will be
consolatory to remember that he survived these
hardships, so nobly borne, when he was considerably
beyond the prime of life, for a period of over another
quarter of a century—in a foreign country, certainly,
but at all events, during his old age, in security,
comfort, and peace.

CHRONOLOGICAL TABLE OF EVENTS MENTIONED OR REFERRED TO.

1506. Island of Sᵗᵃ Apollonia possibly first sighted.

Feb. 9, 1507. Cirne and Sᵗᵃ Apollonia first visited by Diogo Fernandes Pereira.

1509. The name of Don Galopes given to island afterwards known as Rodriguez.

1512. The Mascarene archipelago rediscovered and named by Mascarenhas.

1523. Death of Pope Hadrianus VI.

1527. Mascarenhas and S Apollonia marked on chart of Weimar.

1545. Portuguese settlement on an island south of Madagascar.

1570. Lambarde's account of Queen Mary at Greenwich.

Sept. 20, 1598. Edict of Nantes. Dutch settle in Sᵗᵃ Apollonia, and Mauritius.

1613. An English ship, the "Pearl," visits S. Apollonia, and Captain Castleton names it "England's Forest".

1630. Sᵗᵃ Apollonia named Ile de la Perle.

1638. François Leguat born. Insurrection of Scotch Covenanters against Government of King Charles.

1639. Dutch settlement formed on Mauritius under Pieter de Goyer, who was succeeded by Adriaan van der Stel.

1643. Pronis takes possession of Mascareigne.

1649. Mascareigne or Bourbon formally taken possession of by Le Bourg under orders of De Flacourt, and the arms of France affixed to a tree.

1650. Maximilian de Jong, Dutch Governor at Mauritius.

1653. De Flacourt erects a pillar on coast of Madagascar.

1659. Adriaan Nieuland, Governor at Mauritius.

1664. King of France concedes Madagascar and Mascarene Islands to French East Indian Company. Dirk Janzsoon Smient, Governor of Mauritius.

1668. George Frederick Wreede, Governor of Mauritius.

1669. Sieur Dubois visits Bourbon.

1671. M. Jacob de la Haye, Viceroy of the Indies, visits Bourbon. Hubert Hugo, Governor of Mauritius.

1674. M. de la Haye revisits Bourbon.
1677. Isaac Lamotius, Governor of Mauritius.
1685. Revocation of the Edict of Nantes.
1688. Fort Spielwyk erected at Bantam. First Huguenots leave the Netherlands for South Africa.
1689. Arrival of Huguenots at Cape of Good Hope.
     Marquis Henri Du Quesne publishes " Mémoires" on Eden.
Apr. 26, „ King William III issues a declaration inviting French Protestants to England.
Aug. 6, „ François Leguat passes from France into Holland.
     „ Equipment of *La Droite*, to which Leguat is appointed Major.
     „ *La Droite* and consort, disarmed.
1690. The Frigate *Swallow*, commanded by Captain Anthony Valleau, fitted out.
     Leguat and nine companions, the adventurers, embark as passengers.
July 10, „ The *Swallow* leaves Amsterdam.
     13, „ Arrival in Texel road.
Sept. 4, „ *Swallow* leaves Texel with convoy of 24 sail, English and Dutch.
     18, „ Escape from shipwreck off Schetland Isles.
Oct. 22, „ Arrival at Canary Islands.
     29, „ Arrival at Cape de Verde Island.
     31, „ Island of Salt.
Nov. 6, „ Leave Salt Island.
     20, „ [Revolt of Père Hyacinthe in Bourbon].
Dec. 27, „ Tristan d'Acunha.
Jan. 13,1691. Sight Robben Island.
     26, „ Anchor in Table Bay.
Feb. 13, „ Depart from Cape of Good Hope.
Mar. 15, „ Great storm encountered.
Apr. 3, „ Isle of Eden sighted.
     15, „ Death of John Pagni, one of the adventurers.
     25, „ Diego Ruys sighted.
May 1, „ Leguat lands on Diego-Rodrigo.
     16, „ Capt. Valleau leaves Peter Thomas and takes away Jacques Guiguer and Pierrot, deserts the adventurers.
1692. Roelof Diodati, Governor of Mauritius.
     „ Adventurers employed in building a boat.
Apr. 19, 1693. First attempt to leave the island unsuccessful. The boat strikes on a rock.
May 8, „ Death of Isaac Boyer.

May 21, 1693. Re-embarcation of remaining adventurers. Final departure from Rodriguez.

28, ,, A storm encountered.

29, ,, Arrival on a small bay of Isle Maurice.

June ,, Rest at Black River.

July ,, Visit of the Governor to Black River.

,, Adventurers proceed in their boat to North-West Port.

,, Carry their belongings to Flac, and thence by boat to S.E. port

,, Made prisoners and confined to their hut.

Jan. 15, 1694. Seized by soldiers and put in the *Stombs*.

18, ,, Examined, and put under guard.

Feb. ,, Transported to a rocky islet at entrance of Grand Port.

Mar. 15, ,, Arrival of the Dutch ship, the *Perseverance*.

Oct. ,, Marriage of Governor Diodati. Leguat brought to main land.

Feb 9, 1695. Tremendous hurricane causes a vast amount of damage.

21, ,, Testard brought ashore in irons and placed in the *Stombs*.

Mar. 8, ,, Leguat and Testard sent back to the rocky islet.

,, Fire at Fort Fredrik Hendrik.

,, Arrival of two English ships at North-West Haven.

Jan. 10, 1696. Testard attempts to escape and is drowned.

,, Escape of La Case, and his capture on shore.

,, All the prisoners brought on shore.

Sept. 6, ,, Arrival of the *Suraag*, with orders to take the adventurers to Batavia.

29, ,, Departure from Mauritius.

Dec. 15, ,, Arrival in Batavia. Adventurers put into prison.

16, ,, Examination before the Council.

,, Expedition against Grigriquas by Ensign Schryver.

Feb. 14, 1697. Adventurers detained and enlisted as soldiers.

May 24, ,, Dutch ships wrecked in Table Bay.

Aug. ,, Leguat and companions ordered to prepare for departure to Holland.

Sept. 11, ,, Treaty of Peace, signed at Ryswick, between France, England, Spain, and Holland, ratified by King William at Loo, 15th.

,, Death of the Sieur de la Haye.

Oct. ,, *Placaat* issued by Governor Van der Stel as to trade with Hottentots.

Nov. 28, ,, The Holland fleet of seventeen ships leaves Batavia.

30, ,, Arrival at Bantam.

Dec. 6, ,, Leave Bantam.

17, ,, Leave Straits of Sunda

Jan.   1698. Sight Isle Robben, but driven to sea by a storm.

Feb. 12, ,,   Anchor in Table Bay.

Mar. 8, ,,   Leave Table Bay, homeward bound.

Easter Day,,   Arrival at St. Helena.

Apr. 26, ,,   Leave St. Helena.

May   ,,   Pass near Ascension, do not sight it.
              Pass the Line.

June   ,,   Sight coast of Ireland.
              Off Dungesby Head, Scotland.

June 28, ,,   Arrive at Flushing.

         1701. Le Sieur Luillier's Voyage.

Mar. 8, 1702. Death of King William III ; Accession of Q. Anne.

          ,,   Last elephant killed in Cape flats. Voyage of Macklesfield Frigate.

         1705. Abraham Mommer Van de Velde, Governor of Mauritius.

         1707. Leguat in England dedicates his book to Duke of Kent.

Oct. 7, 1708. Publication of first edition of Leguat's Voyages. Valentyn's visit to the Cape.

         1710. The Dutch evacuate Mauritius.

         1715. Dufresne takes possession of Mauritius for the French.

         1725. Order in Council to occupy Diego Ruys.

         1730. " Relation de l'Ile Rodrigue."

Sept.   1735. Francois Leguat dies in London.

         1760. Pingré at Rodriguez. Kempenfeldt's occupation.

         1763. Admiral Stavorinus at Batavia.

         1769. Bernardin de St. Pierre in the Ile de France.

         1773. M. de Pagés visits the Cape.

         1774. Sonnerat visits the Cape.

         1810. Mauritius and Bourbon captured by the English.

         1814. Bourbon ceded to the French and renamed Ile de la Réunion.

         1843. Wreck of the *Queen Victoria* at Rodriguez.

         1874. Transit of Venus Expedition.

Sep. 11, 1886. Open boat voyage from Rodriguez to Mauritius.

ADDENDA ET CORRIGENDA.

P. 5, note 2, *for* "Andrian VI" *read* "Adrian VI".

P. 6, line 16 and note 2. "*Jean Pagni*, thirty Years old, a Convert and Patrician of *Roan.*" Add to note, "In the above passage is a curious mistranslation. The original text is:—'*Jean Pagni*, âgé de 30 ans, Prosélyte, & Praticien à *Rouen,*' *i.e.*, a Convert and Practitioner (of law) at Rouen."

P. 16, note 1, line 2, *for* "ce font" *read* "ce sont".

P. 21, note 2. *Add,* "Froger and Moore mention the Pelican under this name, saying it is of the size and colour of a Goose. Le Maire describes it as twice as big as a Swan, with a bill a cubit long, and with a craw which lies under its throat like a bag, adding, he swallows fish entire though as large as a middling carp. Cf. Froger's *Voyage au Mer du Sud:* Moore's *Travels into the Inland parts of Africa:* Le Maire's *Voyage to the Canary Isles;* quoted in A new general Collection of Voyages and Travels, by Astley, 1745. Vol. ii, p. 356."

P. 22, note 2. *After* "Eugène Muller", *add* "*op. cit.*, p. 28."

P. 23, note 1. *Add,* "In the Dutch Edition, the taste of the Hollanders has been consulted by substituting for M. Godeau's elegant lines the metrical Dutch version of the well-known verses in the 104th Psalm, beginning at the 24th verse:—' O Lord how manifold are thy works, in wisdom hast thou made them all. . . . . There go the ships, and there is that Leviathan ; whom thou hast made to take his pastime therein.' "

P. 26, note, line 7, *for* "the *Challenger* in 1874" *read* "the *Challenger* touched here in 1874".

Pp. 38-39. Note on *Tramontane, for* "Il ne plus pouvoir", *read* "Il ne plus pouvoit".

P. 39, lines 13, 14. *Add* below, note, "Sweet Odour of Land. M. de Cossigny, who was Governor of the Isle of France in 1791, and (according to Grant) 'a man full of knowledge and philanthropy', states in his *Voyage à Canton* (1799) :—' On approaching the Isle of France, you must keep to windward, because the port, which is frequented by the larger vessels, is to leeward: when the wind is not violent, the air is embalmed with the perfumes of flowers, with which the trees of the island are covered. The same odours are perceived along the island of Ceylon, when the winds blow from the land. This effect was falsely attributed to the cinnamon tree, which forms a part of the forests of this island, as its flowers have a fœtid smell. The effluvia from the land are carried by the winds very far to sea ; and sometimes produce very sudden and unexpected effects. I saw one of this kind, which is not very uncommon. A German soldier, a passenger on board of our vessel, about seven or eight and twenty years old, died suddenly in sight of the little isle of Rodriguez, and about a hundred leagues distant from the Isle of France. He had some slight symptoms of the scurvy, but he was not on the sick-list, nor did he appear to have any unfavourable symptoms.' (Baron Grant's *History of Mauritius*, p. 516.)"

P. 36, line 10, "Idæas of Virgil."[1] *Add* below, in note, "See Virgil's *Æneid*, i, 50 et seq."

P. 45. Quotation ends at "bird" in note 2.

P. 53, line 9, "the Parrots". *Add* note, "In original, 'les Perroquets': *vide infra*, pp. 84, 336, 337, 345."

P. 60. *After* "monsoon", *add* "(more correctly the south-east trade wind)".

P. 65, note 3. *After* "360)." Dele from "But" to "small plum". *Insert* "*Vide* Pref., p. xiv."

P. 66, line 14 from top, "South east monsoon" should *read* "South-east Trade wind". Note 1, *dele* "(*vide* note on p. 65)".

P. 70, note 2. *After* "locality", *add* "(*Vide* Gigantic Land Tortoises, by Dr. A. Günther, p. 2)". *Instead of* "supplementary note", *read* "E, *vide infra*, pp. 376, 377".

P. 77. *After* "See Appendix", *add* "C., p. 352 et seq."

P. 78, note 1, "pour faire le moulinet", *add*, "Sir Walter Scott, when describing the bout with quarter staves between the Miller and Gweth at Ashby-de-la-Zouche, writes: 'The Miller, on the other hand, holding his quarter-staff by the middle, and making it flourish round his head after the fashion which the French call *faire le moulinet*, exclaimed boastfully.'"

P. 79. For "Plate, No. x", *read* "Frontispiece".

P. 80, line 14. "Marriage." *Add* below, note, "*Vide supra*, p. xx."

P. 81, note 3. *After* "*Leguati*", *add* "or *Miserythrus leguati*. Vide *Ency. Brit.*, Art. 'Birds'."

P. 82, note 5. *After* "Part ii" *add* "Appendix B, pp. 326, 329".

P. 104. *After* "in our text", *add* "*Vide* Preface, p. xiv". *Add* "Note 4. '*Vacoa*. This word is not improbably derived from "*Macarequeau*", the French name of the Pandanus, after the Malay name *má-karhi-keyo*.' Vide *Voyage of Pyrard de Laval*, vol. ii, Part II, p. 369 ; Hakluyt edition."

---

[1] P. 36. The famous *Idæas of Virgil* on the storm are expressed in that poet's inimitable description in the 1st Book of the *Æneid*. Virgil represents Neptune as possessed of absolute power over all the waters below the firmament, the *imperium pelagi*, which authority had fallen to his share on the death of Saturn. His elder brother Jupiter ruled over all the powers of the air, and Æolus, the ruler of the storm-clouds, was an inferior deity, whose control of the winds was regulated by fixed meteorological laws (*certo fœdere*), and he lets loose the winds, by striking with his spear the volcanic Stromboli only at the order of Juno, *Jovis et soror et conjux*.

DEDICATION OF THE DUTCH EDITION.

TO HEERE CHRISTIAAN BONGART,

DOCTOR AND ADVOCATE OF CIVIL AND CRIMINAL LAW.

*I*T *is needless to tell one who habitually finds his amusement in the study of books and in its sweet pleasures, that the acquaintance with reliable and truthful travellers and their memoirs brings with it great enjoyment and utility. I make bold to affirm that this knowledge, however much it may be undervalued by the ignorant, will never sink so low in the eyes of those intent on sensible occupations as to be despised; at least not, when with the useful and the agreeable it brings to light facts hitherto unknown, or when it keeps up the attention by curious yet true revelations. However this may be, I flatter myself not to obtrude in respect of either of these points, and take the liberty of dedicating to you this short Voyage, because the discoveries, unimportant as they may seem at first sight, are sure to attract the attention of geographers, and because the perilous yet happy issues of these people who were nearly lost deserve so much attention and pity, that no one will regret the time spent in reading and investigating them. Even should I be wrong in this respect I shall be content to have testified to the world our intimate friendship and the esteem and respect with which I remain,*

Sir,

Your obedient Servant,

W. BROEDELET.

Utrecht, *the* 12*th April* 1708.

TABLE OF CONTENTS FROM DUTCH EDITION.

----

1 " Hitland," in orig.

(PART II.)

Tenth Chapter.

Eleventh Chapter.

Twelfth Chapter.

e

---

[1] *Scheepsraad.*   [2] *Reusvogel.*

[1] Hemelvaarts Eyland.

A New

VOYAGE

TO THE

EAST-INDIES

BY

FRANCIS LEGUAT

AND

His Companions.

Containing their

ADVENTURES In Two Desart Islands,

And an Account of the most Remarkable Things in *Maurice* Island, *Batavia*, at the *Cape* of *Good Hope*, the Island of *St. Helena*, and other Places in their Way to and from the Desart Isles.

Adorn'd with MAPS and FIGURES

LONDON:

Printed for *R. Bonwicke, W. Freeman, Tim. Goodwin, F. Walthoe, M. Wotton, S. Manship, F. Nicholson, B. Tooke, R. Parker, and R. Smith.* MDCCVIII.

To the Most Honourable

HENRY,[1]

MARQUESS OF KENT.

Earl of *Harrold*, and Viscount *Goderich*, Lord Chamberlain
of Her Majesty's Household, Lord Lieutenant of the
County of *Hereford*, and one of the Lords of Her
Majesty's most Honourable Privy Council.

MY LORD,

*T*HE *only Excuse the Translator of this Voyage has to
make Your Lordship, for presuming to put your Name
before it, is that he found it in the Original, and hop'd your
Lordship, who has distinguish'd yourself by your Humanity
and Love of the* Belles lettres, *will be as well pleas'd to see it in
an* English, *as in a* French *Dress. The Original, 'tis true,
has the advantage of being known to more Nations, and the
spreading your Lordship's Fame, was a Justice the Language
of our Enemies ow'd to the many high Qualities that have*

---

[1] Henry Grey, or de Grey, Duke of Kent, succeeded to the title in
1702, and in the third year of Queen Anne was made Lord-Chamberlain of her Household, Lord-Lieutenant of the county of Hereford, and
a Privy-Councillor. In December 1706 he was created Marquis of
Kent, Earl of Harold, and Viscount Goodrich, and in the year 1710,
on resigning his office of Lord-Chamberlain, he was advanced to the
dignity of Duke of Kent. (*The Peerage of England*, 1710, p. 155.)

Nichols, in his *Literary Anecdotes* (iv, 577), mentions that the
Rev. John Laurence dedicated a treatise on the "Usefulness of the
Barometer" to him; and the same author mentions him in connection
with Roger Cotes, professor of astronomy and experimental philosophy
at Cambridge, who was tutor to his sons, Anthony, Earl of Harold, and
Lord Henry de Grey. (*Ibid.*, ii, 127.)—Note by E. Delmar Morgan.

plac'd you in one of the first Posts of the British *Empire, and one of the nearest to Her Majesties Sacred Person and Favour. I cou'd not have forgiv'n my self, if any Foreigner shou'd have shewn more Respect for your Lordship than an* English-man, *or if a Traveller in rude and desolate Islands should be more ambitious of your Protection, than one who has had the honour at other times to frequent the delicious Plains of* Parnassus, *a Region that is immediately under your Lordship's Government, and that has visibly flourish'd, since you have condescended to make it a part of your Care, which is otherwise more nobly employ'd for the Service of the best of Princes, and the best of Countries. Let it be said, my Lord; Notwithstanding our unhappy Divisions,*[1] *against which all your Lordship's moderate Councels have vigorously declar'd, and endeavour'd to unite us all in our Duty to Her Majesty, and Peace among our selves; but Division is so natural to Mankind, that who can hope to see an end of it in his Time? We find the solitary Inhabitants of Rodrigo had their Debates and Disputes; and* 7 *Men united by common Interest, and common Danger, were divided by their Passions.*

May Your Lordship's eminent Worth always meet with the Prosperity it deserves, may it never be wrong'd by Jealousy, nor reach'd by Envy, too Common in this degenerate Age, to the prejudice of the most Heroick Virtue. This my Lord will always be the hearty Prayer of,

Your Lordship's most Humble,

most obedient,

and most Devoted Servant.

[1] This is, apparently, in allusion to the part taken by the Marquess of Kent in the recent Union of the Parliaments of England and Scotland, and to the Tory opposition encountered by the Whig Cabinet of Queen Anne to which he belonged. The Scottish Estates sat for the last time in March 1707, and the Union was effected five months before this dedication was printed.

Maximilian Misson in his preface to the *New Voyage to Italy*,

translated into English by himself, also alludes to the rival factions
of Whigs and Tories, a few years later :—" If the Peace has given any
Calm to our Isles after the bloody Conflicts they have had with our
GREAT neighbour, it has left us involved in such Dissentions and
intestine Animosities that they deprive us of an entire Happiness ; and
these lamentable Misunderstandings seem so to inflame the Minds,
that the most moderate Persons can hardly hinder themselves from
Listing under one of the Banners of this sad Discord.   One is even
look'd upon by the Generality of the People as not being in the
Fashion when he does not take upon himself, and with Warmth too,
one of these factious Names which my Pen declines to set down, of W.
or of T." It may be noticed that Misson here speaks of himself as a
British subject, alluding to "*our* Isles". In a note he explains the
origin of the terms Whig and Tory.

The signature of the anonymous translator is omitted.   In the French
edition the dedicatory epistle bears the signature of François Leguat,
with the date—" Le 7. Octobre, A Londres, 1707." Of course, it
differs considerably from the above wording of the English translator,
who distinctly avows himself to be an Englishman.   In the French
edition the author requests that His Highness will be pleased to grant
his generous and powerful protection in the most flourishing Island of
the world, where good Providence has happily led him, and where,
he adds, he shall never cease to offer his wishes for His Highness'
abundant and eternal prosperity, etc.   It has not been considered
necessary to give this letter *in extenso.*   The arms, crest, supporters,
motto, and heraldic insignia of the Marquess are figured in the French
but not in the English version.

THE

AUTHOR'S PREFACE.[1]

L ET who will say what they please against *Prefaces*, for
my part I always read them with Profit. To deprive
one's self of so necessary a Thing, is to leave off a good
fashion at the peril of Reason and Instruction; He that
exposes a Work to the Multitude, brings himself into such
great Danger, let his Design be ever so just, and the execution of it ever so perfect, that in Prudence he ought to
neglect nothing to prepare the minds of his Readers, and
prevent the ill-effects of Ignorance and Malice; But if the
Author do's this for his own Advantage, the Readers also in
my Opinion benefit by it; for by this he smooths the way
for them. He enlightens them, and makes several things
easy, in which otherwise they would find a great deal of
Difficulty. Be it as it will, I beg the favour of you,
courteous and just Reader, to suffer me to Discourse with
you a little before you turn to the Relation of my Adventures, which I am about to present to you.

When the Companions of my Fortune and my self embark'd aboard our Ship the "*Swallow*" at *Amsterdam*,
abundance of our Friends attended us to the Water-side,
and when they took their leave of us, they cry'd as long as
they could see us; "*Pray let us hear from you, send us all
the News you can, and fill your Letters with the particular
Circumstances of your Adventures.*" From that very Minute

---

[1] According to M. Eyriès, the actual editor and author of Leguat's
narrative was an ex-Benedictine monk named Gabillon. *See* note,
p. lxxxviii, and introduction.

I form'd to myself the design of giving them Satisfaction. But you will find when you have read my History, that my Design could not be executed. After my return, I could neither refuse them the demand they made of seeing my Journal, nor excuse my self from answering a hundred Questions they ask'd concerning things which I had not inserted in it, but which were, however, still in my Memory. I have met no Body ever since who has not been very Inquisitive, and I have endeavour'd to satisfie the curiosity of my Friends to the utmost of my Power. Tho' if I may be so free, I have met with Persons who have been so Importunate, that they became troublesome with their Inquiries.

To save my self answering an infinite number of Questions, and being continually teaz'd by the like importunity, it one day came into my mind that the best way to do it would be to write down a Relation of my Voyage and Adventures, and to shew it to those of my Friends and Acquaintance who desir'd to see it. Accordingly I wrote these *Memoirs*, they were presently seen in the World, and I fancy'd I saw in the looks of those that had read them, when they return'd them, an air of Content, which I took for a very good Omen, and was pleas'd with it. I perceiv'd they interested themselves in every thing that had happen'd to Me, and some of them went so far as to say, ' *Print them,*[1] *fear nothing, the Book will be very Entertaining: A Man shou'd be Modest, but not a Coward. There is something in them very extraordinary and singular, with which all the World will be pleas'd. Take your Friends words for it, and publish them.*' Thus did they perswade me. To which they added one thing that weigh'd very much with me, and help'd to overcome the repugnance I had to Print them; which was their naming to me a great number of false Voyages, and some of them ill-enough related, which, however, went

---

[1] "*Some said, 'John, print it!' others said 'Not so.'*
Some said, 'It might do good,' others said, 'No!'"
(John Bunyan's *Apology*, 1670.)

off. Indeed, said I to my self, there's such a one, and such a one (I can scarce forbear naming fifteen or twenty), such a one, and such a one, have had the Impudence to impose on the Publick, and their ridiculous Falsities have been very well receiv'd. Why therefore is it not lawful for an honest Man to tell things which are true, and of which some use may be made. Wretched Romances, and ill-contriv'd Fables, find a Vent; why may not my true Romance have as favourable a fate?

I expect the Critical Reader shou'd say here, " there's a manner of expressing things": A Story well told, is read with Pleasure, tho' 'tis even a little Romantick or Trivial in its self. People are now more earnest than ever for perfection of Language. As for Example, the little *Nothings* of the Abbot of Choisy[1] in the *Voyage* to *Siam*, have an incomparable Grace in them, and please much more than many other things made of more precious Materials. *" We cast Anchor."   " We made ready to Sail."   " The Wind took Courage."   " Robin is dead."   " We said Mass."   " We Vomited."* Tho' they are poor Words any where else, yet in his Book, which is half compos'd of them, they are Sentences, and the worth of them is not to be told. His Phrases are so fine, so pretty, that we should be more in love with them, than with Discoveries. And what then can you hope for, you a Country Gentleman who relate your Affairs *grosso modo*, and speak plainly without gloss or disguise, what you have seen, or what you have heard: You are in the wrong to imagine your History, tho' true, singular, nay even moral, and as political as you please, can enter into Comparison with a Book that is well Written.

[1] *Journal du Voyage de Siam fait en* 1685-86 (*M. l'Abbé Choisy*), par M. L. D. C. 4to. Paris, 1687. Leguat here writes ironically, but his sarcasm is not undeserved ; for instance, the " Robin " here referred to is a sheep—" un mouton fameux entre les moutons "—and more than a page is occupied in telling how he was cooked, eaten, and discussed at table.

I own all this, I am no Polite Author, nor indeed any at
all.   Neither did I ever believe I cou'd ever set up for one,
till I was as it were forc'd to give way to Importunity, which
lasted five or six years.   'Tis true, and most true, that I am
very far from having the Abbot *Choisy's* rare Talent.   His
Delicacy is without doubt extream.   He writes politely,
and the fine simplicity of his, *"Easter* approaches": *"His
Calm quite flat." "I see nothing but Water." "The same
Song." "To tell you nothing is a new Ragou,"* which pleases
and Charms, tho' I must indeed own, I have not been able
to relish it.   Perhaps it may be too high season'd for me.
Simple and naked Truth, and the singularity of our
Adventures, are the Body and Soul of my Relation.   But
since the Prince of *Roman* Eloquence[1] has commended *Cæsar*
(or the Author of his Commentaries) for writing without
Artifices or Ornament, I hope I shall also find Men of a
moderate Taste, who without lessening the extraordinary
value of the Abbot of *Choisy's* admirable Simplicity, will
readily bear with mine tho' Common.

   There's deceit in this Simplicity, so very simple ; and 'tis
very well known the Inhabitants of the *Republick* of letters,
as well as those of the *Friperie,*[2] make use of several sorts of
Lights[3]: I know also that a *Latin* Cloak is as Convenient as
Venerable, and often proves a great help to such as have
nothing to say, and yet would raise Admiration ; and that
the politeness of a gay gallant Stile, and the Convenience of
Rimes are a good cover for many Authors : *Juvenal* and
Boileau are in the Right to rail at whom they please, as long

   [1] This Prince of Roman eloquence was Cicero, who wrote as follows:
" Cæsar has likewise some commentaries or short memoirs of his own
transactions, and such as merit the highest approbation ; for they are
simple, correct, and elegant, and divested of all the ornaments of
language, so as to appear (if 1 may be allowed the expression) in a kind
of undress." (Cicero, *in Bruto*, c. 74.)
   [2] " A Place in Paris where Second-hand and other Cloaths are sold."
   [3] In orig. : " lustres," *i.e.*, glass or polish.

as they rail in Verse; and the most Scoundrel *Rimers* find also their Account in their Songs and Lampoons. If my Voyage was written in *Hebrew*, I am very well assur'd it wou'd at least succeed as well as that of *Rabbi Benjamin*[1] And if it was only in *Latin* interlarded with *Greek, à la Montfauconne*,[2] with a word or two of *Arabick* to relish it a little, I should without doubt have at least Admirers, if I wanted *Readers*. For who with impunity, and even with Success, would publish a hundred useless sorts of insipid Literature, a hundred Copies of things that have been said again and again by others, a hundred Lyes and Invectives? if they had not been in *Latin*, or in *Verse*, they wou'd never have gone off as they did.

There's a certain Reverend Father[3] of our Acquaintance whose Book is full of Faults, of things ill Chosen, of shocking Repetitions, of Trifles, of Pedantick Insolence, of Injurious and ill-grounded Contradictions; but then 'tis all in *Latin*. This Learned Doctor endeavours to give the World a Relation of his Voyage, in imitation of Father *Mabillon*,[4] whose Scholar he is; and whose Novelty consisting

[1] Rabbi Benjamin, the son of Jonas of Tudela. Travels through Europe, Asia, from Spain to China, 1160-73. From the Latin of Montanus; *vide* Purchas' *Pilgrimes*, vol. ii.

[2] Dom. Bernard de Montfaucon, a distinguished *savant* and Greek scholar, who after taking part in two campaigns under Turenne became a monk of Saint-Benoît at Toulouse in 1675. He died, aged 87 years, in 1741.

[3] According to Bernard this author was Casimir Freschot, the anonymous author of *Remarques Historiques et Critiques, etc.*, but the context further on appears to refer to Mabillon or Montfaucon.

[4] Jean Mabillon was a learned writer and Benedictine monk of the Congregation of St. Maur, born in 1632, a few years senior therefore to Leguat. Mabillon visited the principal Libraries of Italy in 1685 with Michel Germain, and brought back 3,000 volumes and manuscripts for the King's Library. He published an account of his travels, and published the *Musæum Italicum* and many works of deep research. He died, aged 75 years, in 1707. (Weiss, *Biographie Universelle*.)

wholly in Catalogues of *Bulls* and *Decretals*, and of other
Species of base allays, which have been a hundred times
examined, and a hundred times confuted with a Manuscript
of poor *Vacca*,[1] which till now was despis'd by every Body:
What cou'd he do? He cou'd write tolerably in *Latin*, add
Rhapsodies to his Trifles, and give them a *Latin* Pass-port,
and a *Latin* Dress.

But had he not done better if he had written in his own
Tongue, Judiciously, Civilly, Wisely, and Briefly? Or
rather if he had not written at all. What had the *Turba
Eruditorum*,[2] which he explains so ill, and yet with so much
Pomp and Variety, to do with his Journal? There's but
very little in it that deserves to be publish'd; and that that

---

[1] "I have borrowed much, and that not contemptible, from Writers I
lighted on, that have not been made publick, the chiefest whereof is
Flaminius Vacca, a *Roman* Carver. This Man collected many Obser-
vations of his own and Friends on *Roman* Monuments found in his
Time, and before it, and presented them to Anastasius Simonetta of
Perugino, who was compiling a very accurate Work of the *Roman*
Antiquities.

"*Flaminius*' Observations being in no Order, but intermixed as they
happened to occur . . . . I thought fit to translate his Papers. . .
Flaminius was a noble *Roman* Carver, whose Skill is visible in many
Works to be seen in *Roman* Churches and Homes. He flourish'd in the
sixteenth Century and seems to have lived to the seventeenth. His
Tomb is to be seen in the Church of *Santa Maria Rotunda*." (*The
Travels of the learned Father Montfaucon from Paris thro' Italy*, 1698.
Made English. London, 1712, p. 111.)

[2] "This is the place where I design'd to entertain my Reader for some
Time, with certain Passages of the Relation that *D. Bernard de Mont-
faucon* (a Benedictine Monk) has published of his Travels in Italy,
under the Title of *Diarium*, etc. But since he makes a Show of a
Dissertation, with a Sort of Ostentation to the Eyes of the *Turba
Eruditorum*, whom he pretends to inform, after a decisive Manner,
concerning the famous Manuscript which is kept so preciously in the
Treasury of *St. Mark*." (Max. Misson, Pref., *Voyage to Italy*.)

". . . And as I have formerly applied myself with Care to search
after those things which have been the Occasion of his Publishing a
Volume by the Title of *Palæographia Græca*, etc. . . ." (*Ibid.*)

is, may be found in Mess. *Trevoux*[1] and elsewhere. Who is concern'd in his *German* Quarrel,[2] and his Chimerical Triumph about *St. Mark's* Gospel,[3] being written in *Latin* with the Apostles own Hand. If this Fantastick Monk had told his Reasons modestly; if he had not with as much Rudeness as Injustice, offended those who never thought anything of him, good or ill, and who are in a condition to Chastize when they think fit, he had been more Excusable.

As for Me then, I write in *French*,[4] and in plain *French*, not aspiring to any higher degree of beauty of Stile, than what is necessary to be understood, nor to any Supernatural Language. I must desire the Reader to remember, that it

---

[1] " Without retracting what I have just now said of the *Journal of Trevoux*, the *Reverend Fathers* that compose it, will give me Leave to make some Reflections here upon their Article of Tome IV. . . . . This Journal is now (1714) made at Paris by some learned Jesuites under the Title of *Histoire des Sciences & des beaux Arts.*" (Maximilien Misson's Preface to fourth edition, *New Voyage to Italy.*)

[2] Mabillon's Quérelle d'Allemande—his dispute with Père Germain as to the rules of criticism as applied to the authenticity of manuscript characters may perhaps here be alluded to.

[3] " Hence we proceeded to see the Manuscript of the Gospel of *St. Mark*, which is kept in a Cupboard hard by, and we viewed it to Content with D. *Leith* or *Galterius*, the Library Keeper. . . . The characters, tho' scarce legible, are infallibly *Latin*. . . . It is generally said to be *St. Mark's* writing. I do not remember to have ever seen any Manuscript that seems to be of greater Antiquity than this. But that this Book is writ in *Latin* is plainly made out by the story I shall now relate. . . . The letter of Emperor Charles the IVth will inform you that he received from the Patriarchal Church of *Aquileia* two Quires of the Holy Gospel of *St. Mark*, written with his own Hand, which are in this Cathedral." . . . (Montfaucon's *Journey through Italy*, pp. 73-75.)

[4] " As for their Quotations from the *Greek* and *Latin* Poets, which several offer to introduce in great Numbers, into their Writings, there are but very few of them to be found in these *Letters.*" (M. Misson, *l. c.*)

" As I am far from having a perfect Knowledge of the *English* Tongue. . . ." (*Ibid.*)

f

cannot be expected that a Desart Island should furnish me
with such ample Matter, as Travellers commonly meet with
in the inhabited Countries which they Visit. I found
neither Cities nor Temples, nor Palaces, nor Cabinets of
Rarities, nor Antique Monuments, nor Academies, nor Libraries, nor People, on whose Religion, Language, Government, Manners and Customs, I might make Observations.
I have said already, and I say it again, that all that can
make this small Treatise, which I have been encourag'd to
present you with, any way valuable, is in the first place, the
particularity and variety of the Facts and Adventures. To
dwell two years in a Desart; to be sav'd by a Miracle; to
fall from *Charybdis upon Scylla*,[1] as the ancient Proverb
says; to suffer a thousand Miseries for three years together
on a dry Rock, by an unheard of Persecution; to be deliver'd
contrary to Appearance and Hope, and with such strange
Circumstances, must certainly have something very Singular
in it. What is Secondly valuable in this Relation, is the
pure and simple truth of all I have related. It never
enter'd into my Thoughts to adorn my History, to exaggerate any thing at the expence of that Truth, which I have
always Respected. And I will add for your Satisfaction,
that there are living[2] Witnesses of every thing I have reported. Among the things which those that have Travell'd
last in the Countries that are known and describ'd, report,
'tis unavoidable but there must be something which the
first Travellers make no mention of; Be it as it will with
respect to my self, when I talk of the Cape of *Good Hope*,
Batavia, and other Places treated of in other Voyages, I
speak of those things that I thought worth observing, without troubling myself whether others have made any mention

---

[1] "*Incidis in Scyllam cupiens vitare Charybdim*" (*Alexandreis*, lib. v,
301, by Philippe Gaultier. 13th century.)

[2] In orig.: "deux Témoins," *i.e.*, MM. Paul Bénelle, at Amsterdam,
and Jacques de La Case, in America. (*Vide ante*, p. xxxiii, *et post*,
p. 392.)

of them before me or not.[1] If on those occasions I make
some Remarks which have not entirely the grace of Novelty,
it will be some amends for that Deficiency, that they will
doubtless be accompany'd with new Circumstances: For
when did it happen that Men who are not *Copyists*, but Eye-
witnesses and Judges of things, spoke of the same Subject
in the same manner?

I shall conclude with making some Reflection on three
Difficulties that have been started to me. For, Dear Reader,
I will dissemble nothing with you, nor neglect anything to
satisfie you.

I. 'Tis said I have too many Digressions.

Upon this I desire you to consider two things, I confess
that in writing these *Memoirs*, the same thought came often
into my Head, as it did in the Abbot of *Choisy's*, of whom
we have more than once spoken. *I am sorry* (says he from
time to time) *that the Matter did not present it self as I would
have had it—I give what I have—I wish I had something
more pleasant to tell you.* The truth is, I frequently find my
self in the same case; My Desart Islands did not furnish me
with variety enough, and I confess I was sometimes oblig'd
to go a little out of the way for it.

Nevertheless if you do me Justice, I hope you will
approve of the second Answer that I have to make. The
true character of a good Relation, in my Opinion consists in
containing the Remarkable things which the Traveller saw
or heard, or which happen'd to him, and in such a manner,
that the Reader may be as well inform'd of it, as if he had
Travell'd himself, and had been an Eye-Witness of all that
had happen'd. Granting this to be true, the Traveller ought
to Communicate every thing that came to his Knowledge;
his Conversations, Discourses, Adventures, Reflections, pro-

---

[1] For example, Leguat follows very closely Dapper's previous description of the Hottentots. (*Vide infra*, p. 289.)

vided they have so much relation to the Voyage, that they cou'd not be learnt without it. On the contrary, the best and most agreeable thought will come in very *Mal à propos*, in a Relation of this Nature, if 'tis not, as one may say born in the Voyage, and do's not properly and independently belong to it. Pursuant to this Idea, I might report at length, and keep still in my character of a Traveller, all the long Discourse upon the Subject of Women: All that is taken out of the *Golden Sentences*, all that is said on the Rights of Mankind, and almost every thing else which I have spoken of, that seems to go from the Subject.

II. Some advis'd me to put my Name to those *Memoirs* and others were of Opinion that I shou'd not do it. The latter grounded theirs on a Principle of Humility or Modesty, as the thing explains it self: And the former pretend that every Man who affirms Fact, is obliged to make himself known.

I am entirely of their Sentiments. I believe that whoever speaks as a Witness, ought, as we say in *French*, to decline[1] his Name, and to omit nothing that may serve to convince the Reader of his Candour, and the most exact truth of all he says. As to my self in particular, I own I never had any Opinion at all of a Voyage, without the Authors Name to it; nor even of the Relation of a Voyager of an indifferent Reputation, tho' he puts his Name to his Work, if he do's not also produce Witnesses, especially if he comes from a far Country. Who do's not know the Disposition of all Men? A Traveller of an ordinary Character for Fidelity, and one who has no Witnesses to prove what he affirms to be true, is under a great Temptation when he conceals his Name to lace his History a little, to render it the more agreeable. And we have so many proofs of this Truth, that no body can doubt of its being true.

---

[1] In orig. : " décliner," *i.e.*, to state.

I therefore conclude again, that those who tell the World any thing that is Rare, and that they saw in very remote Countries, are under an indispensable necessity to let the Publick know clearly, and distinctly who they are, and even to insinuate without Affectation, all the Particularities which are proper to acquire Credit. From whence it naturally follows, that the Authors of Relations which have no Name to them, are almost always Rogues and Cheats who impose on the Publick, and generally propose some base end to themselves by it.

Such a one most certainly is the Author[1] of a Wretched Book that appeared two years agoe, under the Title of *Historical and Critical Remarks, made in a Journal from Italy to Holland, in the year* 1704. *Containing the Manners of Carniola.* This Impudent Anonymous Author, whom we know, and who forg'd his Collection of Fables according to his common Practice, had no other view, besides a little vile and shameful Profit; but to insult against all the rules of Justice, a Person[2] whom he ought to Honour, and one who has spar'd him too long; 'tis fit sometimes that certain Rascalls should have a mark set upon them, and that the World should know their Villainous Tricks, of which there are very few Persons that wou'd be sensible, if they were not told them.[3]

III. It has also been said to me, when I was once like to die of a cruel Scurvy, at another time persecuted by an Army of Rats; when I have been expos'd to the fury of the Tempests and Hurricanes, or have been the Sport of a little Tyrant; ' Why did you engage yourself in such an Enterprise ? did not you know that there is nothing more uncertain, nor

---

1 Casimir Freschot. (*Vide supra*, p. xxviii.)
2 Max. Misson. (*Vide supra*, pp. xxviii, xxxi.)
3 The whole of this paragraph betrays the hand of Misson.

more difficult, than Settlements in the New World, notwithstanding the fine Colours in which the particular Interests of some Persons will have them Painted ? Cou'd you be ignorant of the great Labour, and the great Danger that attend the execution of such Projects as these ?'

In a word, My Reason was this : After having been forc'd to leave my Native Country, with so many Thousands of my Brethren, to abandon my small Inheritance, and to forsake for ever, according to all outward appearance, those Persons that were dear to me, without finding in the New Country, to which I first Transported my self, that sufficient Relief which my present Necessity demanded, I gave my self up entirely to Providence, and determin'd humbly and patiently to make use of the Means that offer'd for me, perhaps to preserve my Life. Weary of the bustle of the World, and fatigu'd with the Troubles I had endur'd in it, I quitted Variety and Tumult without any regret, and at an Age already advanc'd beyond its Prime, I thought I wou'd endeavour to live in a Place where I might be free from the common and frequent Dangers to which I was expos'd. I had nothing to lose, and therefore risk'd nothing, tho' I had a great deal to hope, at least that I might find that delicious Repose which I never knew ; but for the two years that I remain'd in the Desart Island, where I had without doubt finish'd my Course, if the wicked man[1] who carry'd us thither had not betray'd us, and ruin'd the Design that had been form'd in Holland.

After all, I breath'd an admirable Air there, without the least alteration of my Health. I liv'd like a Prince at ease, and in abundance without Bread, and without Servants. I had there been Rich without Diamonds, and without Gold as well as without Ambition. I had tasted a secret and

---

[1] Captain Valleau.

exquisite Pleasure, and content in being deliver'd from an
infinity of Temptations to Sin, to which Men are liable in
other Places. Collected in my self, I had seen there by
serious Reflection, as plain as if it was within reach of my
Hand or Eye; what *Nothings* the Inhabitants of this
wretched World admire; of this World, I say, where Art
almost always destroys[1] Nature under pretence of adorning
it; Where Artifice worse than Art, Hypocrisy, Fraud,
Superstition and Rapine exercise a Tyrannical Empire over
Mankind; where in short, every thing is Error, Vanity,
Disorder, Corruption, Malice and Misery.[2]

I cannot help adding here by way of Advance, that whatever inconveniences might have attended a longer stay in
this Island, I had never left it, had I not been forc'd to do
it: And nothing but the boisterous Humour, the wild
Precipitation, and the rash attempt of Seven, in *that*,
Inconsiderate young Men, cou'd have constrain'd me to have
abandon'd that sweet Abode.

What do I say,—No, 'twas not Man but Providence that
conducted me thither, and that brought me thence. 'Twas

---

[1] " Too nicely Jonson knew the critic's part,
        Nature in him was almost lost in Art." (*W. Collins,* 1750.)

[2] " These few lines suffice, we believe," writes M. Eugène Muller,
" to characterise the author and the principal hero of the narrative
about to be related. We here recognise one of those pure but rigid
individualities which have so often been engendered by the pious spirit
of enquiry amidst the fires of intolerant persecution." " François
Leguat personifies in all his austerity, imposing yet simple, those
puritans of France, who, obliged by conviction to profess the primitive
faith, openly repudiate with energy all practices both civil and
religious, which according to their ideas are incompatible with ancient
Christian simplicity. Absolutely humble before God, and full of
charity towards their neighbours, they do not regard as vain the
examples of putting away all vanities given by the Divine Saviour;
but freed by the renouncement of the world, they obtain from the
divine revelation the great precept of human equality. A strange
and bizarre type, and we cannot help adding, not without a semblance
of the ridiculous."

Providence that conducted me safely thro' so many Dangers, and has happily transported me from my Desart Isles, to this vast Powerful and Glorious Island of *Great Britain*, where the charity of the Generous Inhabitants has held out its Hand to me, and fix'd my Repose as much as it can be fix'd in this lower World.[1]

---

[1] This preface, according to Jacques Bernard, the successor of Bayle, was not written by Leguat, but by Maximilien Misson. See Introduction and Notice by M. Th. Sauzier therein quoted.

Frédéric Auguste Gabillon, to whom President Bouhier (quoted by M. Eyriès) attributes this volume, was born at Paris in the 17th century. After completing his studies, he joined the religious order of the *Théatins*, but soon repenting of the sacrifice of his liberty, he left their convent and fled to Holland, where he shortly after openly abjured his vows and professed the reformed religion. Being without resources, he worked at compilations for booksellers, but getting into debt, he went over to England, and took the name of Jean Léclerc, a well-known publicist of Holland, thereby imposing on various persons of distinction. The end of the adventurer's career is not very certain according to Moréri's Dictionary. It is, therefore, possible that this refugee was employed by Leguat as an amanuensis or copyist, but there is little doubt that M. Bernard was right, and the President Bouhier wrong in his surmise. Let the reader only compare Leguat's preface with that of Misson's *New Voyage to Italy* (fourth edition), and he cannot fail to be convinced of the identity of the original author. Take, for instance, the first paragraph as to the uses of Prefaces in general. Misson begins:—" Joseph Pamelius, an Ingenious Man, has composed some Dialogues, in one of which he declaims mightily against* Prefaces in general ; but particularly against those who make 'em. . . . . ." This opening, the tirade against false Voyages, and his excuses for publishing his book, have a most wonderful similarity of language and reasoning with the earlier portions of the preface to Leguat's book.

---

* That is to say : *Prefaces are useless to those only who never read 'em ; and are resolv'd to stand fast in their Reproaches and Prejudices. It is in vain to speak to the Deaf or write to the Blind.*

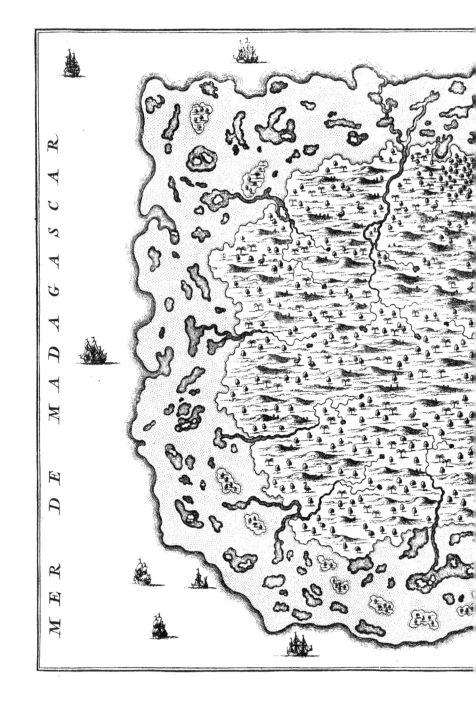

MER DE MADAGASCAR

CARTE de L'ISLE

de *DIEGO-RUYS*, ou *DIEGO-RODRIGO*,
Découverte par les Portugais,
sous le Roi IEAN IV. *l'an* 1645.
Et depuis habitée pendant l'espace de deux
Ans & 20 jours,
par FRANÇOIS LEGUAT, PAUL BE...LE,
IAQ. DE LA CASE, IEAN TESTARD, ISAAC BOYER,
IEAN DE LA HAYE, ROBERT ANSELIN, & PI.
THOMAS, *François Protestans, Fugitifs pour*
leur RELIGION. *Ils y arriverent le* 30 *Avr.* 1691.
Et en repartirent le 20 *May* 1693.

VOYAGE AND ADVENTURES

OF

FRANCIS LEGUAT,

A GENTLEMAN OF BRESSE.[1]

THE State of the Affairs of Religion in *France*, obliging me to seek after some means to leave the Kingdom, I made use of that which Providence furnish'd me with, to pass into *Holland*, where I arriv'd the 6th of *August* 1689.

I had scarce begun to taste the Sweetness of that precious Liberty, which I found in my abode there, and which I had been depriv'd of four whole years, ever since the Revocation of the Edict of *Nants*[2] in 1685, when I understood that the

---

[1] François Leguat, of the Province of Bourgogne, brought up in the Province of Bresse, a small district now represented by the department of Ain.

[2] The Edict of Nantes, which put a temporary end to the religious struggles in France, and assured liberty of belief and safety in worship to the Calvinists, was decreed in 1598.

Louis XIV, under the influence of Madame de Maintenon, having determined for political reasons to re-establish the unity of the Catholic religion throughout his dominions, proceeded by all the means in his power, moral and physical, by cruel persecution, and especially by what were known as *dragonnades*, to enforce his arbitrary acts of despotism ; and finally revoked the Edict of Nantes, eighty-seven years after its original promulgation.

In spite of rigorous prohibitions against emigration, numerous Protestants followed their pastors into exile, and sought in other countries that freedom of conscience denied to them at home. It has been calculated that at least some three hundred thousand Huguenots passed across the frontiers and left France, so that some provinces were deprived of nearly a third of their inhabitants, and many French industries were seriously injured.

Holland, England, and Prussia were the countries which were most benefited by this wholesale emigration, and in fact, at London, a whole suburb (Spitalfields) was peopled by the foreign weavers; whilst at

Marquis *du Quesne*[1] was by the good Pleasure, and under the
Protection of my Lords the *States General,* and Messieurs the
Directors of the *East India* Company, making Preparations
for a Settlement in the Island of *Mascaregne.* To this Purpose two great Ships were equipp'd at *Amsterdam, aboard*
which all the French Protestants, who were willing to be of
this Colony, were receiv'd *gratis.* The Description of this
Island,[2] which was made publick at that time, and the name

Berlin several industries were first established by the Protestant fugi-
tives. More than twelve thousand soldiers and six hundred officers
carried to foreign flags an implacable resentment and sentiments of
vengeance against their mother-country.

[1] " Henry and Abraham, the two sons of the great Duquesne, both
Protestants like their father, the most remarkable of naval commanders
in France during the seventeenth century; and, having already distinguished themselves under his command, they were, like him, excepted
from the rigours of the law pronounced against their co-religionists at
the time of the Revocation of the Edict of Nantes. On the death of
their father, in 1688, being given to understand that they would be
subjected to persecution, they quitted France. Anticipating the
persecutions to which the Calvinists would be subjected, and uneasy as
regards the future of his children, he resolved to prepare a safe refuge
for them by purchasing the property of Aubonne, near Berne, of which
municipality the burgesses granted him the freedom. On hearing of
this, Louis XIV asked him his reason for so doing. " Sire," said he,
" I have been desirous of securing a property of which I cannot be
deprived by the will of a master." It was to this estate of Aubonne
that his sons retired ; but, previous to his death, he made them swear
that, whatever happened, they should never take up arms against
France : an oath which they scrupulously kept. Henri Duquesne, the
elder of the two brothers, promoter of the expedition which Leguat
here mentions, and which was rendered abortive, never more went to sea,
but gave himself up entirely to theological studies, and, in 1718, he
published a volume, entitled *Réflexions sur l'Eucharistie.* The nephew
Duquesne Guiton, with a Dutch squadron, made an expedition to the East
Indies, of which the journal was published in 1721." (*Eugène Muller.*)

[2] *Recueil de Quelques Mémoires servans d'Instruction pour l'Etablisse-
ment de l'Isle d'Eden. A Amsterdam.* M.DC.LXXXIX. (*See* Introduction,
and Appendix at end of volume.) M. Muller believed all trace of
this rare document had been lost ; he has since found a copy in the
Library of the Arsenal, and another copy has lately been reprinted by
M. Sauzier.

of *Eden*[1] that was given it on account of its Excellency, made me conceive so good an Opinion of it that I was tempted to give it a Visit, resolving to end my Days there in Peace, and out of the Care and Confusion of the World, if I found 'twas but in some measure so Pleasant and Commodious as 'twas describ'd to be.

'Twas so easie for a Man to enter himself in this Colony; and the Idea I had of the Quiet and Pleasure I hop'd to enjoy in this lovely Island was such, that I got over all the Obstacles which lay in my way. I offer'd myself to the Gentlemen who were concerned in the Enterprize. They receiv'd me very favourably, and honour'd me with the Post,

---

[1] The island in the Indian Ocean, now known as *Reunion*, the largest of the Mascarene Islands, was first named *St. Appollonia* as early as 1527. It was subsequently called *England's Forest* by the British, and *Mascaregne* by the French in 1613. In 1630 we find it written of as *Ile de la Perle*. M. de Flacourt gave it the name of *Bourbon* in 1649, since which date various names have at different times been applied to it, such as *Eden*, as in the narrative of M. du Quesne ; *Ile Bonaparte*, under the first Republic and Empire ; and finally the present name, *Réunion*.

On the return of M. de la Haye, the viceroy of the Indies, to France, in 1674-75, he advised the French king to send out an expedition with proper officials to take possession of the Island of Bourbon, as it was then called. Accordingly, M. de Vauboulon was despatched there by the Government with a suitable escort, and appointed Governor for the King and the Company (*French East Indian Company*), and Chief Justice of the Island of Bourbon.

M. de Vauboulon took with him a certain Capuchin monk of Quimper, as chaplain, and appointed him Cure of St. Paul. Whether Governor de Vauboulon abused the powers confided in him or not does not clearly appear from the records, but, judging from the conduct of the Dutch Governor of the neighbouring island, the probabilities are that he did ; for, anyhow, a revolution took place on the 20th December 1690, when the rebels, headed by Pere Hyacinthe, the Capuchin, deposed M. de Vauboulon, and kept him in prison until he died in confinement at St. Denis, in August 1692, the Sieur Firelin being installed as Commissioner for the Company by the Cure, who, having accomplished his *coup d'état*, retired to his parish at St. Paul.

or rather Name, of Major of the biggest of the two Ships, which was call'd *La Droite*.

All Things necessary being aboard, and the Masters ready to set sail, waiting only for a fair Wind, we understood that the French King, who had formerly taken Possession of this Isle, had sent a Squadron of seven Men of War that way. The Uncertainty we were in of the Design of that little Fleet, and a just Fear grounded on some advices lately come from *France*, were such powerful Motives with Mr. *du Quesne*,[1] that he disarm'd the two Ships, and disembark'd the Goods and Necessaries, being afraid to expose so many poor Wretches, who were already miserable enough, to Danger ; the greatest part of them being Women, and other Persons who cou'd not defend themselves.   But that he might fully inform himself of the Design of that Squadron, if there was such a one, he resolv'd to set out a little Frigat, and send her away upon Discovery.   Some Persons were chosen to go aboard her, and they had Orders given them concerning the design of the *Voyage :* The substance of which was :

1. To visit the Islands that lie in the Way to the *Cape of good Hope ;* particularly, those of *Martin Vas,* and *Tristan.*

2. Afterwards to pass the *Cape of good Hope,* to learn, if it was possible, more certain News of the Isle of *Eden,* and the Design of the French Squadron, which was said to be at Sea.

3. To take Possession of the Isle of *Mascaregne,* in the Name of the said Marquis, who was authoriz'd to enter upon it, in case there were no *French* there.

4. If it cou'd be done without running any considerable Risk, to proceed as far as the Island of *Diego Ruys,* which the French call *Rodrigue.*

---

[1] The great Duquesne had made his children swear not to take up arms against France, and, therefore, his son wished to prevent the possibility of any aggressive action on the part of the Dutch vessels.

5. If that Island was found to be sufficiently provided
with Things necessary for Settlement, and the Sub-
sistance of those that would live there, then to take
Possession of it, in the Name of the said Marquis.

6. To send the Ship back, after unloading the Things that
were for the use of the Colony, that intended to
settle in this new World.

7. And lastly, to take an exact Account of the Isle, where
those that were left behind staid in expectation of
the rest of the Colony, who were to come after, in
two Years Time at Farthest, and then to possess
themselves of the Isle of *Eden*, under the Protection,
and by the Assistance of *Messieurs* of the Company.

This Project[1] being thus form'd, all Hands were set to
work to forward the Execution of it; and 'twas done with
so much Warmth and Expedition, that the Ship was soon
ready to put to Sea. Care was taken to provide every
Thing necessary for such an Enterprise; and the Vessel was
so little, and so good a Sailer, that she was nam'd the
Swallow. Her Flag had Mons. *du Quesne's* Arms in it, with
this Device, "*Libertas sine Licentia*"; which was us'd by
that wise Pope Adrian VI.[2] Our little Frigate was mounted
with six Guns, and had ten Seamen, commanded by *Anthony
Valleau*, of the Isle of *Rhe*. When 'twas ready to sail,
several of the Passengers, whose Names had been enroll'd
for this Service, shrunk back and chang'd their Opinion;
which was the occasion of the small Number that embark'd;
for the first Complement that design'd to go in her were five

[1] This project is fully described in despatches in the Cape archives.

[2] "They never fail at *Utrecht*, to shew Strangers the House of Pope
Andrian VI, Son of one nam'd *Florent Boyen*, a Brewer in that City;
and I think, the best Man that ever bore the Name of Pope. . . . . .
However, though *Adrian* oppos'd *Luther*, several Bigots of that *Catho-
lick* Religion believ'd they had found out that he favour'd him."—
(Maximilian Misson, *New Voyage to Italy*, vol. i, pp. 66-67). Hadrianus VI, died 1523.

and twenty. The Ten who continu'd in their Resolution to the last were:

Paul Be—le,[1] twenty Years old, a Merchant's son of *Metz*.

Jacques de la Case, thirty Years old, a Merchant's Son of *Nerac*, who had been an Officer in the Elector of *Brandenburgh's* Army.

Jean Testard, a Druggist, twenty-six Years old, a Merchant's Son of *St. Quintin* in *Picardy*.

Isaac Boyer, a Merchant, about twenty-seven Years old, Son of an Apothecary near *Nerac*.

Jean de la Haye, a Silversmith of Roan, twenty-three Years old.

Jacques Guiguer, twenty Years old, a Merchant's Son of *Lyons*.

Jean Pagni,[2] thirty Years old, a Convert and Patrician of *Roan*.

Robert Anselin, eighteen Years old, a Miller's Son of *Picardy*.

Pierrot, twelve Years old, of *Roan*.

And *Francis Leguat*, Esq., above fifty Years of Age, of the Province of Burgundy, who was put over the rest.

Tho' it cou'd not but be a very great Trouble to us to see our selves depriv'd of fifteen of our Companions, when we least expected it, and look'd on them as Persons destin'd to the same Fortune as we were, who perhaps might be a Comfort and Help to us: Yet we cheerfully resign'd our selves into the Hands of Providence, and parted from *Amsterdam* the 10th of *July* 1690. The 13th we arriv'd in *Texel* Road, where we lay till the fourth of *September* following. We then set Sail, in company of 24 Ships, *English* and *Dutch*. We bent our Course Northward, by favour of an East South-

[1] *Paul Bénelle* (or *Bennelle*, according to M. Muller).
[2] Jean Pagni died in April, 1691, on board, off Diego Ruys I.

East Wind, which fill'd our Sails to our Hearts content;
but the next Night it chopp'd about, and became contrary:
there rose also a Tempest, which, however, did us no more
hurt than to make us pay the usual Tribute to the Sea. The
14th the Wind shifting to the South-west, our Admiral fir'd
a Gun, to make us keep our Way Northward. The next
Day we spy'd the Isles of *Schetland*, in the height of 29 deg.
42 min. The 18th we made those Isles, and our Ship
doubled the Cape, but with much difficulty; the Man that
was at the Helm, and had not perceiv'd that our Vessel was
carry'd away by a rapid Current, was surpriz'd when he saw
a flat Rock, which was not above a Foot under Water, and
but seven or eight Fathom distant from us; he cry'd out so
terribly, that we were all frightened, and every Man began
to strip, in hopes of swimming to the Island; but the Water
was deep enough at the side of the Rock for our poor little
Frigat to pass, and we had the good Fortune to escape
being Ship-wreck'd.

Such as have been as far as this End of the World, says
an ancient Author, as far as the famous *Thule*, have a Right
to Lye with Impunity, and to make themselves be believ'd
without fear of being reprehended; and certainly the
Number of those that make use of this Privilege is very
great, conformable to an old Proverb of ours, *A Beau mentir
qui vient de Loin*;—A good Lyer ought to come a great way.
—As for us, we shall say nothing but exact Truth, no more
than if we had never been as far as *Thule*.

This Island makes us still afraid as often as we think of
it, and as we were all of us busie endeavouring to preserve
our selves from this new Danger, one of our Seamen spy'd
a *French* Privateer[1] bearing down upon us with all the Sail
she could make. We went to Prayers, and prepar'd to
defend our selves; but we were so happy as to escape this
Enemy also; for after we had doubled the Cape, we found

---

[1] In original "un *copre*", a Dutch term for a corsair.

she cou'd not gain upon us; however, she pursu'd us six Hours, till Night coming on we lost sight of her, and ran back the false Course we had kept to escape him. We were all of us convinc'd by this double Deliverance the same Day, that we had been under the singular Protection of the Almighty, and we render'd the Thanks that were due to his Divine Favour.

The 22d we took a sort of Curlew by hand, for it came and perch'd upon our Sails: abundance of Purs ["*Allouettes de Mer*"] follow'd us, flying about our Ship.

The 28th an innumerable Army of Porpuses past by us; at which Sight we were very well pleas'd; they seem'd to us to march really along in order of Battel, and they leap'd up and down by turns, still keeping their Ranks; they approach'd so near to us that we struck one; we darted at him with a Trident, fasten'd at the End of a Rope: when they are wounded they grow weak, through loss of Blood, and then may be easily taken up: The blood of these Animals is hot; they bear their Young in their Bellies like Whales, Lamantines, and some other Fish; the inside of their Body is very like that of a Hog, but the Flesh is Oily and has an ill taste.

The 6th of *October* we spy'd a Squadron of 13 great Dutch Men of War, of which one gave us chase; for, not knowing what she was, we made the best of our way from her; when she came up to us, she hung out her Colours; we did the same, and then we both continu'd our several Courses.

The 22d we discover'd the *Canary Islands*[1] by Moonlight, and fell in with the Trade-Winds, which never left us; or, rather, which we never left till we came in the 9th Degree. By our Account we were 50 Leagues to the Wind-ward of *Palma*, between *Forteventura* and the *Grand Canaries.*

---

[1] The archipelago of the Canaries is situated near the polar limit of the north-east trade winds, the prevailing breeze setting from the north-east to north.

We coasted along the Island *Forteventura*, with a Larboard
Tack, a whole Day, and in the Evening, about Sun-set we
perceiv'd the *Grand Canaries;* we past by it in the Night
without meeting with any Ship, tho' commonly they are to
be met with thereabouts, especially *Turks;* they post themselves there to lie in wait for the Ships that come out loaden
with Wines, in hopes of picking up some of them.

The 28th we were in the height of 24 deg. 29 min. and
saw a vast Number of flying Fish about us. I observ'd one
of them very exactly; 'twas about 10 Inches long; there are
few larger, and abundance shorter: Its Back was of a Russet-
brown Colour, speckled with blue Spots, inclining to a
greenish, with a little black amongst it. Its naked Belly
was black, and blue, and its Sides cover'd with little Scales
of dark red. Its long Wings or Fins were brown, with Sea-
green Spots upon them. The young Ones are of a light grey,
and their Tail the same. Its Eye is great and rais'd; the
Sight of it large and blue, the rest black. The Prickles upon
the Head of it are of a greyish Colour, and like a sort of
very rough Chagreen.

Our Books represent this Fish[1] after another manner; and
I doubt not but there are some of them of different sorts of
Figures; for Nature varies in every thing. The *Irish* Horses
are not of a like make with those of *Friseland*, nor *Kentish*
Cows like *Middlesex*, tho' those two Counties are contigu-
ous; much less are they like those of *Iseland*, which have
no Horns. And, without going out of our own Species,

---

[1] "When, for instance, he (Leguat) obtained the first flying-fish, he
examined, described, represented, and compared them with the repre-
sentations of other authors, discovering at once that there exists among
these animals two forms, those now called *Dactylopterus* and *Exocœtus*.
He appends, for this reason, to his drawing the copies of three figures
of these fish taken from other works, and on that of Olearius makes
the true observation that it had probably been drawn from a dried
specimen, and was therefore inaccurate; for he says, ' *quand ces ani-
maux-là viennent à se secher, il est difficile d'en observer la véritable
forme.*'" (Professor Schlegel, *Ibis*, 1866, p. 151.)

one Man is a *Negro*, another a *Dutch* Man, and another a *Chinese*.

To return to our Fish. A certain Naturalist calls that which is mark'd A, a Sea-Swallow, and attributes a great many Properties to it, which I shall not repeat. That which I have mark'd B, is called a Mullet, in *Sanson Mathurin's*[1] Journal; he was a famous Pilot in the *Mediterranean,* and us'd to see them in the *Gulph of Lyons* and elsewhere. The 3rd, mark'd C, was taken from the K. of *Denmark's* Cabinet, where I have some reason to believe 'tis not exactly design'd : For when these Animals grow dry, 'tis a hard matter to observe their true Form. There are some of them that have four Wings. Those we eat tasted something like a Herring.

These poor little Creatures, that may be taken for an Emblem of perpetual Fear, are continually flying and rising to save themselves; they are very often caught in the Ship's Sails: they fly as long as there remains any Moisture in their Wings ; which, as soon as they are dry, turn to Fins again ; and they are forc'd to take again to the water, or else, their Fright is always so great, they would fly to the End of the World.

The Efforts they make to become rather Inhabitants of the Air than of the Water, is to avoid the Persecution of the Goldfish and the Bonita's, who are at eternal War with them. But these wretched Animals fly from one Peril, and are immediately overtaken by another ; for the cruel Birds are their irreconcilable Enemies, and always on the watch in great Flocks to devour them, as soon as they enter the new Element, where they thought they shou'd find an Asylum from their Foes of the Sea. The Porpoises make the same War upon the Goldfish, as the latter do on the Flying Fish : and all this gives us a true Image of human Life ; which is

---

[1] Sanson Mathurin, after whom, probably, Port Mathurin, in Rodriguez, was named.

nothing but continual Dangers, and in which the Weak commonly fall a Victim to the Strong.

Our Ship wanting Balast, we put into the Island of *Salt*, one of the Isles of *Cape Verd*,[1] which we discover'd the 29th of *October*, and arriv'd the next Day in the Road, where we cast Anchor in a Creek to the Southward of the Island, in eight Fathom Water. A great Number of Sea-Birds came to visit our Vessel, and perching on our Yards, let us take them by hand : we eat some of them, but we did not like them. We caught Fools, Frigates, Longtails, and other Birds. Perhaps I shall have room to speak of these Animals hereafter. We had a Swallow ever since we came from the *Canaries*, which we let go every Morning, and it return'd to us at Night; 'twas kill'd here by an Accident.

The 31st we went ashoar, early in the Morning, with our Arms and Dogs to hunt; we found presently a prodigious Quantity of Goats; we cou'd easily see them, tho' at a great distance, for the Island is extreamly dry, without Tree or Bush, producing nothing but a sort of short Grass, at least in the greatest part of what we saw : we kill'd some of them, and left 'em on a Bank, to take them with us when we came back, for we went farther into the Island, and search'd about two or three Hours for fresh Water, but all that we met with was brackish; by which means we were almost dead with Thirst. The Sun shines very hot in this Isle, and there being no Shade, the Heat was very troublesome to us ; we therefore return'd to our Goats, and thence to the Sea-side, where we arriv'd about Sun-set. When we came back

---

[1] The Cape Verde islands are a group of fourteen islands, situated about 320 miles west of Cape Verde. Sal island is the north-eastern-most of the islands; it is seventeen miles long, north and south, and about five miles broad, with rocky shores and mountains, the most northern of which—Pico Martinez—is 1,340 feet high. The only production of this island is salt, which is now brought to the sea-coast on tramways. South Bay or Porte Santa Maria, where Leguat landed, is the only inhabited settlement on the island.

we found there a very handsome Horse, of a reddish bay
Colour, his Main and Tail trailing on the ground; 'twas
fierce, and never had any Horse a better Shape, nor a more
magnificent Chest : he ran away immediately, and let us see
that his Heels were good. I know not what Name to give to
another Animal which we also saw, but were not so near it;
I believe 'twas a sort of Cat, but one of our Company would
have it to be a Fox : And I am mistaken, if he is more
happy in his Conjecture than the Translators of the *Psalms*[1]
into *French*, when they make *David* say, His *Enemies should
be a Prey to Foxes*. We found most of our Companions
ashoar catching Turtles, we went along with them up into
another part of the Country and digg'd, in hopes of meeting
with fresh Water, but all our Labour was in vain, Night
came upon us, and we slept on the Sand, it being a Star-light
Night. Nor were we less weaken'd by Hunger and Thirst,
than tir'd with Hunting. As we lay all of us in a sound
sleep, we were on a sudden waken'd by the braying Musick
of a Rustick Regiment of Asses, of which we cou'd not rid
our selves, but by braying as they did, and firing twice or
thrice a Fuzee at them ; but they had scarce turn'd their
Backs upon us, when another Troop of the same Beasts
entertain'd us with the same Song : They were accompany'd
by above five hundred Goats, which surrounding us, we cou'd
sleep no longer : At last these Animals retir'd, and we
imagin'd if we follow'd them, they might perhaps lead us to
some hidden Spring. As we believ'd, it happen'd, part of
them descended into a little Pit, where there was Water,
which they drank : We rejoyc'd all of us, as if we had found
a Treasure ; but this Water was also salt. These Beasts
having been forc'd to drink of it from their Births, 'tis now
become customary to them.

---

[1] Allusion to verse 11 of Psalm lxiii : " *Tradentur in manus gladii, partes
vulpium erunt*" (" That they may be a portion for foxes"). (*Muller.*)
Probably version by Marot and de Bèze.

Day broke, and Hunger still pressing us, we had a mind to roast a Leg of a Goat, I dare not say of a Kid, 'tis too honourable a Term for it, and I am sorry that ever I should call these Beasts Goats. For want of Wood, we heap'd Asses and Horse Dung together, made a Piramid of it, like one of *Dutch* turfs, hung Pieces of Flesh on Strings, and turning 'em round by a good Fire, our Meat was soon ready. But, alas, such Meat, such a Taste, such a Smell, that I can scarce forbear vomiting when I think of it. There's no Sawce like a good Stomach. Every Man's teeth went to work, we tore it to pieces, chaw'd it as well as we cou'd, and down it went without Water. 'Tis probable the Reader will say here, we were in the wrong to amuse ourselves in this Rascally Island, whereas we might have gone aboard and have eat and drank our fill: He must therefore know, That the Seamen who had set us ashoar, were return'd with their Long boat to the Ship, and, whether we wou'd or not, we were oblig'd to stay till they came for us: They cou'd not think that we far'd so ill; they saw us making good Cheer by a good Fire, afar off, and did not doubt we were very well at our ease. At last they brought the Boat for us about Noon, and we returned to our *Swallow*.

The Isle of *Salt* is not eight Leagues about, 'tis so call'd, because Ships go thither to load Salt, which is there excellent in its kind, and in abundance, lying in the crevises of the Rocks, on the *South* Coast of the Island. 'Tis made without Art by the Sea and the Sun. Here also Sailors come to turn the Turtle, a Term us'd by them for killing it, because they turn the Turtle on its Back when they catch it; all the Shoar is cover'd with these Animals, especially in the Season, when they lay their Eggs. We turn'd some of these stupid and slow Creatures, and amongst the rest, two which, according to the guess of the Skillful, weigh'd 500 Pound each. We Carry'd all that was good of them aboard with us.

There is nothing more to be said of the Isle of *Salt.* We found some *Cow-dung* there, but could see no *Cows;* and all the Birds we met with were Sparrows, they are like ours except in their size, for they are not half so big.

We must not forget the fine Shells that are spread over all the Coast, the variety of them is Charming, and I never saw any in any other Place so beautiful as here; they are certainly the work of an excellent Workman. The shineing of the Enameling, the mixture and diversity of the Colours, the Form, the Delicacy, the Symmetry, every thing Charms, and raises in us a just Admiration of the Great Creator. I was bound for the *Indies,* the *Antipodes,* I did not know whether; for Desert Islands from whence I thought I should never return: And my Head being full of such Thoughts, I could not amuse my self to gather Shells; but had I touch'd at this Island when I came back, I should certainly have furnish'd my self plentifully with them.

I must own, now it comes into my Mind, I was sorry that as I walkt about the Island, I could not meet with any of those great and beautiful Birds call'd *Flamans,* from *Flamboyans* (Flaming), which by relation of Voyagers, are the most considerable of the Place. 'Twas not only a simple desire to see these Birds; the greatest Pleasure I propos'd to my self by it, was to compare the different draughts I had of them with the Original; For all that have describ'd them, except Mr. *Willoughby,* at least all the Authors (and they are not a few in number), which I have seen who have spoke of them, make the beak of these Birds like a Spatula or a Spoon, whereas Mr. *Willoughby* designs them with a sharp Beak.

This curious Naturalist adds, that he believes these Birds had the name of *Flamantes*[1] given them, rather on account

---

[1] " On y voit beaucoup de gros & de menu détail, & particulièrement des boucs : les Isles du Mai, de Bonne-vuë & du Sel, en fournissant assez pour charger des vaisseaux qu'on envoie au Bresil.

" Il n'y a pas une moindre abondance de volatiles, comme de poules de Barbarie, perdrix, cailles, alouëttes, & une sorte d'oiseaux que les Por-

of some of their Feathers, whose colour is like that of flaming Fire, than because they were originally of *Flanders*. And certainly our learned Author is in the Right; for 'tis most sure that such *Flemings* as these are as great Strangers in *Flanders*, as in *England*.

The 6*th of Novemb.* we weigh'd Anchor, the Wind being fair, and sail'd towards the Isle of *Martin-Vas,* according to our Orders.

The 7*th* the Wind continuing still fair, we saw and doubled the Island *Bonavist,* which is as bad as the Isle of *Salt;* 'tis longer and more Mountainous. We could see no more Trees on this Island than we had done on the other.

The 11*th* we the first time made tryal of one of those short but troublesom Tempests, which the Seamen call Gusts,[1] and we had 'em from time to time afterwards till we crost the *Line.* These are a sort of violent Whirlwinds mingled with Rain, which rises at once, but do's not commonly last above a quarter of an Hour. We always prepare to receive them; for we can spy the Gusts afar off: we immediately furl our Top-sails, which otherwise wou'd be carry'd away, and the Masts broken.

tugais appellent *Flamencos*, qui ont sur le corps des plumes blanches, & qui sont de la grosseur d'un cigne, ou d'une cigogne. On y trouve encore des poules communes, de paons, des hérons, quantité de tourterelles & de lapins." (*Ire Voïage des Hollandois.*)

" Not less exact are his observations on the birds which, at that time, were represented under the name of *Flamans.* He says, indeed, that the numerous authors whom he had consulted, except Willughby, attributed to these birds the bill of a Spoonbill; and, in fact, the name of *Flamants* was at that time generally given to large, red Marsh-birds. The true *Flamingo* was figured by Willughby, while many others, Rochefort for instance, whom Leguat respectfully quotes, described and figured the red Spoonbill of America (*Platalea ajaja*) under the name of *Flamant.*" (Schlegel, *Ibis,* 1866, p. 151.)

Franciscus Willughby, *Ornithologiæ Libri tres, in quibus Aves omnes hactenus cognitæ in methodum naturis suis convenientem describuntur* (London, 1676).

1 " *Grains*" in French edition, *i.e.,* squalls.

When the Wind is too strong we lower all our Sails, or
carry as little as we can.   While this Tempest lasts, the Sea
is in an extream agitation, and seems to be all on Fire.
These Gusts often happen several times in the same Day,
during which the Ships Crew is ev'ry Man hard put to it ; a
Calm commonly succeeds in a very little while after the
Storm.   We also escap'd several watry Dragons,[1] and on the
12*th* the Wind ceas'd in the height of 7 Deg. 15 Min.

At Night we caught a Bird something like a Woodcock,
which flew about our Ship all day long ; The Mariners kill'd
her not so much for the pleasure of eating her, tho' that was
worth their while, as to revenge her driving away four
Swallows which had follow'd us·some time, and every Morning and Night entertain'd us with Musick the more agreeable, because it puts us in mind of the dear Land, which is
so well belov'd by all Men that are sailing in the middle of
the vast Ocean.

The 13*th* an hour after Day-light we met with a furious
Gust, which brought our Main-top-mast by the Board, having
broke the Iron Hoop that bound it.   I observe this only because all our Crew were very much amaz'd at it.

The 14*th* we saw a prodigious number of Gold-fish and
Bonitas, of which I have spoken.   These Fish being well
enough known, I did not describe them ; but since I have
occasion to speak of 'em again, I have a great mind to tell
what sort of Fish those were that I saw.

The Gold-fish[2] of *America*, of which Mr. *de Roche-*

---

[1] "C'est un de ces gros tourbillons que les Mariniers appellent Trompes,
Pompes ou Dragons d'eau. Ce font comme de longs Tubes ou Cylindres
formez de vapeurs épaisses, lesquelles touchent les nuës d'une de leurs
extrémitez, & de l'autre la Mer, qui paroit boüillonner tout autour."
(*Voyage de Siam*, p. 49.)

[2] "In his observations on the *dorade bonito*, he (Leguat) quotes" (says
Schlegel) "Rochefort and Rondeletius, the last of whom he subsequently
takes to task severely (p. 89, English edition), and on this occasion it
appears that, at the time of his return, he took an interest in natural,

fort[1] writes, have sharp Heads, I know nothing of such Gold-
fish as these; those that I saw had a round flatish Snout, that
gives them a certain Physiognomy, in which I did not take
much delight. Neither do I believe that any Body values this
Fish for the beauty of its shape, but that of its Colours are
admirable: There are two sorts of Gold-fish, that which I have
giv'n the Figure of, is enammel'd on its Back, with speckles
of a blewish Green on a black Ground: Its Belly is of a
bright Silver Colour, its Tail and Fins as if gilded with fine
Gold; Nothing can be more bright and shining when 'tis in
its Element, or before it begins to Mortifie, which it does presently when 'tis out of it: 'Tis four or five foot long, and not
thicker than a Salmon.[2]　*Rondelet* calls it the Sea-Bream, our
Mariners told me, that the other Species of the Gold-fish
differs from this only in that its Jaw sticks out a little more,
and that its Speckles are a beautiful Azure on a Golden
Ground. The flesh of this Fish is firm, and tasts very
well.

The Bonita is generally three or four Foot long, very thick
and Fleshy, its Back is cover'd with a little Scale, so thin,
that one can scarce perceive it; 'tis of a Slate colour, and a
little upon the Green in some Places. Its Belly is of a grey
Pearl colour, and turns brown near the Back; four streaks of
a yellowish colour begin at the side of its Head, run along
the Body almost at a Parallel distance, and join at the Tail,
which is not unlike that of a Makarel. Its Eye is large and
lively, resembling a Jet-stone set in a Silver Ring. I have

history; for he inserts, for comparison, the figure of a *bonito*, which
one of his friends had drawn and communicated to him from an example, caught in 1702, on the coast of Kent" (*Ibis*, 1866, p. 151). The
French word is " Forade", nowadays commonly called " Dolphins" by
misapplication. N.B.—Dorades and bonitos are very different kinds of
fishes.

[1] *Histoire naturelle et morale des Iles Antilles*, par L. de Poincy et C.
de Rochefort (Rotterdam, 1665).

[2] Rondelet (Gal.), *Libri de piscibus marinis* (1554-55, Lugduni).

C *

design'd the Shape of its Body, and the Disposition of its Fins. Near the Tail of it, there are six little things like square Fins on the Back of it not an inch High, and over against them under its Belly there are seven.

As I was writing this, a Friend of mine, who is always admiring the Divine Wonders of Nature, and very nicely considers them; told me that he had measur'd and design'd a Bonita which was taken in the year 1702 near *Rye*, on the *Kentish* Shoar, and which differ'd in several things from that I have been speaking of. The Reader will, I doubt not, be pleas'd to see the Billet which my Friend wrote me on this Subject, when he sent me the draught of this Bonita.

"The Fish which in the *Indian* Sea is call'd Bonita, is known on the Coasts of *France*, and particularly between the *Loire* and the *Garonne*, by the name of *Germon*. It very rarely enters the Channel, which I note *en passant* is quite contrary to the Makarel; for the Coasts of *Normandy*, especially the *Bessin*[1] and *Costentin* are full of them; whereas they are never, or very rarely, seen about *Rochelle*. *The Germon* or Bonita of our Seas, is certainly a Fish of the same Species with the Bonitas you saw in your Voyages, but the Species varies a little, a thing that may be observ'd in all sorts of Animals, as soon as we change the Country, as you have your self taken notice. The last Bonita which I saw, and which was taken near *Rye* in the beginning of *June* 1702 was just three Foot long, and its Body proportionably greater than that which you design'd in the Figure you shew'd me; for thrice the breadth of it where 'twas broadest, made compleatly its length. I send you an exact draught of it. At the first view one would think that this

[1] " *Bessin* and *Costentin*." " *Costentin* = Cotentin, the large Norman peninsula, the only peninsula in France, which now forms the department of La Manche. *Bessin* is the name of a small district, not now marked on any map, whose principal town is Port-en-Bessin, not far from Bayeux, Calvados." (*Gabriel Marcel.*)

Fish did not open its Mouth very wide, but there's a secret help for that, and it opens it as far as the place mark'd *a*. Its Teeth above and below are so little, so short, and so weak, that one wou'd think they were only made for Scratching: Its Tongue is broad, blackish, and hard at the Root, but soft and a little reddish at the Tip. Its Eye is a good Inch Diameter: The Sight like very white and transparent Chrystal, and the Circle that surrounds it, is more Brilliant than pollish'd Gold.

" The colour of this Fish is the same with that of which you have giv'n us a Description, tho' it has no Scales on its Back, it has nothing but a smooth Skin on its Back and Belly, and on its Side between the Tail and the Fins near the Gills, there's a scaly List two Inches broad, the Scales so little and so fine, that they are scarce perceptible: Its two Fins, if I may call them so, which are mark'd B, are bony and immoveable. In the narrowest part of its Tail, there's a knot on each side, out of which grows a little hairy Tuft that is not above an Inch and a half long.

" Whereas your Fish has but six of those little Fins which you have represented in your Draught, to be upon the Back toward the Tail, and seven under it; this has nine above and eight below. *c.c*, Shews where the Gills are which open one another very easily. And *d.d.*, is like a great Scale, which cannot be but very little lifted up all about it.'

The Trade-winds[1] having left us in the 9*th* Degree, we had nothing after that but Gusts and Calms till we came to the Line, no sooner was one gone, but another came. The Heat was not excessive, we cou'd very well bear our Night-gowns all Night long.

We crost the Line the 23*d* of *November*, and were oblig'd to undergoe the impertinent Ceremony of *Baptism*, at least

---

[1] Sometimes the north-east and south-east trade winds meet, generally somewhere about the meridian of 28°, or 33° west, where a vessel may, by chance, pass in a squall from one trade to the other.

all those who had not assisted at the same Festival before, or would not buy themselves off for a piece of Money.

'Tis an ancient Custom, and will not be abolish'd without difficulty ; 'tis also sometimes done when we pass the Tropicks. I shall in a few words report how this fine Ceremony was perform'd in our Vessel. One of the Seamen who had past the Line before, drest himself in Rags, with a beard and Hair of Hards of Hemp, and black'd his face with Soot and Oil mix'd together. Thus Equip'd, holding a Sea-Chart in one Hand, and a Cutlass in the other, with a Pot full of blacking Stuff standing by him, he presented himself upon Deck attended by his Suffragans, drest as whimsically as himself, and arm'd with Grid-Irons, Stoves, Kettles, and little Bells ; with which rare Instruments they made a sort of Musick, the goodness of which may be easily imagin'd.

They call'd those that were to be initiated into these Rites and Mysteries one after another, and having made them sit down on the edge of a Tub full of Water, they oblig'd them to put one Hand on the Chart, and promise that on the like Occasion they wou'd do to others what was at that time done to them. Then they gave them a mark in the Forehead with the stuff out of the Pot, wetted their faces with Seawater, and askt them if they wou'd give the Crew any thing to drink, promising them they wou'd in such case let them go without doing any further Pennance. Those that gave were presently discharg'd, and some avoided this unpleasant *Præludium* to what was to follow, by giving 'em something Extraordinary : It cost me but a Crown to have the same Privilege with the Latter. As for those who paid nothing they were thrown into the Tub of Water over Head and Ears, and then wash'd and scrub'd every where with the Ships Ballast ; and I believe this scrubbing and washing lasted much longer than those who were so treated desir'd.

Our Frigat and Boat having never past the Line, they were

subjected to the same Law. The Captain was oblig'd to give
something to save the Beakhead of his Ship, the Seamen
alledging, 'twas their Right to cut off the Boats Nose else.
The Money the Men got by it, was laid up to be spent on the
whole Crew when opportunity offer'd. Every Nation practices this ridiculous Custom after a different Manner.

We kept on a straight course towards the Isles of *Martin
Vas*,[1] which are in 20 Degrees *South* Latitude, and we bad
the Captain put in there, that we might go a-shoar and visit
them according to our Orders. He having no design to touch
there, reply'd, That the Round-top of our Fore-Mast was half
broken, and we should have a great deal of trouble to make
those Islands, because we must go near the Wind, and tack
all the Way: He therefore chang'd his Course, notwithstanding all our Entreaties to the contrary, and the Contempt
we shew'd for his false and trivial Reasons. Thus we made
the Cape of the Island of *Tristan d'Acugna*, which is in 37
Deg. of *South* Latitude.

The 10*th* of *December* we past the Tropick of Capricorn,
and enter'd the *Southern* Temperate Zone.

The 13*th* we were visited by several Birds, there were
abundance of those which are call'd Great Gullets, and which
rather shou'd have the name of great Craws,[2] on account of
their great hanging Breasts. They are almost as big as a
Goose, are very tall, but neither handsom nor good to eat; their
Flesh being tough, and having a strange Tast. Their Heads
are big, their Beaks long and sharp, their Bodies white, their

---

[1] Trinidad and Martin Vas form a small but remarkable group of
rocky islets near the usual track of sailing vessels bound for the Cape,
in lat. 20° 30′ S., long. 29° 21′ W. The Martin Vas rocks lie twenty-
six miles from Trinidad; they are three in number, and the largest is
visible thirty miles off.

[2] In the print of the French edition it is named *Grand Gosier*, a well-
known French name for a pelican; but Leguat's figure, entitled *The
Great Throat*, seems to represent a heron of some kind. It is impossible
to specify the bird.

Wings brown or russet, their Neck sometimes short, sometimes long, according as they please, either to stretch it out
or shrink it up. 'Tis a melancholy Bird that passes whole
days on the brink of a Rock, hanging its Head over into the
Sea, like a Fisherman with a Line to catch little Fish.
Though the figure of this Creature was not at first sight very
pleasing to us, they were however very welcome, because we
were weary of seeing nothing but Water, and the least new
Objects diverted us. Like their Highnesses in those little
out-of-the-way Courts where no Company comes to interrupt
their Solitude ; or like the Nuns who are so greedy of Society
in their Solitary Convents.

The 17*th* we heard the Seamen cry a Whale,[1] another
Marine Pleasure ; every Body rose immediately to pay our
Compliment to the Eminency of a great black-Back, which
swam up and down slowly about our ship.

A Moment after we saw fifteen or twenty more, which put
me in mind of what Mr. *de Godeau*[2] says elegantly in his
Poems :—

[1] There are two distinct families of Cetaceans. The first, *Odonto-
ceti*, or toothed whales, include the spouting whales, which subsist on
fish and sepias, representing the carnivorous class, exemplified by the
sperm-whales, porpoises, and dolphins. The second division comprises
the whalebone whales, as the *rorquals* and *mysticetes*, the true or right
whales, provided with filaments of whalebone.

The whales seen by Leguat were probably the sperm-whales, the
largest and most valuable of the southern whales. These are gregarious,
and are found in parties, termed by whalers "schools" or "pods",
according to the size of the association.

[2] "*Monsignor Godeau*, a witty prelate, and an *habitué* of the Hôtel de
Rambouillet, who was one of the first members of the French Academy.
It is related that he owed the bishopric of Grasse to the irresistible
habit of punning possessed by Richelieu. Godeau having written a
paraphrase of the canticle, *Benedicite omnia opera*, presented it to the
Cardinal, who was so pleased with it, that, after having read it over
again in the presence of the author, he said to him : 'You offer me the
Benediction, I offer you in return (*grâces*, thanks) Grasse.'" (*Eugène
Muller.*)

> "Thou, for the Beauty of the Universe,
>   With Monsters various in their Forms
>   Hast Peopled all the Liquid Plains;
>   And wil'st that all within the spatious Deep,
>   To the huge Whales shou'd Homage pay
>   Who look like floating Rocks upon the Sea." [1]

Indeed such as have no more Experience of the Sea than honest *Aloysio Cadamusto*[2] had, and all his Ships Crew imagine, that these huge Beasts seek after to devour them. This celebrated *Voyager* in the I Chapter of the *History* of his *Navigation* tells us, they were all very much afraid of a terrible Monster, whose Fins were like the Sails of a Windmill, which came down upon them, but they escap'd that Danger, by clapping all their Sails to, and flying faster than the Monster could pursue them. As for us, we were so far from being afraid, that we were extreamly delighted to see those Colosses play in the Waves with as much agility, as a Bird flies in the Air. One of these Whales[3] was much bigger than any of the rest, and lookt like a little Isle with a little Mountain in it, on the surface of the smooth Ocean.

I question whether that prodigious half of a Jaw which is

---

[1] " Pour la beauté de l'Univers,
    De Monstres en formes divers
    Tu peuplas les humides plaines ;
    Et voulus qu'en leur vaste enclos,
  Tous rendissent hommage à ces lourdes Baleines
  Qu'on prend pour des écueils sur la face des flots."

[2] Voyages of Cadamosto and Pedro de Cintra, in the Portuguese service, 1454-1463, in the collection of voyages by Vicenza, 1507.

[3] Compare Milton (1665), *Paradise Lost*, Book VII :—

       ". . . . these leviathan,
    Hugest of living creatures, on the deep,
    Stretch'd like a promontory, sleeps or swims,
    And seems a moving land."

When a solitary or lone sperm-whale is observed it almost invariably proves to be an old bull. When two or more schools of whales coalesce and form a very large assemblage, this is technically distinguished as a " body of whales".

thought worthy to be fasten'd to the Wall of the Pallace of
St. James's in *London,* belong'd to an Animal of a more
Monstrous size.[1] Our Seamen who had *Patricius Vartomanni's*
Relation,[2] cou'd not help laughing when they read what that
famous Author writes of Whales that piss'd, as high as the
Clouds.

But if they had read *Pliny* and *Solinus,* venerable for their
Antiquity, with their Whales 960 Foot long, their inclination
to Laugh, had been chang'd into a mortal Fright, for fear of
being all swallow'd, Ship, Anchors, Sails, Masts, Men, and
Goods: For tho' those that are commonly call'd *Naturalists,*
have for a long time us'd themselves to affirm, that *Jonas*
cou'd not be swallow'd by a Whale, because the Throat of
these Animals is so straight, that hardly a Pilcher can go
down it; yet every Body do's not believe what they say, as
a matter beyond all Dispute. There are few Men who have
themselves Dissected Whales, and have seen with their own
Eyes what sort of Throats they have; besides, we must consider there are several different kinds of these Marine
Monsters. And as I cannot refuse believing P. *George
Fournier,*[3] a very curious Man, and very knowing in every
thing which belongs to the Sea, who assures us in his *Hydro-
graphy,* that two Men were found in the Belly of a Whale
that was thrown a-shoar at *Valentia,* on the Coast of *Spain,*
a Jaw of which is preserv'd in the Escurial, so I am satisfi'd
a Whale of the size *Solinus* speaks of, wou'd have swallow'd
us up as easily, as they do Sack and Loaches in *England.*

---

[1] In Max. Misson's *Memoirs and Observations* in his travels over
England, 1697, translated by Mr. Ozell, 1719, p. 359 :—
"Whale.] In one of the Courts of St. James's Palace, there is the
Rib of a Whale twenty feet long. *Jonas* would certainly have had
Elbow-room enough in the Belly of such a Fish, if the Monster's Throat
(or the Gate of the House) was proportionable to the rest; that Point
s to be examin'd."

[2] *Navigatio Vartomanni ;* see *Novus Orbis* of Hervagius, 1537.

[3] *Hydrographie,* par M. George Fournier, Paris, 1667.

Signior Cadamusto says that his *Leviathan* was bigger than
the Whale, but the Dispute concerning the *Whale* and the
Leviathan, is about a word only ; for the Animal that in all
Languages is call'd a Whale, is the biggest of all Fish, and
even of all Animals.   And from thence Mr. *Bochart*[1] writes
(*Phal.* Vol. II. Book I. Chap. I.) that the word *Baleine* or
Whale is a Syriaque word, which signifies Lord of Fishes.

I cou'd willingly say one word more on this Article, to
confute the Error of those who imagine the Whale-bone which
Women use in their Stays and Gowns, is taken out of the
Tail and Fins of this Fish ; for what I say, I know very well,
and that is, the Whale-bone we speak of is never found any
where but in the Mouth of several kinds of these Animals
which have no Teeth : Enough of this, 'tis time to keep on
our way, and that I may not be accus'd here of loving Digressions, I shall say nothing of the Battel between the Sword-
fish and the Whale, which our Mariners told us of, tho' it
cou'd not properly be call'd a Digression, and the thing is
curious enough, much more so than the fighting of Cocks, or
that of Dogs and Bears, in which whole Nations take
delight.

The 21*st* we again met with abundance of Whales, and
there was one which I believe scratch'd her self against our
Ship,[2] but so rudely, that she was flead with it ; she found
some Fracture which rub'd off the Skin, for when she was
at a Distance from us, we perceiv'd she was all bloody, and
her scratching had giv'n our Vessel a little *shake.*

[1] *Hierozoicon sive Bipartitum opus de Animalibus S. Scripturæ, Geogr.
Sacra, seu Phaleg et Canaan,* 3tia editio, Samuel Bochartus, 3 vol. in 2,
fol., Lugduni Batavorum, 1692. *Balæna* is derived from φάλλαινα.

[2] A male sperm-whale of the largest size, and probably the guardian
of a "school", rushed repeatedly at an American whaling ship, the
Essex, and stove in the planking of her starboard bow, in 1820.—This
was a case of assault, which, however, there is nothing to show that
Leguat's was. The whale that "scratched" herself against his ship was
more likely trying to divest itself of barnacles, with which, like most
whales, especially in the South Seas, it was probably beset.

Arriving in the height of the Isle *Tristan* we sail'd *East-ward* to endeavour to gain it, but we cou'd not succeed because of the Fogs and hazy Weather, which we had for five or six days; we lay by all that while, that we might not go beyond it, nor come too near it. The Weather not clearing up, we were afraid of losing our time there, and resolv'd to take hold of the opportunity of a fair Wind which then presented, and might bring us in a few days to the *Cape of Good Hope;* But we had not kept on our Course thither six Hours, before the Wind shifted again, and was in our Teeth, which oblig'd the Captain to tell us, he must make a new effort to put into the Isle of *Tristan.*[1] His pretended design succeeded in some sort, we saw that Island *Thursday* the 27*th* of *December*, about six in the Morning, and coasted it from the *North*, to the *South* and by *East*, but we cou'd find no place to cast Anchor, we were always Sounding, but never reach'd the Bottom.

We perceiv'd plainly enough that the Captain's Chart was false, because there was a Bay mark'd to be in that part which we saw, where there certainly was none at all; and having no intention that we should land there, he wou'd have perswaded us the Isle was inaccessible: But we were sure Ships had formerly anchor'd there, and were confirm'd in that Opinion by a good Chart of the Sieur *Testard's*, where a Bay was mark'd in another place to the *Westward*, and it represented the Coasts that were before us, to be, as indeed they were, very high and steep.

---

[1] The Tristan d'Acunha Isles are three in number : Tristan, the largest, to the north-east; Inaccessible, the westernmost and smallest; Nightingale Island, to the south. The N.W. extremity of Tristan, near the settlement, is in lat. 37° 2′ S., long. 12° 18′ W. The people now living in the village on Tristan form a very interesting community in what is called Falmouth Bay. The Duke of Edinburgh landed here in 1867, the *Challenger* in 1874. It is dangerous to range along the margin of the island nearer than two miles, on account of the baffling eddies, which leave a ship in the onset influence of the swell.

We observ'd a little Island *to the Southward*, but we did not come near it. That Coast of the Isle of *Tristan* which we saw, was about two Leagues long; it seem'd to be extreamly agreeable, tho' very steep, as I have said; and tho' we had Mists from time to time, which depriv'd us in part of the sight of it, and sometimes hid it all entirely from us, yet we could see the Hills from the top to the bottom, were adorn'd with the most beautiful verdure in the World, and we saw the Sun with Pleasure thro' tall and straight Trees, with which the tops of the Mountains were cover'd, Birds were every where flying about, the running Waters flow'd abundantly in several places, from Bason to Bason, making admirable Cascades; and from the foot of the Hills, to which they rapidly rowl'd, they fell precipitately, into the Sea. All the different Beauties of this charming Prospect, made us more desirous to have a nearer view of it, and refresh our selves in so delicious a Place; but we desir'd it in vain.

The Sea was almost cover'd with Whales and Sea-Wolfs, which swam to the very Shoar of the Isle playing with the Water, and some of them ran against our Frigat; about which flew a great number of Sea-fowl of several kinds, some as big as our Geese, others no bigger than Ducks. The sight of them fill'd us with new Joy, as did every thing that brought the much desir'd Land to our Remembrance: 'Twas to no purpose for us to flatter our selves with hopes of Landing on the lovely Isle that lay before us, and perhaps we might have stay'd there too long if we had. There was the greater likelihood of it, inasmuch as our Healths were very much impair'd, the most Vigorous finding his Strength extreamly decay'd, but we cou'd discover neither Bay nor Port, our Captain not having done all that was in his Power to search after one: We durst not stay near the Shoar in the Night-time; besides, we were too much expos'd to violent gusts of Wind which blew off Land from between the Mountains, so we pursu'd our Voyage towards the Cape.

In the Night the Wind rose so high, that all our Hands found business enough to employ them. The Waves flew up to the top of our Masts, and there fell so much Water upon Deck, that our young Lad had been drown'd if he had not been very nimbly assisted.

On *New-Years-Day*, 1691, we were entertain'd with the sight of a Sea-Cow, of a russet Colour; sometimes her whole Head, and sometimes above half her Body appear'd above Water; she was thick and round, and seem'd to be more bulky than the bigest of our Cows.[1] Her Eye was large, her Teeth or Tusks long, and her Muzzle swell'd out a little: One of our Mariners assur'd us, this Animal had Feet the same as you see in this Figure.

The 11*th* and 12*th* we saw abundance of Birds as big as Partridges, and very near of the same Colour, which our Ships Crew call'd by the Name of *Grissards*[2] or grey Birds: There were several other sorts, and all of them different from those of our Continent. You may imagine these new Objects were not disagreeable to us; but what pleas'd us most was, that they were a certain sign of our being near Land.

[1] The figure given by Leguat's publishers of the *Vache Marine* is all but identical with that figured by Père Tachard, who writes of it:—" On voit dans les grandes Rivieres un Animal monstrueux, qu'on apelle Vache-Marine, & qui égale le Rhinocéros en grandeur, sa chair ou pour mieux dire son lard est bon a manger, & le goût en est fort agréable. J'en ay mis icy la figure." (*Voyage de Siam*, liv. ii, p. 89.)

There is much confusion as to the synonyme of so-called sea-elephants, sea-lions, sea-bears, sea-leopards, sea-wolves, etc., which names have been more or less misapplied to all seals with ears, so that it is impossible to form any conjecture as to what this "*Vache marine*" was. The figure given by Leguat is clearly meant to represent a hippopotamus; but he could not have met with a hippopotamus at sea! All we can say is, that it was probably not one of the sea-wolves he found at Tristan d'Acunha.

[2] " Des grisets ce sont oyseaux gros comme Pigeons qui vivent de pesche, ils sentent trop le marescage" (*de Flacourt*). " *Grissard*" seems to be any grey sea-bird. Leguat, doubtless, met with " Cape Pigeons", but he would hardly call them " Grissards": more likely "*Pintades*".

The 13*th* in the Evening we saw and knew the Cape of *Good Hope*, but lost sight of it again in a great Fog, which rose on a sudden, and oblig'd us to keep to Sea all that Night.

The next day we drew near and saw the Isle *Robben*,[1] which is at the entrance of the Port. This little Island is flat, and has no Dwellings upon it but some Hutts where the *Lime-burners* live, when they are sent thither to make it.

All of us had a long while earnestly desir'd to arrive at the *Cape*, for we all wanted Refreshment extreamly, being almost eaten up with the Scurvy, and the Grapes beginning to ripen, the Season, was very favourable to us. After having Coasted along the Cape two days, sometimes with a Larboard, and sometimes with a Starboard Tack, because of the contrary Wind and Current, we at last enter'd the Bay the 26*th* of *January* 1691 and cast Anchor about four in the Afternoon.

Tho' this seems to be an admirable Bay, its vast Bason being enclos'd on one side by a ridge of Mountains, and on the other by a long tract of Earth, which seems instead of a Mole for it. 'Tis however very often dangerous to ride in, the

---

[1] Robben (so called from the seals which used to inhabit it) or Penguin Island lies five miles N.E. from Green Point, at the entrance to Table Bay, and three miles from Blaauwberg beach, the northern boundary of the bay. A constantly northern current sets out between Robben Island and the mainland: added to which the wind blows with great violence from the S.E. In dark or hazy weather many ships have sailed right upon Green Point, without seeing land, whilst their masts were seen over the fog from the elevated ground, so it is a prudent course for a stranger not to beat into the bay in thick weather, but to keep off until it is clearer.

" On laisse sur la gauche en entrant une Isle assez basse nommée l'Isle Robin, au milieu de laquelle les Hollandois ont arboré leur Pavillon. Ils y releguent ceux du païs, & même ceux des Indes qu'ils veulent punir de banissement & les obligent d'y travailler à la chaux, qu'ils font des coquillages, que la Mer y jette." (*Père Tachard*, 1686.)

reason of which is, partly for that one of those Mountains which ought always to be a shelter to it, is sometimes, and even frequently a fatal Source of those impetuous Gusts, that presently put all the Ships into a terrible Disorder; besides, the Sea-winds are very furious, they blow with a frightful force, and the Anchorage not being very good, Ships are in great danger of running a-shoar, or oversetting, and no Boats are then suffer'd to come off to them. This bad Mountain is near the Point of the Cape, and call'd the *Devil's Mountain*, on account of the mischief it do's. 'Twas in the year 1493 that *Bartholomew Diaz*[1] was sent by *John* II, King of *Portugal* to discover this Cape; but he says, the dreadful Winds that always blow there, hinder'd him from Landing, and for that Reason he gave the Place the Name of *Tormentado*, the Tempestuous. The story adds, the King reply'd they shou'd not be so soon discourag'd, and that he wou'd himself give that Land the Name of the Cape of *Good Hope*.[2]

[1] A Portuguese expedition under Bartholomew Dias was despatched by King John II, from Lisbon, in 1487, along the west and south coasts of Africa, to find a route to the Indies, and successfully reached the Cape, named *Cabo Tormentoso*, afterwards Cabo de Boa Esperança, which name, some say, was given it instead of Agesingue, its proper designation, because that was the farthest the Portuguese King hoped to extend his explorations and conquests, or because this Cape gave expectation of better countries and discoveries beyond it. (*Weise*.)

[2] The southern promontory of Africa, commonly called the Cape of Good Hope, is a peninsula twenty-eight miles in length, composed of a vast mass of mountainous and rocky land. The north end of this promontory forms the west side of Table Bay, on the south coast of which stands Cape Town, having near it, on the west, the Lion's Mountain, 2,180 feet high; at two miles from it, to the south, the Table Mountain, 3,550 feet, eastward of which is the Devil's Berg, 3,270 feet, and other elevations.

The Cape, on approaching, either from the east or west, has the appearance of a large island. Of all the land the most remarkable feature is Table Mountain, which appears to have a flat, level summit with perpendicular sides. It is composed of a sandstone and quartzose rock resting on a granite base.

When the S.E. wind blows at the Cape, a remarkable phenomenon

There are two other Mountains near the *Devil's*, one call'd
the *Lyon's Mountain;* for that when we see it from the Bay,
some Men fansie it looks like a Lyon Couchant. On the top
of it there's always a Guard, and ten pieces of Canon: And '
when any Ships are discover'd at Sea, notice of it is giv'n to
the Port.

The other Mountain is call'd the *Table Mountain,* and with
good reason : for its Summit being cut off Horizontally, it
naturally enough represents the figure of a Table.   There's
a little Lake or Pond at the top of it, which supplies part of
the cultivated Lands in the bottom with Water: We had
several *Charts,* and took several views of the Bay, but this[1]
seem'd to us to be the best.

We found four Ships there, two *Dutch* (the *Black Lion* and
the *Mountain of China*), one *English,* and one *Danish.*   Our
Guns being still in the *Hold,* we cou'd not Salute them at
first according to Custom.   'Twas the next day before they
were ready, and when fir'd, it had been better we had let it
alone, unless we cou'd have come off more luckily ; though,
as it happen'd, 'twas well it was no worse ; for one of our
Guns which was loaden with Ball ever since we came from
the *Texel,* and had not been discharg'd, was forgotten to be
loaden, and being fir'd struck the Wall of the Fort, after

attends it, in that a dense, continuous mantle of cloud rests upon the
summits, and pouring down the precipitous sides like a cataract, dissolves
in vapour at about 1,000 feet.   This majestic white cap is called by the
inhabitants " the table-cloth", and by the French *La perruque* (cf.
Findlay, op. cit., p. 211).

[1] Vide *Voyage de Siam, des Pères Jesuites, envoyez par le Roy aux Indes
& à la Chine.   Avec leurs Observations Astronomiques, et leurs Remarques
de Physique, de Géographie, d'Hydrographie & d'Histoire.   A Paris,*
M.DC.LXXXVI., *par Guy Tachard de la Compagnie de Jesus.*   Plate of *La
Baye du Cap de Bonne Esperance,* p. 62, qto. edition; p. 53, 12mo
edition, 1687.   *C. Vermeulen fecit.*   The only difference between Tachard's
charts and that in Leguat's volume is the difference of size, with the in-
sertion of four ships and the omission of four large fish, meant perhaps
for whales, in the Jesuit's drawing.

having past through the middle of thirty Persons, and brush'd
a little the Beard of the Serjeant, who return'd us our Bullet.
We were chid for our Negligence, and that was all. I
remember to have read in *Lambard's*[1] Description of the
County of *Kent* in *England,* a like violent Salutation of a
Bullet which was shot thro' the Palace of *Greenwich,* and
whistl'd in the First Queen *Mary's* Ears. Kings don't love
such sort of Honours, and our Serjeant was of the same mind
with Kings.

The next day we went to deliver our Letters to the
Governour,[2] who check'd us for the Blunder we had made in
entring the Port, and indeed we deserv'd it. However, he
receiv'd us very civilly out of respect to the Treaty[3] Monsieur

---

[1] Lambard's *Perambulation of Kent,* 1576, p. 339. " One accident
more touching this house, and then an ende ; it hapened in the reigne
of *Queene Marie,* that the Master of a Ship, passing by whilest the
Court lay there, and meaning (as the manner and dutie is) with saile
and shot to honour the Princes presence unadvisedly gaue fyre to a
peice charged with a pellet in sted of a tampion, the which lighting on
the Palaice wall, ranne through one of the priuie lodginges, and did no
further harme."

[2] Herr Simon van der Stel was *Commandeur* at the Cape from 1679
to October 1691, when he was promoted Governor and, in 1692,
Gouverneur en Extraordinaar Raad, till 1699, when he retired to Con-
stantia. Herr Willem Pat was the Militaire Hoofd at the Castle from
1689-93.

[3] A few French refugees took service with the Dutch in South Africa
before 1685, when the Company decided to send out a French pastor and
some Huguenots as colonists, providing free passages and farms without
payment as inducements, in order to improve the cultivation of vines and
olives at the Cape. In 1688 several parties of French emigrants were
dispatched from Holland, whom the Commander, van der Stel, received
and treated kindly ; but, in 1689, when these French settlers requested
permission to establish a separate church at Drakenstein, he, being
anxious to blend the nationalities, contested their right. He therefore
viewed with pleasure the project of the Marquis du Quesne for drawing
French emigrants to the Island of Mascaregne, as thereby the proportion of French refugees introduced into Cape Colony would be lessened.
(*Cape Quarterly Review,* vol. i, p. 385.)

du Quesne had made with *Messieurs* the Directors of the *East-India* Company, from whom we also brought Letters of Recommendation. We afterwards made the necessary Inquiries for the prosecution of our Voyage, particularly if the *French* had again taken possession of the Island of *Mascaregne*, and if there was any news of their Squadron at the *Cape?* But we cou'd meet with no certain account of either the one or the other.

Some told us, the Squadron of Seven Men of War had put three hundred Men a-shoar there, in their way to the *Indies:* Others said, the *French* who were driv'n out of *Siam*, had seiz'd the Isle. And others assur'd us, that Squadron never touch'd there, and that there were only a few Families at *Mascaregne*, who had dwelt there a long time. These Reports being all different, were of no use to us. All agreed, that nothing cou'd compare with the Island of *Mascaregne* for Beauty and Fertility. That Corn, Grapes, and every thing else proper for the Nourishment of Man, grew there in abundance, and almost without Cultivating. This made us resolve to depart with all convenient speed for *Maurice* Isle which is not far from that of *Mascaregne* or *Eden*. We might expect there to be better inform'd of things, and enabled to concert our Measures better, to follow the Orders that were giv'n us in *Holland*.

Those of us that were sickest Landed at the Cape, as soon as we arriv'd, to cure our selves of the Scurvy, staying at Land being the only true and sovereign Remedy for that Distemper.

The Grapes were just beginning to grow ripe when we came there (which was an excellent Refreshment for our selves, and our Ships Crew :) We stay'd three Weeks at the *Cape*, as well to recover our Health, as to refit our Ship. Since my design is to speak more largely of the Cape of *Good Hope* in the sequel of this Relation, and to give an account of what Remarkable things I saw there in my Return,

I shall not detain the Reader any longer about it now, our good *Swallow* having been refresh'd as well as we, and all our Company being in a good state of Health, we weigh'd Anchor the 13*th* of *Feb.* 1691, after three Weeks rest a-shoar. We Saluted the Fort with five Guns, and so set Sail, tho' the Wind was not quite fair for us. After having tack'd to and again some time, we went on in a straight Course to double Cape *Needles*[1]; we came into 40 Degrees, and the Wind continu'd changeable till the 15*th* of *March*, when we had all the Prognosticks that fore-run a terrible Tempest.

The Wind became Impetuous in a very little time, and the Sea foaming and lifting up its Waves, form'd Mountains that seem'd higher than our Masts: the Air appear'd to be all on fire, Lightnings struck us almost blind, and the Waves rowl'd dreadfully in upon us. But our Crew were most of all terrify'd at the sight of *St. Elme's*[2] Fire, which stuck to our

---

[1] During the Southern summer, October to April, the passage round the Cape is a simple and easy one to make, the track lying within the region of the anti-trade winds. The chief difficulties are the strong gales which are encountered further to the south, at this season, than they are in winter, when they occur near the latitude of Cape Colony. Besides the adverse winds in the summer near the Cape, there is the Agulhas current to be encountered, setting to the west along the edge of the Agulhas bank. To avoid this a high latitude should be chosen, and the parallel recommended to run down the easting as far as the longitude of eastern Madagascar, is that between lats. 38° and 40°. After reaching longitude 54° or 55°, turning northward, the route carries between Mauritius and Réunion. This track, which was known and used from early time, has been named by the French "the Boscawen passage", in consequence of Admiral Boscawen, with a convoy of twenty-six sail, making a quick passage by this route in 1748.

All that part of Africa of which Cape Agulhas is the southernmost point is surrounded by a bank of soundings, which is called the bank of Agulhas. This bank begins at 32° 30' of S. lat., near the coast, in long. 29° E., and continually increases its breadth to the southwestward, till it exceeds 135 miles, then, extending north-west, it contracts to the Cape of Good Hope, and finally terminates near St. Helena Bay. (*Findlay.*)

[2] "Dans l'une de ces Travades parurent deux diverses fois sur les mats, sur les vergues & sur le canon de notre Navire, de ces petits feux

Masts: Our Ship was so little, that People were amaz'd at the sight of it at the Cape, and 'twas now driv'n along with inconceiveable swiftness: All things were in Confusion, and horrible Disorder. Our Tackling broke, our Chests, our Arms, Beds, the Mariners and Passengers were tumbled *Pell-mell*, from one side to t'other: The Heavens which appear'd at first to us to be all on fire, were now hid from our Eyes by black Clouds, from whose profound depths issu'd such Torrents of Water, as threaten'd to overwhelm those that handled the Ropes with present Destruction.

Our Deck was always a Foot deep in Water, for the Sea threw it in faster than it cou'd run out; and it added to our Terrors, that no body there had ever seen the like before, so extraordinary was this Storm; the same Wind encreas'd still to a certain Point: after which all the others blew successively, and sometimes mingled together with equal fury to make Sport with our poor little Vessel, which this Minute they tost up to the Skyes, and the next sunk down to the Earth. During the ten hours that this Tempest lasted, all the Winds conspir'd to make an entire *tour* of the Compass; and it being impossible to handle the Ropes and Sails to work the Ship regularly, we were all that while oblig'd to abandon our selves to the caprice and fury of the Waves.

At last the Storm decreas'd by little and little, we recover'd Hope in the midst of Despair, and heartily Congratulated one another on our common Deliverance, each of us feeling a secret Joy, which none can be sensible of, that has not escap'd the like Danger, and been deliver'd out of so great and so just a Fright. We therefore return'd thanks

de figure piramidale, que les Portugais appellent le feu de saint Telme & non pas Saint Helme. Quelques Matelots les regardent comme l'ame du Saint de ce nom, qu'ils invoquent alors de toutes leurs forces, les mains jointes & avec beaucoup d'autres marques de respect. . . . . . Ce sont ces mêmes feux que les Payens adoroient autrefois sous le nom de Castor & de Pollux; & il est surprenant que cette superstition se soit ainsi introduite parmy les Chrêtiens." (*Voyage de Siam*, 1686.)

to him, that had preserv'd us in the midst of it thro' his infinite Mercy.

When we were a little come to our selves, we lookt upon
those dreadful Billows which threaten'd still to swallow us
up, as if they only play'd with us, and concluded that the
Tempest in which we had been, cou'd be nothing less than a
Hurricane. We found a true and lively Description of it in
the CVII Psalm, which we read with great Pleasure and
Admiration, as we did also the XXIX.

Let who will boast of the famous *Idœa's* of *Virgil* on the
same Subject: What he says, do's not come up to the
Sublime of these two Psalms. And, indeed, all the Places
admir'd by the Pedants in the *Greek* and *Latin* Poets, are
but Trifles, in Comparison with the Magnificent and Inimitable Canticles of *David*.

We Discours'd a long time on the terrible and almost in-
credible effects of the Matter of Air, which is in appearance
so soft, so weak, so light, so invisible, and like to nothing,
and which in the impetuous Agitations of these Whirl-winds,
tear up the greatest Trees by the Roots, break Ships to
pieces, throw down Houses, and in a few Minutes cause such
great Disorders.

What's most to be admir'd in it, is, that the surest Presage
of a Hurricane[1] (an *Indian* Word which we have adopted)

---

[1] *"Ouragan"*. The winds and weather between the Cape and the
meridians of Madagascar or Mauritius are certainly very peculiar, being
a sort of debatable ground between the trades and the anti-trades,
a region alternately affected by both.

Lieut. Bridet, Director of the Observatory at St. Denis, Réunion,
attributes the rotatory gales or cyclones, which are encountered as far
south as lat. 40°, to the recurving of those true cyclones which com-
mence in the northern margin of the trade winds. These cyclones turn
from left to right, like all others in the southern hemisphere, but
with an angular velocity less than that of the cyclones of the torrid
zone.

These extra tropical gales, which are most violent from May to
August, invariably travel to the eastward. They last from one to

is a perfect Calm; the Sea puts on a deceitful Mien, she smooths all her Furrows, and leaves not the least wrinkle on her Brows, but looks on you with a gay and smiling Air.

I wish those Gentlemen whom we call Philosophers, wou'd shew us distinctly the secret Springs of these several wonderful Movements; instead of filling their famous Writings with their little superficial Reasons, which are almost always false. True sages humbly confess that Nature has her unsearchable Depths, and that to speak properly, all these are things Divine. They acknowledge also, that one of the greatest Sciences of true Philosophy, is not to be ignorant of ones Ignorance.

It has been thought that the Rain is salt when the Hurricane is at the height; several Voyagers have written as much, but tho' I will not positively deny the matter of fact, I am very apt to believe they confound the sprinklings of the Waves with the Rain: If 'tis said that the Rain has been found to be Salt a-shoar, in the middle of certain Islands, I answer in the first place, that I doubt it, and add, that the same Whirl-winds that lift up the greatest Vessels, may also raise up great quantities of those broken Waves, and scatter them to a vast distance, in these Isles or other Places far from the Sea, where, falling down in drops, they may easily be mistaken for Rain.

I shall say one word only of *St. Elme's* Fire, which I saw sticking to our Masts when the Storm was at the strongest, because I did not make any particular Observation of that

seven days, and travel at the rate of from four to twenty miles an hour. These storms are generally limited within a few degrees to the latitude of 40°.

The gales most to be dreaded are those which are preceded by heavy black clouds, rising from the N.W. and W., sometimes with lightning. The old Dutch commanders were directed by the East India Company to wear and shorten sail when this occurred, as a gale might be expected.

Phænomena. I saw it but by chance, and my Mind was
then so employ'd about things of another Nature, that it had
no time for matters of Curiosity. I observ'd a Body of
blewish Light, as it were curl round one of our Masts, and I
did not look to see if there was any more; what makes me
believe there was but one, is, our Seamen were frighted at
the sight of it; Whereas, had there been two, these poor
Wretches wou'd have taken it for a Happy Omen. 'Twas
without doubt according to this Idæa, that the Name of one
of these two Fires only, is not mention'd by *St. Paul* speaking of the Ship he was in, but of both together: I say of
both, because two was then spoken of. The two Children
that came out of the same Womb with *Hellen* and *Clytem-
nestra*, the two Eggs of *Læda*, which some have transform'd
into the Constellation of *Gemini*, and others adore under
their Primitive Name of *Castor* and *Pollux*, as Gods of the
Sea, because they support Pirates: But I know there sometimes appear four or five together, and perhaps more. As
for Monsieur *St. Elme* succeeding Monsieur *St. Castor*, and
Monsieur *St. Pollux*, 'tis a question that I leave to some
Seraphick Doctor to decide how it came about.

The 3d of *April* we saw Land, great News! What it was
we cou'd not tell, for we had lost our *Tramontane*[1]; Nevertheless we flatter'd ourselves with Hopes that 'twas the Isle
of *Eden;* and we made Merry with the thoughts of setting
foot on the Land we so much desir'd as design'd for the

---

[1] *Tramontana* or *Tresmontaine* = the Pole Star, thus alluded to in a
document among the Ashburnham MSS.:—

> "La tresmontaine est de tel guise
> Qu'ele est el firmament asisse
> Où ele luist et reflambie
> Li maronier qui vont en Frise
> En Gresse, en Acre, ou en Venise.
> *   *   *   *
> Pour bise, ne pour autre afaire
> Ne laist sen dout servise à faire,
> La tresmontaigne clere et pure

place of our Habitation. The Wind seem'd to have a spirit
of Contradiction, and wou'd not let us approach it, however,
we disputed that Matter so effectually with it, that, in spite
of its Obstinacy, we drew so near it as to perceive, after a
strict Examination, 'twas the same we sought after, and had
now found with equal Surprize and Joy.

We discover'd several Beauties in this admirable Country,
from the place where we stopt to view it : All that part of it
which presented it self to our View appear'd to be a Level,
with Mountains rising in the Middle; and we cou'd easily
discern the agreeable mixture of Woods, Rivers and Valleys
enamell'd with a charming Verdure : If our Sight was perfectly well pleas'd, our Smell was no less ; for the Air was
perfum'd with a Delicious Odour that ascended from the
Isle, and that plainly arose from the abundance of Limons
and Oranges which grow there. This sweet Odour struck us
all alike, when we came at a certain distance from the Island :
some agreeably complain'd, that the Perfume hinder'd them
from sleeping, others said they were so embalm'd with it,
that 'twas as much a Refreshment to them, as if they had
been fifteen days a-shoar.

The Account[1] which Monsieur *Du Quesne* order'd to be
publish'd of this Island, has not this Particular, but Mr.
Delon[2] did not forget it ; and he even writes, that he believes

Les maroniers par son esclaire
Jete souvent hors de contraire
Et de chemin les asséure."
(*Lais inédits*, M. F. Michel, Paris, 1836, quoted by Wm. Chapell
in *Nature*, June 15, 1876.)

Perdre la Tramontane, equivalent to lose reckoning. "Il ne plus
pouvoir s'aider de la boussole à cause d'agitation du vaisseau" (*Littré*).
In fact, they knocked about so much that the compass-bearings could
not be depended on.

[1] *Vide ante*, p. 2, and Appendix.

[2] *Relation de Voyage*, par M. Dellon, 2 vols. in 12, Paris, 1685. M.
Dellon writes : " For the rest, there is neither Serpent nor Scorpion, or
any other reptiles or Venomous Insects to be found in this Island, the

the Reason why there are no Serpents, Rats, nor Venomous
Insects in that Isle, is, because the great number of Odori-
ferous Flowers with which it is cover'd, are Poyson to those
Animals, which he says he has experienc'd. We cou'd not
help praising this Paradise, all of us extoll'd it but the Captain, who affected to speak the quite contrary, whatever
Disposition he then shew'd to it, and however positive his
Orders were to Land on that Island, he never intended it;
and 'twas pure chance that brought him so near it, for he
thought he was above forty Leagues off when we discover'd
it. He seem'd to be amaz'd when the Pilot told him he
spy'd Land, and believ'd 'twas that we sought after. I shall
not pretend here to give this Man's secret Reasons for what
he did, because I know nothing but by Conjecture, and besides, 'tis not to our purpose, be it one way or t'other. (Alas,
I can hardly hold my Pen in my Hand to say it); this Cheat,
this Rascal, took hold of the weak Condition we were in,
drew farther off from the Island by little and little, and
sail'd directly to *Diego-Ruys*. His Ships Crew were all at
his Disposal, and we, the Passengers, being all Sick, cou'd
not pretend to force him to execute his Commission. 'Tis
easie to imagine how we were surpriz'd and troubled.

As for the Description of this Amiable Country, since I
was not so happy as to visit it my self, which the Reader
has expected I should do from the beginning of the Voyage:
I believe he will not be displeas'd, if I have recourse to a
means to procure it for him that will in a great measure
make amends for my disappointing him. To this end I will
abridge the Relation[1] of the most Remarkable Rarities of this

goodness of it being such, as to be quite contrary to these Creatures, as
it has been found by several Experiments which the *French* have made
upon Rats." (*A Voyage to the East Indies*, 1698, p. 12.)

[1] "Now that I have compared Leguat's extracts from Du Quesne
with the tract found and reprinted by M. Sauzier in 1887, I feel very
doubtful whether M. Sauzier has got hold of the right thing. I don't
doubt that his prize is the work of du Quesne, but it reads like an

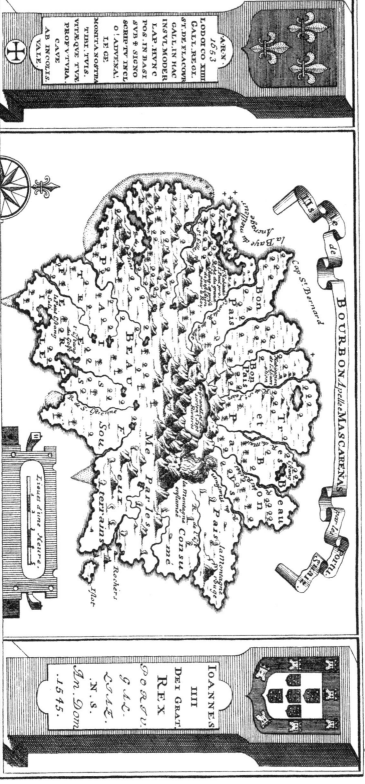

Island, which Monsieur *du Quesne* made publick before our
departure from *Holland*. 'Tis true, this Relation may be
suspected by those who think 'twas his Interest to pre-
possess the World with an advantageous Opinion of the new
World which he was going to Inhabit: But tò this I shall
first reply that Monsieur *du Quesne* was so very far from
adding to the truth, that he wou'd not suffer any thing to be
inserted in the Book he order'd to be Publish'd, which had
the least air of Exaggeration: And in the next place I add
that at *Maurice* Island, *Batavia* and the *Cape*, I can my self
Witness, every Body allow'd there was nothing in that Relation, which was not exactly conformable to Truth.

"This Island was at first call'd *Mascarenas*, by the *Portuguese*, who took Possession of it in the Reign of their King
John IV,[1] in the Year 1545. M. *de Flacour* set up the
Standard of *France* there, one hundred and eight Years
afterwards, in the Name of Lewis XIV. now reigning, and
gave it the Illustrious Name of *Bourbon*. What he wrote
concerning it is to be seen. He put the Arms of *France* on
the very Monument where he found those of *Portugal*, having
done the same at *Madagascar*.

"I believe the *French* have as good as abandon'd this little
Island. Others that have since landed there, have found it
to be so excellent and so beautiful, that they look'd upon it
as a Terrestrial Paradise, and gave it the fine Name of *Eden*;
that is, *The Country of Delight*."[2]

The Relation out of which I have taken this Abstract

abridgment of some book which Leguat had before him. If Leguat had
had only the tract which M. Sauzier found he would never have inserted
so many particulars which it does not contain."—N.

[1] This is an error of du Quesne; it should be John III. In 1661
M. de Flacourt described Bourbon, and gave a map showing the rivers
and the volcano. The rivers are named and the habitation of the
French settlers is shown at St. Paul. M. du Quesne evidently drew
upon M. Flacourt's account for his description of Mascaregne.

[2] De Flacourt wrote : "Ce seroit auec juste raison que l'on pourroit
appeller cette isle un Paradis terrestre."

says, no Body ever went quite thro' the Island, which was for want of good Information. The Map I have plac'd here, was taken from a Description given by Persons that visited it all over, and liv'd there several Years.

Monsieur du Quesne adds, " Be it as it will, 'tis certain the Isle of Eden is of a sufficient Extent, to contain easily a long Descent of Generations, of whatever Colony will settle there.

" 'Tis most true, *says our Author*, That Voyagers have not made mention of any Country where the Air is more healthy than in this Isle; which is a very important Article. 'Tis well known abundance of sick People have gone ashoar there, and have recover'd their Health in a very little time. The same have those said, who have remain'd there much longer; tho' they wanted several Conveniencies, and were but too much expos'd sometimes to the Sun, and sometimes to the Dew. The Sky is clear; the Exhalations of the Earth, as well as those of the Aromatick Plants and Flowers, with which 'tis cover'd, perfume the Air, and they breath'd in a Balmy Spirit equally wholesome and agreeable.

" This charming Isle[1] lies between 21 and 22 deg. of S. Latitude, and has one Advantage in common with other Countries near the *Line*, that the Heats are temper'd by certain cool and regular Breezes, which Providence, admirable in all its Ways, has so dispos'd to render these Countries more Commodious for Habitation.

" The abundance of Springs that are found in this Isle, is

---

[1] Réunion, as the island is now called, is situated in lat. 20° 51', long. 55° 26' (*St. Denis*). It was captured by the British in 1810, but restored to France by the treaty of Paris in 1815, and is now an important colony of the Republic. It is 138 miles in circumference, and 48 miles long, east and west, by 34 miles broad, north and south. The island is a mass of volcanic mountains, the ridges rising to a height of 10,169 feet between the extinct crater *cirques*, whilst an active volcano forms the extremity of the island, whose summit is 8,613 feet in height. Its area contains about 610,000 acres, of which nearly one-third is cultivated.

one of its Rarities. The Water is clear and wholesome, and
some of it Purgative. From these Springs flow Rivulets,
and even some Rivers, which water all the Plains, and are so
full of Fish, that Voyagers affirm, *Those who ford them find
it so slippery, they can hardly stand for the Number of Fish.*[1]
There are several Lakes, and one among the rest, so plentiful
of Springs, that seven great Rivulets run out of it into a vast
and rich Plain.

"There is no venomous Creature upon it, neither in the
Water, neither on the dry Land; whereas almost all other
hot Countries are full of Snakes, and such sort of Animals,
whose Sting or Bite is dangerous, if not mortal. The same
thing is affirm'd of the Plants and Fruits here.

"I shall say nothing of the admirable Shells that are
pick'd up on the Sea shoar, nor of the Coral and Ambergreese
that are found here, tho' they are both valuable and useful
Things. But I must declare that the Sea is full of Fish, and
that its Turtles only wou'd abundantly and deliciously subsist
the Inhabitants. The Land Turtles are also some of the
Riches of the Island. There are vast Numbers of them: Their
Flesh is very delicate; the Fat better than Butter or the best
Oil, for all sorts of Sawces. Some of the Sea turtles weigh
above 500 Pound weight. The Land Turtles are not so big;
but the great ones carry a Man with more ease than a Man
can carry them. This Oil of Turtle, for 'tis a sort of Fat,
which do's not congeal as other Fat do's, is an excellent
Remedy in several Distempers.

"The Forrests are not so thick but one may easily go thro'
them, and the Shade do's not hinder the Fruit from ripening.
There is abundance of Cedars, of Ebony, and Timber for
Carpenter's use, Palm-Trees, Fig-Trees, Plantanes, Oranges,

[1] "Les estangs & riuieres y fourmillent de poissons, il n'i a ni cro-
codilles dans icelles, ni serpens nuisibles à l'homme, ni insectes facheu-
ses, ainsi que dans les autres iles, ni pulces, ni mouches, ni mousquites
picquantes, ni fourmis, ni rats, ni souris." (*De Flacourt*, 1661.)

Limons, etc. We might name 20 other different kinds of Trees that bear Fruit good to eat, and the variety of their Tastes are enough to content those of all Men. Aloes, Indigo, Sugar Canes, Cotton, Ananas, Bananas, Tobacco, Potatoes, Pumpkins, Land and Water Melons, Cucumbers, Charibbean Cabages, Beans, Artichokes, a certain sort of Pease, and a hundred other Plants. Fruits or Roots of this nature grow naturally every where. 'Tis experienc'd that Indian Corn, Millet, Rice, Wheat, Barley, and Oats grow very well there, and that one may have above one Crop a Year of all these several sorts of Grains. People have had the Curiosity to sow some of each sort of our Pulse and Garden Herbs (which I shall not particularise, for fear of being tiresome), and they all came up to a wonder. The reason is, 'tis an excellent Soil, and the Father of Nature has render'd it admirably fruitful. Since we find very good Grapes there, we have reason to believe one may have very good Wine; and, no doubt, might with the same success raise any of the Fruit-trees peculiar to our Continent.

"The black Cattle,[1] Hogs and Goats, that were formerly left there by the *Portuguese*, are so multiply'd that we meet with them in Droves in the Forrests; and one may reasonably expect that. Dear, Sheep, and all Animals that we find any where else, in the same Climate, wou'd in the same manner succeed there.

"The Fowl that are most plenty in this Island, are Partridges, Doves, Ducks, Wood-Pigeons, Woodcocks, Quales, Black-Birds, Puets, Thrushes, Geese, Coots, Ducks, Bitterns, Parrots, Herons, Peacocks,[2] Fools, Frigats, Sparrows, and

---

[1] "En cette année mil six cens-quarante-neuf, i'y ay fait passer quatre genisses et un toreau, afin d'y multiplier. Et en l'année mil six cens cinquante-quatre, i'y en ay enuoyé autant, lesquelles on trouua qu'elles estoient multipliées jusques à plus de trente." (*De Flacourt.*)

[2] "In the English translation the word 'Géants' is here given as 'peacocks', as though it had been '*paons*'; but at p. 171 by 'giants'" (*Strickland*). "Les oiseaux de terre sont : le solitaire (comme une

abundances of other small Birds, as also Birds of Prey, and other Birds. There are Batts whose[1] Bodies are bigger than a Hen's, and the Flesh of them very pleasant to eat, when a Man gets over that Aversion to 'em which is begot by Prejudice. The Parrots are also excellent Food. The Pea-cocks are great Birds mounted upon Stilts; they frequent Lakes and Rivers, and their Flesh tastes much like that of a Bittern. The Partridges are all grey, and half as little again as ours. The Males of the Sparrows have red Breasts,[2] and when they make Love, redder than ordinary. But these little Animals, which, like Flowers and Butter-flies, seem to be made only to embellish Nature, multiply so fast, that, to say the Truth, they are troublesome. They come in Clouds, and carry away the Corn that is sown, if great Care is not taken of it; which is doubtless an Inconvenience; but a little Gunpowder soon frightens 'em away. There are also Caterpillars and Flyes, which are a little vexatious. And lastly (for we must say all we can, if we wou'd give a true and entire Idea of Things) those dreadful Tempests, that are

grosse oie), blanc, avec noir à l'extremité des ailes et de la queue, où il y a des plumes pareilles à celles de l'autruche, col long, bec de bécasse, mais plus gros, pieds de poule d'Inde, se prennent à la course et vollent peu. C'est un des meilleurs gibiers de l'île. Les oiseaux bleus, gros comme les précédents, avec bec et pieds rouges, faits comme pieds de poules, ne volant pas mais courant très-vite." (*Dubois*, 1669, quoted by *Maillard*, p. 10.)

[1] *Collet rouge*, or flying fox, is a large species of bat, *Pteropus Edwardsii*. Some specimens measure over three feet from tip to tip of the wings. "Il y a aussi beaucoup de tortues de terre et de mer, et des chauve-souris, grosses comme des petits chats." (*Dubois*.)

[2] These "Sparrows with red breasts" belonged to a species of weaver-bird, *Foudia Bruante* (*P. L. S. Müller*), of which Sir Edward Newton says (*Trans. Norfolk and Norw. Natural Soc.*, iv, p. 543) that "it was described in the last century by Buffon and figured by Daubertin. The specimen which provided the description and figure no longer exists, so far as I can ascertain. I have never heard of anyone now living who has ever seen an example of the bird. Its place on the island is now taken by the kindred species, *Foudia Madagascariensis*, introduced from Madagascar." See Appendix for list of Bourbon birds.

known by the Name of *Hurricanes*, are a dismal Article. However, we are assur'd they are much less violent than those of *America*; and, after all, do not last above four and twenty Hours. Besides, these terrible Tempests never happen but once a Year, and there are infallible ways of providing against them: to which we may add, that for one bad Day there are three hundred and sixty-four wonderfully fair ones. And this Consideration is very comfortable. Wise Men, who have had a little Experience of the World, and travell'd a little, know that no perfect happiness is to be expected in it, neither under the *Line* nor under the *Poles*. Every Thing has its For and Against, and the best is but the least bad. All that can be done therefore on this Occasion, as well as in others, is to take the Balance and weigh Things before we determine what to do. If some Inconveniencies in our *Eden* trouble you, says Mr. *du Quesne*, Put the Catterpillars, the Flyes and the Sparrows of this Isle, together with one *Hurricane* a Year, in one Scale, and add *Health, Liberty, Safety, Abundance*, and *Peace*. To counterbalance these three sorts of little troublesome Animals, put all those strange Beasts that our famous *Molière* calls Harpagons,[1] Purgons,[2] Macratons, Mascarils,[3] Metaphrasts,[4] Trissotins,[5] Town-Fops, all the Race of Misers, Cheats, Coxcombs, and Blockheads, add to that Dragons and Beetles, Cellar-Rats, Barn-Rats, Slavery, Poverty, Alarms, and a thousand Miseries, and see which Scale is the heaviest!"

I must again declare, 'twas to our great Regret, that we saw our selves leaving this Island behind us, this charming Island, so much desir'd by us. We were so weak and so troubled, that we consented to what we could not help; and

[1] *Harpagon*, the miser in *L'Avare*, by Molière (1667).
[2] *Purgon*, the conventional doctor in *Le Malade Imaginaire*.
[3] *Mascarille*, the sham marquis in *Les Precieuses Ridicules*, by Molière (1659).
[4] *Métaphrast*, a critic, *l'auteur qui l'explique*.
[5] *Trissotin*, a *bel esprit* in *Les Femmes Savantes*, by Molière (1672).

English Bay.   The Peak.

ISLAND

LOOKING

J.Wiggon del., C.D.M^cS. lith.

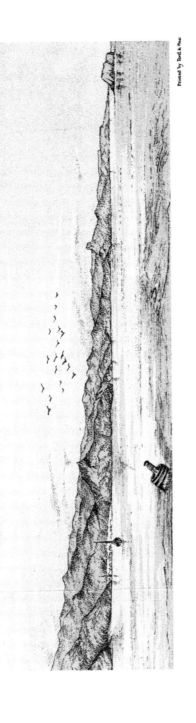

Printed by Ford & West

Waterfall Glen. Port Mathurin Castle Hill Oyster Bay. Friar's Hood. Diamond Island.

R O D R I G U E Z.

SOUTH.

2 & 3. miles.

the Commander of our *Swallow* endeavour'd to persuade us
he wou'd carry us to a Place every whit as good as that of
which we were so fond. 'Twas but one hundred and fifty
Leagues from this Island, but the Wind was so contrary,
that we' were forc'd to tack to and again for a Month
together.

Poor *John Pagni*, one of our Companions, dy'd between
the Isle we had found, and that we were seeking. He cou'd
no longer resist the Violence of the Scurvy and the Oppression
that tormented him.

On Saturday Morning, the 25th of *April* 1691, Old Stile,
we spy'd *Land*, which was the little Island *Diego Ruys*, where
our Captain resolv'd to carry us; we came very near it, by
the Eastern Point sailing Southward. It appear'd to us to
be difficult of access, it being surrounded with Rocks call'd
Shelves,[1] which run very far out into the Sea. We did not
at first perceive either Port, or Bay, or any Place where we
might land. In the Evening we sounded and met with
the Bottom, three Leagues from Shoar. We cast Anchor,
'twas a Calm, and we stay'd there till Monday the 27th. for
what reason I know not. That and the next day we spent
in examining the outside of the Isle as much as we cou'd,
to endeavour to discover some Place that was accessible.
The 28th, about four in the Afternoon, we perceiv'd an
Opening, which seem'd proper for our Design: But the
Night following we were driv'n out to Sea, and beat there
till the next Day. About 11 a Clock in the Forenoon a
Calm took us, and brought us into great Danger; for a rapid
Current plainly carry'd us among Rocks, that run out above
a League into the Sea. We were so near that there was no

---

[1] *Shelves*, the coral reefs which encircle the island. "*Brisans*" in the
French edition, rocks on which the sea breaks in heavy surf. Glorious
old John Dryden used the word *shelves*:

"Three ships were hurried by the southern blast
    And on the secret shelves with fury cast." (*Æneid*, i, 154.)

likelihood of avoiding them, when by the special Mercy of
Heaven there sprang up a brisk and fair Wind that drove us
back.   We then made the *Cape* towards the North Point, and
at Noon the Captain put out his Boat to seek for a Place to
enter.   In the Evening we sail'd towards the Northeast Point,
and the Boat gave us a Signal that it had found out good
Anchorage: We were then on the Rock in eight Fathom
Water only, which oblig'd us to be always sounding.   We
cast Anchor in nine Fathom, a sandy Mud at Bottom; our
Ship was tow'd along by the Boat; We lay there till the
next Day, when we intended to look out for a better Place.
Accordingly, early in the Morning, the 30th of April, we
cast Anchor in nine Fathom Water, a good Bottom of Ouzy
Sand, and shelter'd from the East and South-East Winds,
which blow always in that Country.

     The Island afar off, and near at hand, appear'd to us very
lovely: The Captain, who had his Reasons for not landing us
at *Tristan* or *Mascaregna,* desir'd nothing better than to
leave us at *Rodrigo,* and with that Design he highly extoll'd
the Beauty and Advantages of this Island; and indeed this
little new World seem'd full of Delights and Charms.   'Tis
true we did not see so many Birds flying about as at *Tristan,*
and our *Road* was not so perfum'd with the *Odours* of the
neighbouring Shoar as at *Eden,* from whence we had been
come about a Month.   But we cou'd not thence conclude
there were no Birds in the New Island, nor no Flowers to
send up grateful Sweets.   Besides, the Face of it was extreamly Fair.   We cou'd hardly take our Eyes off from the
little Mountains, of which it almost entirely consists, they
are so richly spread with great and tall Trees.   The Rivers
that we saw run from them water'd Valleys, whose Fertility
we cou'd not doubt of; and, after having run thro' a beautiful
Level, they fell into the Sea, even before our Eyes.   Their
Banks were adorn'd with Forrests; and some of us, at the

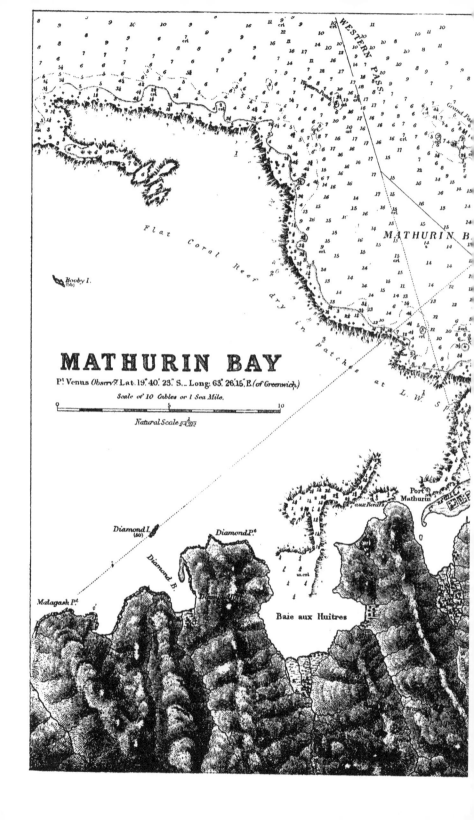

MATHURIN BAY

P.^t Venus *Observ.^y* Lat. 19.° 40.′ 23.″ S. — Long. 63.° 26.15.″ E. *(of Greenwich.)*

Scale of 10 Cables or 1 Sea Mile.

Natural Scale $\frac{1}{74,273}$

WESTERN PASS.

MATHURIN B.

Booby I.
(55)

Flat Coral Reef dry in patches at L. W. S.

Diamond I.
(50)

Diamond P.^t

Diamond B.

Malagash P.^t

Baie aux Huitres

Port
Mathurin

aux Boeufs

sight of this Lovely Isle, call'd to mind the famous *Lignon*,[1]
and those several enchanted Places, so agreeably describ'd
by Mr. *d'Urfé* in his Romance; But our Thoughts were immediately carry'd away by other Contemplations. We
admir'd the secret and wonderful Ways of Providence,
which, after having permitted us to be ruin'd at home, had
brought us thence by many Miracles, and now dry'd up all
our Tears, by the sight of the Earthly Paradise it presented
to our view; where, if we wou'd, we might be rich, free and
happy; if contemning vain Riches, we wou'd employ the
peaceable Life that was offer'd to us, to glorifie God and save
our Souls.

We were all of us more busy'd with these sweet Medita-
tions, than possess'd with Transports of Joy, when the Boat
was put out again, and we were ask'd who wou'd go ashoar?
Upon which every one rose up hastily, tho' there was not
one but was sick. All my Companions got into the Boat,
but seeing it was full, I made no great haste after them. I
was older by much than any of them, and consequently more
Master of my self; and being full of I know not what,
mixtures of Grief and Joy, I spent the rest of the Day in
profound Silence.

In the Evening the Captain return'd, and told me Wonders
of the Country, which he exaggerated much beyond the
Truth, as I had time enough to discover. He talk'd to me
of Animals and Fruits that were never seen in that Island.
'Tis true, he brought back several sorts of great and good
Birds: I experienc'd the Truth of that by making an agree-

---

[1] A small stream in the department of Loire, which, taking its rise
in the hills of Forez, flows through Boen and by the family château of
the celebrated d'Urfé (who has there placed the scene of his romance
l'Astrée), and enters the river Loire near Feurs. It is not surprising to
find Leguat quoting this romance, first published in the reign of Henri
IV, for it continued a popular book down to the days of J. J. Rousseau
(born in 1712), with whom it was a favourite volume during his youth.
(Note in Eugène Muller's version of *Leguat's Voyage*, p. 60.)

able Meal on this new and unknown Dish. The next day (the 1st of *May* 1691) I follow'd my Companions, and went ashoar.

This Isle, which is call'd either *Diego-Rodrigo*, or *Diego-Ruys*, or *Rodrigo*, is situated in nineteen Degrees of South Latitude. 'Tis about twenty Miles (*lieues*) in Circuit. Its Length from East to West, and its Shape, are as may be seen in the Map.

We seated our selves near the Sea, on the North North-West Shoar, in a lovely Valley, by the side of a great Brook, the Water of which was clear and good. We went all over the Island, and chose this Place as the most convenient, and that which Providence design'd for us, by conducting us first to it.

I have observ'd that every one to whom I have told my Adventures, have had a great Curiosity to know the Disposition of our little Habitations ; 'tis for that reason I now lay down a Plan of them. For by my own Experience, I know very well that when the Reader by this means conceives any Idea of the Places where Things happen'd, he is the more concern'd about the Things themselves.

Let him therefore cast his Eyes on the *Map* I set before him, he will see I distinguish it from the General Plan of the Island, because Things cou'd not have been so distinctly mark'd there. I desire he wou'd pardon my deficiency in *Designing*, which I profess not to understand, I give him what I have, and I can do no more. As I have made but an imperfect Relation of Things, so I have drawn but an imperfect Design, in this small Delineation of our poor Settlement. And I hope my Defects will not be found to be so great, but he may himself easily supply them.

The little River he sees, comes from the middle of the Island, and at four or five thousand common Paces below our Cabbins, it forms several Cascades, falling from Rock to Rock, and several Basons (*et napes d'eau*), that wou'd adorn a Prince's Garden. In a hot and dry Time it receives very little Water from its Fountain ; But in all

Plate IV. p 5

E. Higgin Del. C. D. M. S. Lithog.

PORT MATHURIN.

(RODRIGUEZ.)

Looking west.

Times the Tide fills it to the Brink of the Banks. The little
Space which I have mark'd towards the Left, and at the
Mouth of it, is low Ground, which the Sea covers as often
as it rises. This side of the Water is in general lower than
the other, and subject to frequent Inundations by the Floods
in *Hurricane* time.

Peter Thomas, one of our Pilots, of whom I have made
mention, chose to inhabit a little Island form'd by the River.
He built his Cabbin there, and made a little Garden with a
double Bridge. He was a very pretty Lad, and us'd to perch
upon a Tree in an Inundation; which brings to my Remembrance the glorious Monarch *Charles* II when he was
mounted up in the famous Oak at *Boscobel,*[1] whose Relicks
are Venerable to this Day. But whereas that King durst not
say a Word, or only Whisper to Captain *Sans-Soucy,*[2] the
Companion of his Fortune, Master *Peter Thomas*[3] play'd on

[1] After the battle of Worcester Charles heard, at the house of John
Penderell, near the Boscobel Wood, that Colonel Careless was hiding
in the vicinity. At his suggestion the prince passed the third day of
his wanderings in concealment with Colonel Careless, among the
branches of an oak tree, which was called the Royal Oak, and remained
standing as late as the middle of the last century, when it was mentioned by Dr. Stukeley in his *Itinerarium Curiosum,* published in 1776.
  The reference to the Oak of Boscobel seems a favourite allusion of
Max. Misson, who in his *New Voyage to Italy* writes : " This is no ill
Thought ; and puts me in Mind of some of our Friends in *London,* who
have precious Snuff-Boxes, made of the *Royal*-Oak known as Boscobel."
[2] " The Name of the Captain that accompany'd the King in the Oak
at *Boscobel* was *Careless,* an English Word which signifies Negligence,
or without Care. But the King thought fit to change his Name from
Careless to *Carlos.*" (See Sylvanus Morgan's *Spheres of Gentry,* and
Dr. Chamberlain's *Present State of England,* vol. i, ch. 4.)—Note by
the editor of the original edition. The translator has retained the
French equivalent for Careless—*Sans-souci*—in the text as it stands in
the French edition.
[3] This Peter Thomas is not mentioned in the list of Leguat's companions on p. 6 (*supra*). He appears to have been one of the crew of
the ship, and to have made up his mind to remain at Rodriguez at the
last moment when the ship sailed. See note in Muller's 1883 edition,
p. 71, and p. 55 *infra.*

the Flute, or sung, or chatter'd freely with his Friends.   He
was the Only Man of the Company that smoak'd Tobacco :
He was also a Mariner.   When his Tobacco was gone he
smoak'd Leaves.

The next Cabbin to the Isle on the Right-hand towards
the Sea, was Mr. *de la Haye's*.   He was a Silversmith, and
had built a Forge, so that he was oblig'd to make his House
a little bigger than the rest.   *La Haye* was always singing of
Psalms, whether he was at work or walking.

The Cabbins were ten or twelve Foot square, some more
some less, according to the Fansie of the Builder.   The Walls
were made of the Trunks of Plantanes,[1] and the broad Leaves
of the same Tree serv'd to cover them.   The Dotts about
every Cabbin shew where the Pallisado's stood, which enclos'd our Gardens.   The Doors are also mark'd by the void
Spaces.

The Plan shews at what distance these Hutts (*maison-
ettes*) were one from the other.

Near poor *la Haye's*, on the same side of the River, and
not far from the Water, was the *Stadt-House* (*Hôtel-de-
ville*), or, if you please, the Place of Rendezvous for our
Republick, whose chief Councils concern'd the Affairs of
the Kitchen.   This Edifice was about twice as big as the
others, and *Robert Anselin* lay in it.   'Twas there we
prepar'd the Sawces for our Dishes, but we eat under a
tall and great Tree, on the Bank of the Rivulet, over-
against the Door of that Cabbin.   This Tree afforded us
a very fine Shade, and defended us from the burning
Rays of the Sun.   'Twas in the Trunk of this Tree, which
was very hard, that we cut a sort of a Nich, to leave there
the Memorial and Monuments, of which I shall speak
hereafter.   On the other side of the Water, opposite to the
Common *Hall* (*Hôtel*) was the Common *Garden :* 'Twas
fifty or sixty Foot Square, and the Pallisado's that encom-

---

[1] Palm-trees ; see *infra*, note on p. 63.

pass'd it of a Man's height and very close: Insomuch that the least Turtles cou'd not go between them. For that, as may be imagin'd, was the only reason which oblig'd us to enclose our Gardens.

But let us re-pass the Bridge, and come back to *Francis Leguat*, the Author of this Relation's Cabbin; you see 'twas between two Parterres, and upheld by a great Tree, which also cover'd it on the side of the Sea. This Tree[1] bore a Fruit something like an Olive; and the Parrots lov'd the Nuts of it mightily.

A little lower and nearer the Water on the same side of the Brook, stood Mr. *de la Case's* Lodge. This brave Man, who is now in *America*, had been an Officer in the *Brandenburgh* Troops, and knew already what it was to live in Tents. He was a Man of good Presence, Ingenious, full of Honour, Courage and Wit.

On the other side of the Rivulet between the Islet and the great Garden, was the Cabbin of poor Mr. *Testard*, whose sad Destiny we shall see in a short time. He was a stout (*brave*) Man, and one whom I very much regretted the loss of.

Mess. *B—le*[2] and *Boyer* liv'd together, and built their Hutt a little farther from the Brook, and nearer the Sea. The Reader will find a true Picture of honest *Isaac Boyer* in his Epitaph; for I must tell him before hand, that this dear Companion of our first Adventures, laid his Bones in *Rodrigo*. And since I have giv'n a Character of those whom I have spoken of, I shall add concerning Mr. *B——le* (who is, thanks be to God, now alive and in Health), that we all lov'd

---

1 From this tree, cons'dered by Professor Balfour to be the so-called "Bois d'olive" (*Elæodendron orientale*), exudes an enormous quantity of gum in the form of tears, which soon harden and form large masses in the crevices of the stem or on the ground around. It is the most frequently met with of all the trees in the island. (*Phil. Trans.*, vol. clxviii, p. 334.)

2 M. Bénelle; *vide ante*, p. 6; also Introduction.

him for the good Qualities with which he is adorn'd.   I
observ'd with pleasure in this young Man (for he was not
above twenty years old) an honest and upright Soul, good
natur'd and lively : He had by his Studies acquir'd more
Knowledge, than the generality of Mankind can pretend to.
He was always Gay, and in good Humour,[1] and 'twas chiefly
owing to his faculty of Invention and Address, that we built
the rare Vessel, of which we shall say more hereafter ; as
also that we Manufactur'd certain little Hatts, which were
very great Comforts to us in our great Distresses.   To conclude, I must inform the Reader, *en passant*, that except *P.
Thomas* and *R. Anselin*, Men of mean Fortunes, all the rest
of our Friends were not driv'n out of *Europe* by Misery, nor
did they desperately cast themselves on Desert Islands,
because they knew not where to set their foot in the World.
They were Men of good Families, and of no contemptible
Estates ; but Mr. *du Quesne's* Colony made such a noise (*&
qu'ils étaient jeunes, sains & gaillards*), that having no ties
of Families or Affairs to detain them, they had a mind to
make this Voyage.

I believ'd, Reader, you wou'd be better pleas'd with the
Continuation of our Adventures, after I had given you some
light into the Characters and Circumstances of the Adventurers.

You see Trees scatter'd up and down in our little Town,
they are Remainders of a much greater Number, which we
thought fit to fell, and 'twas no hard matter to do it ; for the
Ground is extreamly light, and the Roots were easily taken
up : I don't doubt, you Laugh to hear us talk of our little
Town, but what I pray you was the famous *Rome* in its
beginning ?   Had there been Women amongst us, 100 years
hence, instead of seven Hutts, one might have reckon'd seven
Parishes.

---

[1] " Il étoit toûjours gai, toûjours obligeant, & du meilleur naturel
du monde."   Bénelle was living at Amsterdam when this was written.
(See Introduction.)

When we had finish'd our Preparations for building our
little Houses, the Captain who stay'd fifteen days in the
Road weigh'd Anchor, after having deliver'd us the greatest
part of the Necessaries we brought for a Settlement, and
taken fresh Provisions Aboard. We sent Letters by him to
our *Friends* in *Holland*, wherein we had set out his Panegy-
rick as he deserv'd, but he was not such a Fool as to deliver
them, as we understood afterwards, and, indeed, as we expected from him. What he left us was chiefly—

Biskets, Fuzees,[1] and other Arms, Powder and Bullets,
Tools for Husbandry and building our Cabbins, as Saws,
Hatchets, Nails, Hammers, and Sheers, Household-stuff, a
Turn-broach, Fishing-Nets and Lines ; in short, every thing
except *Drugs*, which I believe, the Captain rather forgot,
than maliciously kept from us : Besides this, every Man had
his particular Goods, Necessaries and Provisions.

Peter Thomas, whom I have mention'd, having quarrell'd
with the Captain, and fearing to return with him, resolv'd to
stay in the Island, and that wou'd have made up the loss of
one of our Companions who dy'd at Sea near *Mascaregne*, if the
Captain, the Night before he left us, had not taken away two
of our Company (*Jacques Guiguer* and *Pierrot*) so that we had
but eight left.

When the Ship was gone, and each of us were well recover'd of the Fatigues of the Sea, we made the *tour* of the
Island to see whether we cou'd discover any better Place to
settle in, than that where we first Arriv'd ; but we found
'twas much the same all over it, and even tho' there were
about twenty several sorts of level Land, and almost as Commodious as Ours, yet we met with none that was not somewhat Inferior to it in Beauty and in Goodness ; so that we
resolv'd to stay in the place where we first sat down.

As soon as we had clear'd the Earth as much as was necessary for Tillage, we dug it, and sow'd our Grain. We had

---

[1] Fusee, a small, light musket or firelock, commonly written " fusil".

abundance, and of all sorts ; but that which we brought from *Holland*, was spoil'd by the Air of the Sea, we having forgot to put it into Earthen Pots, and Seal them down well. We furnish'd our selves with other Seed at the Cape of *Good Hope*. Only five Seeds of Ordinary, and as many of Water-Melons came up ; three of Succory,[1] three of Wheat, some Artichokes, Purslain, Turnips, Mustard, Gilly-flowers and Clover-grass. The Gilly-flowers rose high, but they did not blow, and at last they all perish'd.

The Turnips did the same, and were entirely destroy'd by the Worms before we cou'd eat them. The Melons which I call *Land*, to distinguish them from *Water*-Melons, came up almost without Culture in abundance, prodigiously Large, and excellently well tasted. I do not believe there can be better anywhere, and we found by Experience they had this rare Quality, that tho' one did eat of them a little to Excess, no Inconvenience happen'd afterwards.

We put 'em into all our Sauces, and they were admirable in all ; We might have had them all the year long, but we observ'd that those which came up in the Winter, that is, when 'twas not so hot as at other times, towards the Months of *June* and *July*, were a great deal better than the others.

We thought at first we must expose them to the Sun, as we do in *France*, but we soon found they wou'd thrive better in the Shade, which we may suppose is caus'd by the difference of the Climate and Soil.

Among our five Plants of Water-Melons, there were two sorts, Red and White ; the first were the best. The Rind was Green, and the inside Red ; they are very Refreshing, and never do any hurt no more than the others : They are so full of Water, that one may easily go without Drink when they are eaten : Sometimes they were so big, that all Eight of us cou'd hardly eat up one of them.

---

[1] Or chicory (*C. intybus*), extensively used for adulterating coffee.

These several kinds of Melons grew without taking Pains about them, as I have said already, and produc'd Fruit in great Abundance. When we mingled a little Ashes with the Earth in the Place where they were Sown, it made 'em grow and fructifie extraordinarily, and the Fruit was more than ordinarily delicate. We had great hopes of our Artichokes. We cou'd almost see them grow. They spread very much, but they yielded very little Fruit. Indeed we cou'd not be sure that the Seed was true Artichoke Seed, tho' it had the figure of it, and the Plant was like that of an Artichoke. We brought it from the Cape of *Good Hope*, without knowing what it was. We did our utmost to make the sides of it whiten, but to no purpose, tho' we were not ignorant of the several ways of doing it. And we had as bad Success with the Succoury (*Chicorée*): It came up to a wonder, so did the Purslain and the Mustard-Seed; but do what we cou'd, we cou'd never take off its bitterness. Of three Grains of Wheat that came up, we cou'd preserve but one Plant: It had above 200 Ears, and we were full of Hopes that it wou'd come to something, but it produc'd only a sort of Tares,[1] which very much troubled us, as you may imagine; because we found our selves depriv'd of the Pleasure of eating Bread.

However we shou'd not from hence conclude, that Wheat Corn will always turn to Tares here, since in *Europe* such like Degenerations are often to be met with. And if our young Men instead of precipitately sowing all our Seed in one Place, and in one Day, had kept some for other Soils, and other Seasons, perhaps we might have had an ample Harvest, and better luck with all our other Grain.

The Air is very clear and healthy at *Rodrigo*, and none of us having been ill all the while we liv'd there, is a very good proof of it, considering the great difference of the Climate

---

[1] Professor Balfour suggests that this grain was not wheat, but might have been millet. (*Phil. Trans.*, vol. clxviii, p. 304.)

and Food. He who dy'd just as we were about to leave it, as I shall relate in the sequel of these Memoirs, was perfectly born down by the violence of Fatigue.

The Sky is always fair and serene, and the heats of the Summer very Moderate ; because precisely at Eight a Clock in the Morning there rises every day a little North-East or North-West Wind, which agreeably cools the Air, and tempering the hottest Season, causes a perpetual Spring all the year round, and a continual Autumn, no part of it deserving the Name of Winter, insomuch that one may bath one's self at any time. The Nights are cool and refreshing ; it seldom Rains, at least we saw no Rain, except for four or five Weeks after the Hurricane ; that is, in *January* and *February*.[1] There fall great Dews, and frequently, which serve instead of Show'rs. As for Thunder,[2] which is so formidable in our *Europe*, and in several other parts of the World, I believe it was never heard in this Island.

'Tis as I have hinted, compos'd of lovely Hills, cover'd all with fine Trees, whose perpetual Verdure is entirely Charming. These Trees are very rarely entangled (*de broussailles*) one in another by the nearness and thickness of their Branches. They naturally form Ally's to defend us from the Sun's Heat ; and the Prospect is every where adorn'd by the sight of the Sea, thro' the Boughs which are almost in all Places open enough, to admit a View of the vast Ocean between them.

At the foot of these Hills are Valleys, the Soil of which is the most excellent in the World, as we may easily conceive, if we consider it consists chiefly of rotten Trees ; whose Matter being reduc'd to dust, is driven by the Floods

---

[1] "Une heure après que l'eau est tombée, on peut se promener comme à l'ordinaire." Omitted by translator after word *February*. The translator frequently makes such omissions.

[2] Thunder is rarely heard throughout the regions of the trade-winds.

down the Hills. This Mould is very light, and produces almost without Cultivating. It abounds in fruitful Juices.

The Valleys are cover'd with Palm-Trees, Plantanes (*Lataniers*), Ebony's, and several other sorts of Trees; the Beauty of whose Leaves and Branches may compare with that of the finest of our *European* Trees. In the low parts of these Valleys we frequently meet with Rivulets of fresh Water, whose Springs are all in the middle of the Island. These pure Streams are never dry, and so conveniently dispos'd for watering all this little Country, that nothing can be more Commodious. What pity 'tis that a Place so Delicious in all things, shou'd be useless to the Inhabitants of the World. I insist the more on these charming Rivulets, because there are a great many Islands that have none; and 'tis doubly a wonder to find so many here, and all so happily distributed.

Several of the other Rivulets besides that near which as I have said we built our Cabbins, form (*des Napes &*) Cascades by falling from the top of Rocks: I reckon'd seven Basons, and as many Cascades all together, and all form'd by the same River.[1]

There are abundance of Eels in these Rivers, some of

---

[1] The reviewer of Leguat's book in the *Nouv: lles de la République des Lettres*, for December 1707 (p. 611), calls attention to the very small rainfall being insufficient to supply the sources of the streams. This circumstance, and the fact of the remoteness of the island from any continent, would apparently. he adds, disprove the theory of those who maintain that all springs are dependent on rainfall, for the dews, though frequent, would not supply enough moisture for these perennial rivulets. Recent accounts give a somewhat different account of the climate. " The island," says Prof. Balfour, "is comparatively dry, the soil is parched and arid, and during the warm season many of the streams are dried up. But the size of the water-courses and the enormous boulders filling their beds indicate large torrents in the rainy season. In some places, issuing from the clay, springs occur, of which the water is brackish, has a very disagreeable taste, and is slightly tepid, but has no smell. As a rule the water of the streams is

them very big, and all excellently well tasted. We have
taken some so Monstrous, (I am afraid to tell it) that two
Men cou'd hardly carry home one of them; 'tis easie to
catch them, for you can scarce put your Bait into the
Water, before the Fish bite. This Water is seldom deep,
and being very Transparent, we cou'd easily see these huge
Eels creeping at the bottom; and if we pleas'd, might have
taken them with a Harping-Iron (harpoon) : We have sometimes shot them with a Fuzee[1] and Hare-shot.

The Valleys I am talking of, Water'd and made fertile by
these little Rivers, extend themselves Insensibly as we draw
nearer the Sea, and form a Level, which in some Places is
two Miles[2] broad, and two long. The Soil of these little
Plains is excellent eight or ten foot deep, and there those
great and tall Trees grow, between which one may walk at
ease, and find such refreshing coolness in their shade at
Noon; so sweet, so healthy, that 'twou'd give Life to those
that are dying. Their spreading and tufty Tops, which are
almost all of an equal height, joyn together like so many
Canopy's and Umbrello's, and jointly make a Cieling of an
eternal Verdure, supported by natural Pillars, which raise
and nourish them. This is certainly the Workmanship of a
Divine Architect.

What is more Remarkable, is the greatest part of the

good and safe to drink, but that of some rivers, notably the river
Saumâtre, is most unpalatable, and apt to cause slight catharsis.

"The climate is much like that of Mauritius, where the average annual
temperature is 78° Fahr. During the north-west monsoon, from
November to April, the weather is wet and warm, and frequently in
the first months of the year the island is visited by severe hurricanes.
From May to October the south-east monsoon prevails, and then the
weather is cool and dry.

"The rainfall is exceedingly irregular, the hills being hardly high
enough, and not sufficiently wooded, to arrest clouds; hence, also, fogs
are rare." (*Philosophical Transactions*, vol. clxviii, p. 292.)

[1] Cf. p. 55.

[2] In original, "two thousand paces". The breadth of these level
valleys near the sea would, therefore, be one mile, *not* two, as in text.

Trees of this little *Eden*, are not less useful or necessary for the Conveniences of Life, than pleasant to the Eyes or the Mind. For Example, the several sorts of Palm-Trees and Plantanes are Admirable Magazines of Necessaries for those Sages, who Believe and Practise what *St. Paul* says. The Fruit of them is excellent, and the Water which the Trunks of these Trees yield, and which runs from its Spring without Preparation, is a kindly and delicious Liquor; some of the Leaves are good to eat, others serve instead of Silk or Linen. There are abundance of these wonderful Trees all over our Isle. Perhaps the Reader may expect that I shou'd explain my self a little on this Head.

I shall not undertake to give a Description of Palm-trees and Plantanes (*Lataniers*), a Thousand and a Thousand Men having written of them, and I know there are above thirty[1] several sorts of them: Neither shall I enlarge in the Description of those I am speaking of, but give a small *Idæa* of them, for the sake of such as do not know what sort of Trees these are.

Our Palm-trees are commonly thirty or forty Foot high; their Trunk is straight, and without Leaves, but 'tis cover'd with a sort of prickly Scales, whose prickles stand out a little: Some have a smoother Bark than others. On the top of the Trunks grow those Boughs of Palm, of which no Man ever saw a lively Picture. These Boughs form a great Knot (*bouquet*), and fall down all about it in Plumes: Below these Boughs, or rather below the Trunk from which they grow, are produc'd long Bunches, each Fruit or Grain (*est verd*) as big as a Hens Egg, and of the same shape, known by the Name of *Dates*.[2]

[1] Botanists have now distinguished considerably more than a thousand species of palms, divided, according to Sir J. Hooker, into 132 genera.

[2] It is a difficult matter to decide what particular species of palm is referred to by Leguat. Prof. Is. Bayley Balfour, who visited Rodriguez with the Transit of Venus expedition (1874-5), made a special

In the center of this great Knot (*bouquet*), and at the
Summet of the Trunk, is what we call the Cabbidge. One
cannot see it, being hidden by the Boughs that rise a little
all about it. This Summet consists of tender Leaves, which
closely embrace each other, joyn together, and form a Mass
something like that of a Cabbage Lettice, or common Cabbage; 'tis about two Foot high if the Tree is large, and of
the same bigness with the Trunk. The large outside Leaves
of this Mass are white, soft, pliable, and as strong as Buff,
which it resembles. They will serve also for Linen, Satin,
for Napkins, Table Cloths, and anything what you please.
The Membrana or inside leaves are tender and brittle, like
the Heart of a Lettice: They are good to eat raw, and
tast like a Filberd; but we made an admirable Ragout of
them when we Fricasi'd them with the Fat and Liver of a
Turtle. We put them also in our Soops.

We come now to the Liquor, or rather the Nectar of the
Isle of *Rodrigo.* 'Tis call'd Palm-Wine all over the *Indies :*
There are two ways of drawing out the Juice. We make a
hole in the Trunk of the Tree at about a Mans height, as
big as ones two Fists. We presently put a Pot or other

study of the botany of this island. He says that Leguat probably
included in his description two kinds of palm—*Dictyosperma album*,
now very abundant in the island, and *Hyophorbe Verschaffeltii*. Part of
his remarks would apply to one of these and part to the other, while
his allusions to the fruit as big as a hen's egg, and the prickly scales
on the trunk, would agree well with neither. "As pointing in this
direction, I think," says Balfour, "we may take his remark, 'some have
a smoother bark than others,' for the bark *Hyophorbe Verschaffeltii* is
much smoother than that of *Dictyosperma album*."

This palm, *Hyophorbe Verschaffeltii*, called Palmiste marron (*i.e.*, wild
Palmiste) by the Creoles, grows to a height of 25-30 feet and is spread
over the whole island, but never occurs on the coralline limestone. It
begins with a stem 6-12 ins. diameter at the base, bulging after a few
feet, reaching 12-24 ins. in the middle, thence contracting upwards.
If the tree be lofty, there may be a second ventricosity. (Cf. *Philosophical Trans. of the Royal Society*, vol. clxviii, p. 375 *seqq.*; *Flora
of Mauritius and the Seychelles*, by J. G. Baker, F.L.S.,1877, p. 383.)

Vessel there to receive the delicious Liquor, which runs out
fast enough, otherwise we dig (*creusions*) the Cabbage, and
make a little Cistern at its Head. We need only go twice or
thrice a Day, and draw this rare Wine at the Fountain Head,
and we may be abundantly supply'd with it. The Wine of
the Trunk, and that of the Cabbage, are in my Opinion
of an equal goodness.

But those who wou'd be good Husbands of their Trees
(for as for us we were lavish enough of them), the first way
is the best, because after the Cabbage has yielded its Liquor
for about a Month, it Withers, and the Tree decays and dies.
'Tis the same thing if you tear off the Cabbage, when its
Head and Brain are gone it dies almost suddenly.

Whereas if you only pierce its Side, the Tree do's not die,
provided the Wound is not too deep; but the Liquor will
not run out at that Hole above four Days : The wounded
Tree must afterwards have time to recover. I do not know
what is done elsewhere, but I can tell by Experience what I
have said here, we having made trial of it daily for two
years together. The Bark of this Tree is very hard, 'tis an
Inch thick, Porous and Tender in the Inside. If one make
the Hole on the side of the Trunk too wide, there is reason
to fear 'twill weaken the Tree there, and that then the next
Hurricane will break it.

The Plantane[1] (*Latanier*) is a sort of Palm-tree, and the
Arborists place it in the same Class. Our Plantanes have a

<hr />

[1] The word " Latanier" in the original has been throughout the
narrative mistranslated " plantane". It is evidently the fan-palm
(*Latania Verschaffeltii*) that Leguat is describing here. Prof. Balfour
says it is found in every part of the island, where it is put to a variety
of uses. The wood is very hard and durable, of a rich mottled black
appearance, and used for building huts, though now this is interdicted,
as the trees are becoming more scarce. The leaves are chiefly used
for thatching huts, and are also made into baskets. The fibres of
the petiole form a very excellent material for cordage, and the reti-
culum is also put to various uses. (Cf. *Phil. Trans.*, vol. clxviii. p. 374.)

straight Trunk, which seems to be form'd of large Rings at an
equal Distance. They have no such prickly Scales as I have
talkt of. At the top of the Trunk is a Cabbage, very like
to that I have describ'd. At the foot of this Cabbage
instead of Palm Boughs are broad Leaves, with Stalks about
six or seven Foot long: These Leaves are strong and thick,
and like a Fan when 'tis open ; the Sticks of which come a
little out of the Circumference, and are pointed at the end.
Some of these Leaves are eight Foot Diameter, insomuch
that they serv'd to make rare Coverings for our Cabbins.
We cut 'em out into little pieces, and made Hatts and
Umbrello's (*parasols*) of them. The Stalk is four Inches
broad, an Inch thick and a little roundish at the sides ; at the
bottom where it joyns to the Tree, it widens, and grows like a
flat Shell which sticks to the Trunk, and in part embraces it.
This wide and hollow Plate (*patte*) is sometimes above a
Foot Diameter, and of the thickness of a Crown-Piece. We
made use of it for Dishes, Plates and Sawcers. The first
Rind of the Stalk serv'd us instead of Ropes, and the Fibres
of the second made good Thread to Sow with. One might
have wove Stuffs with it, had it been prepar'd.

We could not perceive any difference in the Tast, or in any
other qualities (*entre le vin*) of the Palm-tree or Plantane. This
Liquor is whitish like white Whey, and so sweet, that no
other sweetness, if I may judge of it, can compare to it:
The newer it is, the more agreeable. In three or four days
it begins to turn Sowre, and in seven or eight, 'tis as sharp
as the strongest Vinegar without changing its Colour.

The Dates of the Plantane (*Latanier*) are bigger than
those of the Palm-tree. Having abundance of better things
to feed on, Fish and Flesh, Fruits, etc., we left the Dates for
the Turtles and other Birds, particularly the *Solitaries*, of
which we shall hereafter make mention.

About the Cabbage of the Plantane, near the bottom of it

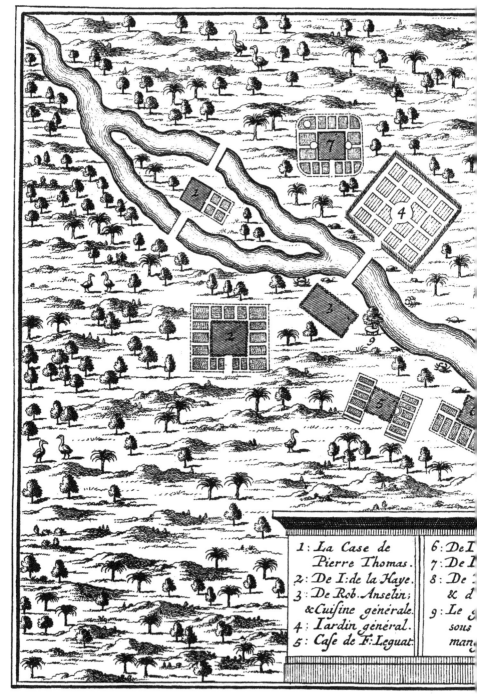

1 : La Case de
    Pierre Thomas.
2 : De I: de la Haye.
3 : De Rob. Anselin;
    &Cuisine générale.
4 : Iardin général.
5 : Case de F: Leguat.

6 : De I
7 : De I
8 : De
   & d
9 : Le
   sous
   man

ABITATION

la Caſe
tard.
B: ✳✳✳
Boyer.
Arbre.
el on

M E·R

D E S

I N D E S

and between the Stalks of its broad Leaves, is a sort of Cotton of a Limon Colour, which all thro' *India* is known by the name of *Capoc*.[1] We made very good Quilts (*matelas*) of it. It may be Wove, and Manufactur'd for all the Uses that Cotton is put to: Perhaps we might have thought of making a sort of stuff, both of the *Capoc* and the Fibers of our Plantane Leaves; but we had Stuff enough of our own to serve a long time, and the Air is so mild, so sweet, that we did not make much use of our Cloaths. Happy for us had we sav'd them ; for the time when the Persecution of a New *giv'n of God*,[2] whom we shall speak of expos'd us to a thousand Miseries on the fatal Rock, whither that wicked Man banish'd us.

There are several other kinds of Trees in this Island, which yield tolerable Fruit. Those that bear a sort of Pepper,[3] are not a little like Plum-trees of a moderate size : Their Leaves are much like that of the Jessamine ; they bear their Fruit in little Bunches, and it did very well in our Sauces.

The Sea having thrown us up some Cocos which began to bud, we planted some of that Fruit some Months after our Arrival, and when we left the Place, the Trees were four Foot high.

I leave it to the Reader to guess how these Cocoes,[4] some

1 *Capoc*, a sort of cotton so fine and so short that it cannot be spun. It is used in the East Indies to line palanquins, and to make beds, mattresses, cushions, pillows, etc. (Rees' *Cyclopædia*.)

2 A play on the name of Diodati, or Deodate, the Governor in Mauritius, who subsequently persecuted and imprisoned Leguat.

3 Professor Balfour supposes this plant to have been either *Capsicum frutescens*, abundant everywhere in the island, or *C. cordiforme*, not common (*l. c.*, pp. 3C3, 360). But it seems scarcely probable that Leguat's pepper was a capsicum, which bears a long, pod-like fruit or seed, whereas he compares that of his plant to a small plum.

4 A few trees of *Cocos nucifera* occur in the compound of Government House at Port Mathurin. Leguat's remark that the cocoa-nuts thrown up on his island came from St. Brandon, better known as the Cargados

of which weigh'd five or six Pound, can be thrown on the
Coasts of *Rodrigo*, and come three or four score Leagues by
Sea without Corrupting. For we are very certain they come
from the Isle of *Ste. Brande*, which is to the Windward, to
the North-East of Ours, and at least as far off as I have
said.[1]

The Sea brings in nothing but from that side, from
whence we may conclude, there are certain Currents which
contribute very much together with the Wind and Tide
to throw abundance of things on the Coast.[2] We may
therefore suppose, these Fruits were blown off from the

Garajos, in lat. 16° 25′ south, and between long. 50° and 60° east, is
difficult to reconcile with the circumstance of the prevailing south-east
monsoon setting the current in an opposite direction, *i.e.*, towards this
group from Rodriguez. There are, however, more singular instances
of drift on record, *e.g.*, the Keeling Islands, whose flora is almost
wholly derived from islands in the Indian Archipelago, though the
direction of the winds and currents would hardly seem to render such
a thing possible. Compare Darwin's remarks on this subject in *Voyage
of the Beagle*, vol. iii, p. 542, and Chamisso, in Kotzebue's first voyage
(vol. iii, p. 155).

[1] Here our author is in error; the Cargados Garajos (*vide* note on
p. 65) are to the *north-westward* of Rodriguez, and about 300 miles distant
from it. These islets, of which there are said to be sixteen in number,
lie off a dangerous bank of coral sand. It was with reference to their
position that an acrimonious controversy raged, towards the end of the
last century, between the Abbé Rochon and M. d'Après de Manevil-
lette, a well-known hydrographer, the Abbé having placed St. Brandon
fifty leagues to the eastward of Cargados Garajos. Later surveyors
have, however, succeeded in establishing their identity. According to
Sir E. Belcher, who visited the group in 1846, the fishermen there have
a way of calling every white stone above water a St. Brandon. The
southernmost of these isles, Coco Island, owes its name to its having
been formerly covered with these trees, of which only two remained
in a perishing condition at the time of his visit. St. Brandon is noted
for the beautiful scarlet coral, the *Tubifora musica*. (Cf. Findlay's
Sailing Directions for the Indian Ocean, p. 454; Pike's *Sub-tropical
Rambles*, pp. 423-4; *Voyages à Madagascar*, par Alexis Rochon, 1802,
tome i, ch. xlvi.)

[2] "Dans la saison de l'Ouragan, on pourroit dire que le tourbillon
auroit enlévé ces fruits dans l'isle de Ste. Brande."

Isle of *Ste. Brande,* very far into the Sea ; and from thence
brought to us by the Tide and the Currents.

There's a wonderful fine Tree at *Rodrigo,* whose Branches
are so round, and so thick, 'tis impossible for the Sun-Beams
to penetrate thro' it : Some of these Trees are so big, that
two or three hundred People may stand under them, and be
shelter'd from the Sun or the Weather.[1]

The vast Extent of it is occasioned thus. Some of the
great Branches naturally tend downwards, and reaching the
Ground take Root, and become new Trunks themselves,
which make a sort of little Forest.

The first time I saw this Tree, I remember I had read in
some Voyages, that they are to be met with every where in the
Indies, and in the Continent and Isles of *America.* I do not
think there's any of them in *Europe.* The Eastern Idolaters
have a great Respect for them, and commonly build their
Pagods under them.

---

[1] There can be little doubt that Leguat's description and the authors
he cites point to the banyan (*Ficus indica*). Its great height and the
vast area it covers with its interlacing branches, the curious way these
have of taking root and forming new stems, are all characteristic of this
remarkable tree, which has been a favourite theme of writers in prose
and verse in all ages, from the days of Pliny to our own times.

But, though indigenous to India, Southern Persia, and Ceylon, the
banyan is foreign to the Mascarene flora. We may suppose, therefore, either that it was formerly extant and has become extinct in
Rodriguez, or that Leguat referred to some other species of *Ficus.*
Balfour describes two—*F. consimilis* and *F. rubra*—found by him on
that island, where they are both common, but adds that neither of
them is the one described by Leguat. Baker mentions these and
several other species in his *Flora of Mauritius* (pp. 283 *seqq.*), and Sir
Henry Barkly informs the writer that there is a large tree of *F. consimilis* in Seychelles, and that the bats feed on its fruit precisely as
Leguat describes at Rodriguez ; but the size of the leaves and fruit is
much smaller than his species. (*Phil. Trans.*, *l. c.*, p. 368 ; Balfour's
Timber-Trees of India, p. 117 ; Helmsley's *Vegetation of Diego Garcia*,
in *Linn. Soc. Journal*, vol. xxii, p. 334.)

La Boulaye le Gouz writes,[1] that this sacred Tree is call'd *Kasta*, and that the *Indians* say, 'tis cherish'd by the Saints ; because their God *Pan* diverts himself with playing upon the Flute, under the shade of its broad Leaves.

The same Author adds, that no Man dares pull off one of those Leaves for fear of dying within the year ; and refers his Reader to what *Herodotus* and *Quintus Curtius* have said on the same Subject. *Tavernier*[2] also speaks of it, and tells us the *Persians* call it Lull, but that the *Franks* have giv'n it the Name of the *Banians* Tree ; because the Penitents of the *Faquors* and *Banians* dress their Meat, and pay their Devotions under this Tree. Mr. *de Rochefort* calls it *Pare-*

---

[1] *Les Voyages et Observations du Sieur de la Boullaye-Le-Gouz, etc.*, Paris, 1653, 2nd ed., 1657. This author, whose tour in Ireland in 1644 was edited in English by Croker in 1837, was born in the early part of the seventeenth century. He travelled extensively in the East, and died in Persia in 1668. The genuineness and impartiality of his remarks on men and things earned for him the reputation of "a very honest fellow". The passage in his above-mentioned work referring to the banyan-tree is in chapter xvii (pp. 183 *seq.* of 1st edit.). He figures the tree with a native Indian seated below, a cow and a pagoda, while above is a quaint representation of the sun. He mentions camping several times under its shade while on the journey from Surat to Goa, and remarks that Rama or Brahma taught the Indians to venerate it. The followers of this divinity, however, mingling superstition with their worship, declared that anyone plucking its leaves would die within the year. Milton described it as follows :—

> ". . . . there soon they chose
> The fig-tree, not that kind for fruit renown'd,
> But such as at this day to Indians known
> In Malabar or Deccan spreads her arms,
> Branching so broad and long, that in the ground
> The bended twigs take root and daughters grow
> About the mother tree, a pillar'd shade
> High overarch'd, and echoing walls between."
>
> (*Paradise Lost*, Book ix.)

[2] Cf. Tavernier's *Persian Voyages*, Book v, ch. xxiii, 1682 ed., vol. i, p. 614. This traveller also figures the banyan, stating that the Persians call it *Lul*, the Portuguese "arbre de Reys", and the French "l'arbre des Banianes".

tuvier[1] in his *Natural History of the Antilles*,[2] and says, its Leaves are broad, thick and long, without saying any thing of the Fruit :   And the two Voyagers before mention'd, tell us nothing either of the Fruit or of the Leaves.

The *Rodrigo Kastas*[3] (for I ought to keep the *Indian* Name at least in the *Indies*) bear Leaves as broad as one's Hand, pretty thick, and somewhat like that of a Lilach or a Heart in shape, they are softer than Satin to touch.   Their Flower is white, and smells well :   Their Fruit is red and round, and as big as a black Damask Plum.   Their Skin is hard, and within it is a thin Seed, a little like that of a Fig.   The Fruit is not prejudicial to Health, but 'tis insipid.   The Batts commonly feed upon it, and multitudes of them nest in the tufted Branches of this Tree.

The Wood of all the Trees in this Island, is generally hard. We made this Observation in building our Cabbins; The Timber we us'd about them, in a few Weeks after 'twas cut, wou'd be full of Worms, till to prevent that Inconvenience, we let it lie three Weeks in the Sea, and then the Worm never came into it.

There is a Tree we call the *Nasty* Tree,[4] because it stunk :

1 *I.e.*, *Paletuvier*, the mangrove, a very different tree.

2 The title of this rare book is given on page 17, *supra*.

3 The name *Kasta*, to which Leguat, following La Boullaye-Le-Gouz, attributes an Indian origin, is Portuguese, meaning no more than our word "caste", which is derived from it.   Of course, the caste-tree would not be an inappropriate name for the *Ficus religiosa*, which has always been an object of superstitious reverence among the Hindus. (Cf. Dr. Brewer's *Dictionary of Phrase and Fable;* Yule's *Anglo-Indian Glossary.*)

4 Prof. Balfour has no doubt but that the tree referred to by Leguat as the "nasty tree" is *Clerodendron laciniatum*, the *Bois cabri* of the Creoles, a small tree easily recognised by its disagreeable odour, which has occasioned its popular name.   The wood is very white and close-grained, but is not put to great use, save for burning, probably on account of the odour.   Some have thought that Leguat referred to the Bois puant (*Fœtidia Mauritiana Lam.*), but the odour of that tree, though exceedingly objectionable, is only apparent when the sun shines

'Tis the best Wood of all for Carpenters use, but 'twas of no Service to us; for it stinks so, that it makes all the Places about it smell of it, and the Smell is very Offensive.

We did not find in this Island any Plant, Tree, Shrub, or Herb, which grows naturally in any part of *Europe*, that was known to us, except Purslain,[1] which is small and green, There's plenty of it in some Places of the Valleys, and that which we sow'd having brought some of the Seed from the *Cape*, came up exactly like the Purslain of the Island.

We saw no four-footed Creatures, but Rats, Lizards, and Land-Turtles,[2] of which there are different sorts. I have

upon it, and is evanescent, and not at all like the persistent odour which the Bois cabri emits. (Balfour, in *Phil. Trans.*, vol. clxviii, p. 364, and Plate xxxii ; and cf. Baker, *l. c.*, pp. 255 and 120.)

[1] *Portulaca oleracea*, Creole name *Pourpier*, is common in waste ground, and especially abundant on the barren ground towards the west of the island. (*Balfour, l. c.*, p. 328.)

[2] According to Admiral Kempenfeldt, who visited Rodriguez in 1761, the land-turtle was the best production of the island. Small vessels were constantly employed in transporting them by thousands to Mauritius for the service of the hospital. The principal objects of interest in Rodriguez then were : First, the house of the Superintendent appointed by the Governor of Mauritius to direct the cultivation of the gardens and to overlook the park of land-turtles ; secondly, the park for the land-turtles, which is on the sea-shore, facing the house. As long as Rodriguez was in the hands of the French, these tortoises were protected. (*History of Mauritius, etc.*, by C. Grant, Viscount de Vaux, 1801, pp. 100-101.) " But early in the present century the work of extermination appears to have been accomplished," remarks Dr. Günther, "and there is at present of the Rodriguez tortoise not a single living example in the island or in any other locality.

" In 1874 the Presidents of the Royal and Geographical Societies addressed a memorial to the Governor of Mauritius, Sir Arthur Gordon, requesting him to preserve the last remnants of the nearly extinct race of Mascarene tortoises, which still survive in the island of Aldabra.

" Among the bones collected by the naturalist of the Transit of Venus Expedition, 1874-5, some, far exceeding in size the majority of their kind, are not rare, and prove that the Rodriguez tortoise was quite equal in bulk to *Testudo elephantina*, many individuals having had a carapace four and a half feet long." (A. Günther, in *Phil. Trans., l. c.*, pp. 452 *seqq.* See Appendix and supplementary note.)

seen one[1] that weigh'd one hundred pound, and had Flesh
enough about it, to feed a good number of Men. This
Flesh is very wholsom, and tasts something like Mutton,
but 'tis more delicate : The Fat is extreamly white, and
never Congeals nor rises in your Stomach, eat as much as
you will of it. We all unanimously agreed, 'twas better
than the best Butter in *Europe*. To anoint one's self with
this Oil, is an excellent Remedy for Surfeits, Colds, Cramps
and several other Distempers. The Liver of this Animal is
extraordinarily delicate,[2] 'tis so Delicious that one may say of
it, it always carries its own Sauce with it, dress it how you
will.

The Bones of these Turtles are Massy; I mean they have
no Marrow in them. Every one knows, that these Animals
in general are hatch'd of Eggs. The Land-Turtles lay theirs
in the Sand, and cover them,[3] that they may be hatch'd[4] : The
Scale of it, or rather the Shell, is soft, and the Substance
within good to eat. There are such plenty of Land-Turtles
in this Isle, that sometimes you see two or three thousand of
them in a Flock ; so that one may go above a hundred Paces
on their Backs ; or, to speak more properly on their *Cara-
paces*, without setting foot to the Ground. They meet together in the Evening in shady Places, and lie so close, that
one wou'd think those Places were pav'd with them. There's
one thing very odd among them ; they always place Sentinels
at some Distance from their Troop, at the four corners of
their Camp, to which the Sentinels turn their Backs, and

---

[1] In orig. : " J'en ai vu qui pesent," etc.

[2] " Et fort gros à proportion de l'animal ; car une tortue qui n'a que
quinze livres de chair, a le foye de cinq à six livres," omitted in translation.

[3] In orig. : " & les en couvrent, pour les faire éclorre doucement au
Soleil."

[4] " Ces œufs sont ronds en tous sens, comme des billes de billard,
et de la grosseur des œufs de poules," omitted in translation.

look with the Eyes, as if they were on the Watch. This we
have always observ'd of them; and this Mystery seems the
more difficult to be comprehended, for that these Creatures
are uncapable to defend themselves, or to fly.

We have also great plenty of Sea-Turtles here: Their
Flesh tasts like Beef, that of the Breast is admirable. The
fat is as good as Veal Marrow, but being green, it has something the Air of an Ointment, which at first renders it
Nauseous. This fat is not only delicate, but wholsom, and
purges gently. The *Indians* make use of it as a Soveraign
Remedy in the Venereal Disease.[1]

The Sea-Turtles are prodigious big, we have seen some
that weigh'd above 500 Pound. When we wou'd take them,
we turn'd them on their Backs by strength of Arms, or with
Leavers; and when they are overturn'd, 'tis impossible for
them to get up again. They lay their Eggs in sandy Places
near the Sea, and always in the Night-time; they make a
hole about three Foot deep, and a Foot broad for that purpose: The greatest of them will lay near two hundred in less
than two Hours. They cover them with Sand, and in six
Weeks time the Sun hatches them: As soon as they are
hatch'd, all these little Animals which are not so big as a
Chicken, just coming out of the Shell, go directly to the Sea,
do what you will to hinder them; they are generally hatch'd
in an Hour's time. We have often, to divert our selves,
carry'd some of them a quarter of a League off on the Mountain, and as soon as we put them on the Ground, they immediately went directly to the Sea. They then go faster than
when they are grown bigger.

The Fools, the Frigats, and several other Birds which lie
in wait for them upon Trees, destroy abundance of them
when they are so young; insomuch, that hardly ten in a

---

[1] "Quand on a mangé de cette graisse (voudra-t-on bien que je
le dise?) l'eau qu'on rend est d'un verd d'émeraude admirable,"
omitted by translator.

Hundred of them are sav'd. Yet there are such prodigious Numbers, that 'twou'd have amaz'd one if we had not consider'd, every Turtle lays two thousand Eggs a year at times, that they have multiply'd thus from the beginning of the World, and perhaps have not met with any Destroyers but our selves.

Their Eggs are not quite so good to eat, as those of the Land-Turtles, neither is their Flesh so Delicate. They are of the same shape, and the white both of the one and the other cannot without a great deal of difficulty be chang'd ; but in length of time it changes so entirely, that it turns quite yellow.[1] The Liver of the Sea-Turtle hath not at all the Tast of that of the Land; besides, 'tis very unwholsome, it smells offensive like bad Oil[2] : 'Tis Rank, and rises in the Stomach a good while after it is eaten.

These Animals feed upon Weeds at the bottom of the Sea, and never come a-shoar but to Lay. And I must observe here, *en passant*, that before that time they couple for nine days together without Disjunction.

Their Fat remains Liquid when 'tis melted, and tasts Admirably, as well as that of the Land-Turtles. It may be made use of in all sorts of Sauces, either for Flesh or Fish.

The Turtle is a dull, heavy sort of a Creature.[3] It can live without eating a whole Month, provided 'tis discharg'd of the burthen of its Eggs, and you water it from time to time with some Pails of Sea-Water.

---

[1] In orig.: " et le blanc des uns et des autres ne se cuit que très difficilement; et même à la longue il se dissipe absolument de sorte qu'il ne reste proprement que le jaune." The translator's rendering of this passage is nonsense.

[2] " Ou une espèce de sauvagin," omitted in translation. " Sauvagin" is applied to the smell of whale-blubber.

[3] In original : " La Tortue a le sang froid." This evidently applies to the actual temperature of the blood, and not to the phlegmatic disposition of the animal, as the translator makes it appear : later on Leguat distinguishes the Lamentin as having hot blood. (*Infra*, p. 74.)

The Lamentins,[1] which other Nations call *Manati*, that is *having Hands*, abound in the Sea about this Isle, appearing often in numerous Troops. Its Head is extreamly like that of a Hog, whatever is said in Mr. *Corneille's*[2] *Dictionary of Arts and Sciences;* for in the Article of this Fish, of the difference of Palm-Trees, and several other things that have fallen within my Knowledge; he is apt to erre frequently and grosly, as is the least imperfect Dictionary that ever was. He borrows the Heads of an Ox, of a Mole, of a Horse and a Hog, to Compose that of a Lamantin ; and in this case falls into the same Confusion, which happens to all that undertake to describe things they never saw, and have no distinct *Idæa* of. As for my self, I have seen, and carefully and nearly examin'd several ; wherefore I say again, that not only I, but my Companions also found the Head of a Lamentin was altogether very like that of a Hog, excepting that its Snout was not so sharp.

[1] This animal was evidently the *Halicore dugong*, now extinct in the Mascarene waters, an innocuous herbivore, without fear of man, easily captured, and therefore soon extirpated by the sailors in want of fresh meat. (See supplementary note.)

"Where is the *Rhytina* of Behrings' Island? Absolutely abolished from the face of the earth ! Where are the *Manatees* that played in the waters of the Antilles ?   . . .   Where are the Dugongs of Rodriguez, so charmingly described by Leguat ? Vanished ! Where are the Sea-elephants of Ascension, Tristan d'Acunha and the Crozettes ? So hunted down that it is not worth a skipper's while to seek them ! Where are the countless and mighty Otaries that Péron found in Bass's Straits ? Not there assuredly !   . . .   Surely it is time to stop such wanton, such short-sighted destruction." (Professor Newton on " Extermination of Marine Mammalia", *Nature*, December 11, 1873, p. 112 ; *Mammalia, Recent and Extinct*, by A. W. Scott, Sydney, pp. 52 *et seq.*)

[2] This M. Corneille was Thomas, the younger brother of Pierre, the great Corneille. He composed this *Dictionnaire des Arts et des Sciences* at the request of the French Academy, as a supplementary work to the Academy's *Dictionary*. The article on Lamentins, by Thos. Corneille, was solely concerned with the American Lamentin, and not with the Dugong described by Leguat. (Muller's note on p. 92 of modern French ed.)

The greatest of them are about twenty Foot long, and have no other Fins but the Tail and two Paws. The Body is pretty big down to the middle, and a little below it, the Tail has this in Particular with the Whales[1]; that its breadth is Horizontal, when the Animal lies on its Belly. The Blood of this Creature is hot, its Skin is Black, very rough and hard, with some Hairs, but so few, they are scarce perceivable. Its Eyes are small, and it has two holes which it opens and shuts, and for that reason may be call'd (its) Gills and its Ears. Because it often draws in its Tongue, which is not very great, several have assur'd me it has none. It has Hind-Teeth,[2] and even Tusks like a Boar, but no Fore-Teeth: Its Jaws are hard enough to bite Grass,[3] its Flesh is excellent, and tasts something like the best Veal: 'Tis very wholsom Meat.

The Female has Tets like Women's; Some say it brings forth two young ones at a time, and gives them Milk together, carrying them both at its Breast with its two things like Hands[4]: But since I have never seen it hold but one, I encline to believe it bears no more at once.

I never saw this extraordinary Nurse,[5] without remembring with double Reason my own Condition, that of an

[1] This remarkable order of aquatic mammalia, now known as *Sirenia*, was formerly classed with *Cetacea*, with walruses and seals by others, and even with elephants by De Blainville. (See supplementary note.)

[2] In orig. : " Il a des dents mâchelières," *i.e.*, molars.

[3] In orig. : "pour arracher et pour brouter l'herbe."

[4] In orig. : " avec ses deux espèces de mains."

[5] This habit of the female *Lamentin*, described by Leguat, confirms the opinion, before mentioned, that it is the *Halicore Dugong*. When the female Dugong is nursing her young one, she carries it on one flipper and takes care to keep the head of her offspring, as well as her own, well above the surface of the water, thus presenting a strangely human aspect. These creatures are most affectionate, and if one of a pair be captured, the other falls an easy prey, as it refuses to leave the dead body of its companion. Some of these animals attain to a length of over seven feet in Ceylon. (See Sir Emerson Tennent's *Ceylon*, 2nd edit., ii, pp. 557 *et seq.*)

Exile, and that Passage of the Prophet *Jeremy*, in his Lamentations, where he there Complains thus. *Even the Sea-Monsters*[1] *draw out the Breast, they give suck to their young ones; (but) the Daughter of my People is become cruel like the Ostriches in the Wilderness.* (Lamentations, iv, 3.)

This Fish is very easily taken, it feeds in Herds like Sheep, about three or four foot under Water; and when we came among them did not fly, so that we might take which we wou'd of them, by either Shooting them,[2] or falling upon them two or three at a time upon one without Arms, and pulling it a-shoar by main force. We sometimes found three or four hundred together feeding on the Weeds at the bottom of the Water, and they are so far from being Wild, that they wou'd often let us handle them to feel which was fattest. We put a Rope about its Tail, and so hale it a-shoar. We never took the greatest of them, because we cou'd not master them so easily, and they might perhaps have master'd us: Besides, their Flesh is not so Delicate as that of the little ones.

Their Lard is firm and excellent, no body that ever saw and tasted the Flesh, took it for any thing but Butchers Meat. This poor Animal dies as soon as it has lost a little Blood. We discover'd that they were to be met with in these Seas, by finding one dead on the Shoar some Months after our Arrival on the Island. We did not observe that this Creature ever came to Land: We imagin'd it might be thrown there, for I do not take it to be Amphibious.

We found several other sorts of Fish, and all different from those of *Europe*, except Oysters and Eels.

We easily caught Sea-Eels with a line, as well as Fresh-Water. Between the Shelves,[3] and the dry Land, there

[1] The *Halicore tabernaculi* was well known to the Jews, as its *habitat* was in the Red Sea, on the coral reefs, described by Rüppell. See Tristram's *Natural Hist. of the Bible*, pp. 44, 152.

[2] In orig.: "le tirer à bout touchant avec un fusil."

[3] In orig.: "brisans," reefs.

are certain spaces of Ground which are cover'd when the Tide is in, and dry when 'tis out. In this Extent there are Ditches or sorts of Reservatories, which the Sea has dug, and which remain always full of Water, and also full of Fish. 'Tis there that we fish'd with Ease and Pleasure; for the Water being very clear, we cou'd see the Fish catch greedily after the Bait; and sometimes there wou'd be a kind of Battel about it, who shou'd bite first; insomuch that we might catch abundance in a very little time.

The fishing with a Net is not less Diverting, for we had the pleasure of taking a great number of Fish, whose Variety was very agreeable.

About a thousand Paces from our Lodges there was a Creek, which was full of Sea-Water (at high tide), and at its entrance we cast our Net; so that when the Sea went out, abundance of Fish remain'd dry, and we took up what we pleas'd, letting the rest go, as long as there was Water enough to carry them.

We had also another Creek on the other side of our Cabbins, and full of Oysters, sticking to the Rocks. We went often to Breakfast there, and brought some home, with which we made an excellent Ragout with Palm-Tree-Cabbages and Turtles fat.

Of all the Birds in the Island, the most Remarkable is that which goes by the Name of the *Solitary*,[1] because 'tis very seldom seen in Company, tho' there are abundance of them. The Feathers of the Males are of a brown, grey Colour: The Feet and Beak are like a Turkeys, but a little more crooked. They have scarce any Tail, but their Hindpart cover'd with Feathers is Roundish, like the Crupper of a Horse, they are taller than Turkeys. Their Neck is straight, and a little longer in proportion than a Turkeys, when it lifts up his Head. Its Eye is black and lively, and its Head without Comb or Cop.[2] They never fly, their Wings

[1] See Appendix.
[2] In orig. : " sans crête ni houpe."

are too little to support the weight of their Bodies; they
serve only to beat themselves, and flutter[1] when they call one
another. They will whirl about[2] for twenty or thirty times
together on the same side, during the space of four or five
Minutes: The Motions of their Wings makes then a noise
very like that of a Rattle; and one may hear it two hundred
Paces off. The Bone of their Wing grows greater towards
the Extremity, and forms a little round Mass under the
Feathers, as big as a Musket Ball: That and its Beak are
the chief Defence of this Bird. 'Tis very hard to catch it
in the Woods, but easie in open Places, because we run faster
than they, and sometimes we approach them without much
Trouble. From *March* to *September* they are extremely fat,
and tast admirably well, especially while they are young,
some of the Males weigh forty five Pound.

The Females are wonderfully beautiful, some fair, some
brown; I call them fair, because they are of the colour of fair
Hair: They have a sort of Peak like a Widow's cap[3] upon
their Breasts, which is of a dun Colour. No one Feather is
stragling from the other all over their Bodies, they being very
careful to adjust themselves, and make them all even with
their Beaks. The Feathers on their Thighs are round like
shells at the end, and being there very thick, have an
agreeable effect: They have two Risings on their *Craws*,[4] and
the Feathers are whiter there than the rest, which livelily
Represents the fine Neck of a Beautiful Woman. They
walk with so much Stateliness and good Grace, that one cannot help admiring and loving them; by which means their
fine Mein (*i.e.*, mien) often saves their Lives.

Tho' these Birds will sometimes very familiarly come up

[1] In orig.: " pour faire le moulinet."

[2] In orig.: " Ils font avec vitesse vingt ou trente piroüettes tout de
suite, du même côté, pendant l'espace de quatre ou cinq minutes."

[3] In orig.: " bandeau."

[4] Craw—Dutch *Kraag*, Swed. *Kräfva*, Germ. *Kragen*—the crop of
fowls.

near enough to one, when we do not run after them, yet they will never grow Tame: As soon as they are caught they shed Tears without Crying, and (obstinately) refuse all manner of Sustenance till they die.

We find in the Gizards of both Male and Female a brown Stone, of the bigness of a Hens Egg,[1] 'tis somewhat rough, flat on one side, and round on the other, heavy and hard. We believe this Stone was there when they were hatch'd, for let them be never so young, you met with it always. They have never but one of 'em, and besides, the Passage from the Craw to the Gizard is so narrow, that a like Mass of half the bigness cou'd not pass. It serv'd to whet our Knives, better than any other Stone whatsoever.

When these Birds build their Nests, they choose a clean Place, gather together some Palm-Leaves for that purpose, and heap them up a foot and a half high from the Ground, on which they sit. They never lay but one Egg, which is much bigger than that of a Goose. The Male and Female both cover[2] it in their turns, and the young is not hatch'd till at seven Weeks end: All the while they are sitting upon it, or are bringing up their young one, which is not able to provide for its self in several Months,[3] they will not suffer any other Bird of their Species to come within two hundred yards round of the Place: But what is very singular, is, The Males will never drive away the Females, only when he perceives one he makes a noise with his Wings to call the Female, and she drives the unwelcome Stranger away, not leaving it till 'tis without her Bounds. The Female do's the same as to the Males, whom she leaves to the Male, and he drives them away. We have observ'd this several times, and I affirm it to be true.

The Combats between them on this occasion last some-

---

[1] See Appendix, and Plate No. x.

[2] In orig. : "le couvent."

[3] In orig. : "qu'après plusieurs mois."

times pretty long, because the Stranger only turns about, and
do's not fly directly from the Nest : However, the others do
not forsake it, till they have quite driv'n it out of their Limits.
After these Birds have rais'd their young One, and left it to
its self, they are always together, which the other Birds are
not, and tho' they happen to mingle with other Birds of the
same Species, these two Companions never disunite.[1] We
have often remark'd, that some days after the young one
leaves the Nest, a Company of thirty or forty brings another
young one to it ; and the new fledg'd Bird with its Father
and Mother joyning with the Band, march to some bye Place.
We frequently follow'd them, and found that afterwards the
old ones went each their way alone, or in Couples, and left
the two young ones together, which we call'd a *Marriage*.

This Particularity has something in it which looks a little
Fabulous, nevertheless, what I say is sincere Truth, and what
I have more than once observ'd with Care and Pleasure :
neither cou'd I forbear to entertain my Mind with several
Reflections on this Occasion. I sent Mankind to learn of the
Beasts. I commended my *Solitaries* for marrying young (a
piece of Wisdom practis'd by our *Jews*) for satisfying Nature
in a proper time ; and when she wants to be satisfy'd according to the state of the same Nature, and conformable to the
intention of the Creator. I admir'd the Happiness of these
innocent and faithful Pairs, who liv'd so peaceably in constant Love : I said to my self, if our Pride and Extravagance
were restrain'd, if Men were or had been as wise as these
Birds, to say all at once, they wou'd marry as these Birds do,
without any other Pomp or Ceremony, without Contracts or
Jointures, without Portions or Settlements,[2] without subjec-
tion to any Laws, and without any Offence, with which

---

[1] "Mais ils demeurent toujours unis et compagnons quoiqu'ils aillent
quelquefois se mêler parmi d'autres de leur espèce," omitted in translation.

[2] In orig : " Sans Mien sans Tien."

LE SOLITAIRE

Nature wou'd be most pleas'd, and the Common-Wealth most benefited; for Divine and Human Laws, are only Precautions against the disorders of Mankind. Know, kind Reader, that my chief Employment in this Desart Island was thinking, and suffer me therefore sometimes to speak my Thoughts. I have already giv'n you notice, that you were not to expect a Dissertation on the *Antiquity* of *Greek* Accents, nor on Manuscripts of our *Eden*, nor on the Medals found there, any more than Descriptions of its Amphitheaters, Palaces and Temples.

Our Wood-hens[1] are fat all the year round, and of a most delicate Tast. Their Colour is always of a bright Gray, and there's very little difference in the *Plumage* between the two Sexes. They hide their Nests so well, that we cou'd not find 'em out, and consequently did not tast their Eggs. They have a red List[2] about their Eyes, their Beaks are straight and pointed, near two Inches long, and red also. They cannot fly, their fat makes 'em too heavy for it. If you offer them any thing that's red,[3] they are so angry they will fly at you to catch it out of your Hand, and in the heat of the Combat, we had an opportunity to take them with ease. We had abundance of Bitterns,[4] as big and as good as

[1] In orig. "Gelinotes", an extinct form of *Rallidæ*, closely allied to the *Aphanapteryx* of Mauritius. Cf. *Recherches sur la faune ancienne des îles Mascareignes*, par Alph. Milne Edwards in *Ann. des Sc. nat. Zool.*, 5me série, t. xix, art. 3, and, by the same author, *Sur les affinités zoologiques de l'Aphanapteryx, etc., op. c.*, x, 325.

[2] In orig.: "ourlet rouge autour." Anglo-Saxon *List;* Icel. *listi* or fillet ; a list of cloth is the outer edge or border.

Cf. Shakespeare, "Gartered with a red and blue list." (*Taming of the Shrew*, iii, 2.)

[3] M. Milne Edwards proposes the name *Erythromachus, i.e.*, "Hostile to red," for this genus, and has named the species here described after our author, *E. Leguati*. But Messrs. Günther and Newton prefer looking upon the Rodriguez bird as a smaller species of *Aphanapteryx*, and to treat of it as *A. Leguati*. Cf. *Phil. Trans., op. c.*, p. 431. *Vide* App.

[4] In orig. "Butors". The bitterns mentioned seem to have been night-herons, *Nycticorax megacephalus*. This night-heron was clearly

G

Capons; they are more familiar, and more easily to be caught than Woodhens.

The Pigeons[1] here are somewhat less than ours, and all of a Slate colour, fat and good. They pearch and build their Nests upon Trees; they are easily taken, being so Tame, that we have had fifty about our Table to Pick up the Melon-Seeds which we threw them, and they lik'd mightily. We took them when we pleas'd, and ty'd little Rags to their Thighs of several Colours, that we might know them again if we let them loose. They never miss'd attending us at our Meals, and we call'd them our Chickens. They never built their Nests in the Isle, but in the little *Islets*[2] that are near it. We suppos'd 'twas to avoid the persecution of the Rats, of which there are vast Numbers in this Island, as I shall report in the Sequel of this Relation. The Rats never pass into the Islets. The Fools,[3] the Frigats[4] and perhaps some other Sea-Birds who live upon Fish only, build their Nests on Trees; but[5] there are some other

"of much more cursorial habits", write Messrs. Günther and Newton, " than its congeners, chasing rather terrestrial animals (lizards) than aquatic." (*Phil. Trans., l. c.*, 436.)

"The effect of the prolonged isolation on the two vertebrate-hunting birds of Rodriguez, the owl and the night-heron, was precisely the same. Without losing the power of flight, they became brevipennate; but the increased development of the legs compensated for the reduction of this power, and enabled the one to destroy animals of larger size when the smaller kinds become scarcer, and the other to chase its swift-running prey." (*Philosophical Transactions, op. c.*, p. 436.)

[1] *Columba rodericana*. This pigeon, now extinct, was probably of the genus *Erythræna*, being of a slate colour (*ardoise*), and not the *Turtur picturatus* of Madagascar, Réunion, and Mauritius, as suggested by M. Milne Edwards. (*E. N.*)

[2] These islets all received names subsequently. See p. 86, *infra*, and a later account of Rodriguez (1730), *Ann. des Sc. nat. Zool.* (6), ii, art. 4.

[3] The "Booby", probably *Sula piscator*, a species of gannet.; but cf. Alph. Milne Edwards, in *Ann. des Sc. nat. Zool.*, 6me série, t. ii, art. 4.

[4] " Les Paille-en-queue," omitted in translation. See next page.

[5] In orig: "les ferrets et quelques autres." These birds are described later, in Part II.

Birds that sit on the Land, in the same Isles where the
Pigeons nest. All these Birds have a rank Taste, which is
not agreeable; to make amends their Eggs are very good.
The Fools come ev'ry Night, and Roost in the Island;
and the *Frigats* which are larger, and so call'd because
they are light, and admirable Sailers,[1] lie in wait for
them on the top of the Trees, from whence they flounce
down upon them like Falcons on their Prey, not to kill
them, but make them bring up the Fish that is in their
Craw, which the Fool as soon as it is thus struck, is forc'd
to do. The Frigat catches it always before it comes to the
Ground. The Fool cries, and sometimes is very unwilling
to part with its Prog, but the Frigat who is a bolder and
stronger Bird, laughs at its Cries, mounts into the Air, and
down he flounces again upon it, seizes upon the Throat, and
do's so till he has compell'd it to obey.

The Frigat[2] is blackish, and about the bigness of a Duck.
Its Wings are very large, 'tis a sort of Bird of Prey; for it
has Talons, and its Beak which is above half a Foot long, is
a little crooked at the end. The old ones of the Males, have
a kind of red Flesh like a Comb under its Neck, as our
Cocks have. The *Fools* are so call'd because they incon-
siderately come about Ships, Perch on the Ropes, and
innocently suffer themselves to be easily taken. Their
Simplicity is so great, that they judge of others by themselves, and do not take Men to be Mischievous Creatures.
Their Backs are of a Chesnut Colour, their Bellies whitish,
their Beaks sharp, four Inches long, and big towards the
Head, a little indented at the Edges. Their legs are short,
their feet like those of a Duck, and of a pale Yellow.

There's another sort of Bird[3] as big as a Pigeon all over

---

[1] In orig.: "bons Voiliers."

[2] The Frigate, or man-of-war bird (*Tachypetes aquila*, or *T. minor*).

[3] *Le Paille-en-queue*, the Tropic bird (*Phaethon candidus*); according
to Milne Edwards, *P. Phœnicurus* and *P. flavirostris*. These birds are

white, its Beak is short and strong, it has a Feather at its Tail a Foot and a half long, from whence it takes its Name being call'd *Straw-Tail*. These Birds made a pleasant War upon us, or rather upon our Bonnets; they often came behind us, and caught 'em off our Heads before we were aware of it: This they did so frequently that we were forc'd to carry Sticks in our hands to defend our selves. We prevented them sometimes, when we discover'd them by their shadow before us: we then struck them in the Moment they were about to strike us. We cou'd never find out of what use the Bonnets were to them, nor what they did with those they took from us.

I shall speak of the *Tag* and the *Pluto* in *Maurice* Island. There's but one sort of small Birds[1] at *Rodrigo*, they are not much unlike Canary Birds; we never heard them sing, tho' they are so familiar, that they will place themselves on a Book which you hold in your hand.

There are abundance of green and blew Parrets,[2] they are

still very abundant in those regions (*Ann. des. Sc. nat. Zool., op. cit.*, 5me série, xix, art. 3, and 6me série, ii, art. 4). Another red-tailed species (*Phaethon rubricauda*) breeds on Round Island, near Mauritius.

[1] Two indigenous species of small birds were collected by Sir E. Newton on Rodriguez in 1864. These were described by him as *Foudia flavicans* and *Drymæca rodericana*, and specimens of both were brought home by the naturalists of the Transit of Venus Expedition in 1874. Sir E. Newton identifies Leguat's small birds with *Foudia flavicans*, but notices that they had "a very pleasant song", in contradiction to his statement that "we never heard them sing". M. Milne Edwards, however, laying more stress on Leguat's words, is of opinion that his small birds were neither *Foudia flavicans* nor *Drymæca rodericana*, and that these may have been of more recent introduction. Leguat's canaries, he thinks, have shared the fate of the solitaires and woodhens—*i.e.*, become extinct. (Cf. *P. Z. S.*, 1865, p. 47; *Ibis*, 1865, pp. 147 *et seq.*; *Phil. Trans., l. c.*, p. 459; *Ann. des Sc. nat. Zool.* (5), xix, art. 3, and (6), ii, art. 4.)

[2] M. Milne Edwards has shown, in a memoir published some years ago, that there were great parrots at Rodriguez of a species which neither exists there nor in any other part of the globe. These were distinct from *Agapornis cana* and *Palæornis exsul*, and furnish additional proof

$\frac{2}{5}$

PALÆORNIS EXSUL

of a midling and equal bigness; when they are young, their
Flesh is as good as that of young Pigeons.

There are Purrs[1] and a few Swallows.[2]

The Batts[3] fly there by day as well as other Birds; they
are as big as a good Hen, and each wing is near two Foot
long. They never Perch, but hang by their Feet to the
Boughs of Trees, with their Head downwards, and their
Wings being supply'd with several Hooks, they do not easily
fall tho' they are struck.[4] When you see them at a Distance,
hanging thus wrapt up in their Wings, you wou'd take them
rather for Fruit than Birds. The *Dutch* whom I knew at
Maurice Island, made a rare Dish with them, and preferr'd it
to the most Delicate Wild-Fowl. Every Man has his Tast;
As for us, we found something in these Batts that we did
not like, and having a great many things that were much

of changes having taken place in the fauna of that island. See his
Mémoire sur un Psittacus fossile de l'ile de Rodrigue (*Psittacus roderi-
canus*) in *Ann. des Sc. nat. Zool.* (5), viii, 145. The parrots, however,
referred to in our text were of moderate size, and may probably have
been *Palæornis exul*, of which a living specimen was seen in the island by
Mr. Slater in 1874. (Cf. *Phil. Trans. R. S., l. c.*, pp. 430 and 459.)

[1] Purrs, probably a species of sandpiper, or perhaps small plovers, for
Leguat could not distinguish them.

[2] In orig.: " Il y a des allouettes de mer et des Becassines. Nous
n'avons vû que très-peu d'hirondelles."

[3] Flying-foxes, *Pteropus Edwardsii*. Pingré, who touched at Rodriguez in 1761, during his voyage for the observation of the Transit
of Venus, gives some interesting details on these flying-foxes. Those
he saw were the size of a pigeon, but longer; the head like that of
a fox; the skin reddish, darker on the head and neck than on the rest
of the body; the wings dark grey; when extended they may have
measured a foot or a foot and a half. These animals are still extant
at Rodriguez, but no materials have hitherto been accessible for their
identification. M. Milne Edwards is inclined to think they are not
Pteropus Edwardsii, a much larger species inhabiting Madagascar, nor
Pteropus vulgaris of the island of Mauritius, also a larger type. (*Ann.
des Sc. nat. Zool.*, 5me série, xix, art. 3.)

[4] " Elles demeurent toujours attachées par quelque crochet," omitted
by translator.

better, at least in our Opinion, we never eat any of these filthy Creatures. They carry their young about with them[1]; We observ'd they had always two.

The Palmtrees and Plantanes are always loaden with Lizards[2] about a foot long, the Beáuty of which is very Extraordinary; some of them are blue, some black, some green, some red, some grey, and the colour of each the most lively and bright of any of its kind. Their common Food is the Fruit of the Palm-Trees. They are not mischievous, and so Tame, that they often come and eat the Melons on our Tables, and in our Presence, and even in our Hands[3]; they serve for Prey to some Birds, especially the Bitterns. When we beat 'em down from the Trees with a Pole, these Birds wou'd come and devour them before us, tho' we did our utmost to hinder them; and when we offer'd to oppose them, they came on still after their Prey, and still follow'd us when we endeavour'd to defend them.

There's another sort of Nocturnal Lizards[4] of a grayish

[1] " & ne les abandonnent que lors qu'ils peuvent voler," omitted by translator.

[2] Possibly, Dr. Günther thinks, a species of *Phelsuma*, a genus well represented in the Mascarene region. (*Phil. Trans., l. c.*, p. 454.)

[3] The fact of there being lizards at Rodriguez is another proof of its being zoologically distinct from Hindustan, for though several kinds of these reptiles are found in Ceylon, there are none in the adjacent continent. With reference to the tameness of lizards, Sir E. Tennent relates the following anecdote : "In an officer's quarters, a gecko had been taught to come daily to the dinner-table, and always made its appearance along with the dessert. The family were absent for some months while the house underwent repairs ; but on the return of its old friends, at their first dinner, the little lizard made its entrance as usual as soon as the cloth had been removed." (Sir E. Tennent's *Ceylon*, i, 186.)

[4] Probably, according to the authority quoted above (n. 2), the species of which Mr. Slater collected, with remains of the solitaire and tortoise, several bones. He recognised them as the remains of a lizard, possibly belonging to the family of Skinks. In Dr. Günther's opinion it is a geckoid lizard, which cannot be separated from the genus Gecko. He concurs in the proposal of Mr. Slater to name it, after Sir E. Newton, *Gecko Newtonii.* (*Ibid.*)

Colour, and very ugly; they are as big and as long as ones Arm, their Flesh is not very bad, they love Plantanes. We found Salt enough in holes on the Rocks upon our Coasts, and had the Island been full of Inhabitants, they might have been supply'd there. The Waves throw up the Sea-water in their Agitation, and the Sun, that admirable Workman of all the Metamorphoses of Nature, turns it into Salt. The Sea brings yellow Amber and Ambergreece.[1] We found a great piece of the latter, which we did not know, and which prov'd the cause of all the Misfortunes that happen'd to us afterwards, as will be related in the sequel of this History. We found also abundance of a sort of black Bitumen, to which we gave the name of Amber, but I believe 'tis properly Jet.

There's a certain admirable Flower[2] in this Island, which I shou'd prefer to *Spanish* Jessamine, 'tis as white as a Lily, and shap'd something like common Jessamine. It grows particularly out of the Trunks of rotten Trees, when they

---

[1] "La mer apporte de l'ambre jaune, & de l'ambre gris." The Arabic term *Amber* was first given to the remarkable secretion formed in the intestines of the spermaceti whale, and subsequently to the fossilised gum now generally known by that term. These two substances, both mysterious products of the sea, were, in the seventeenth century, distinguished only by their colour as *ambre gris* and *ambre jaune*. Ben Jonson asks—

     "Why do you smell of ambergrise,
      Of which was formed Neptune's niece?"
                  (*Neptune's Triumph.*)
Whilst Milton speaks of game—
     "In pastry built, or from the spit or boiled
      Gris-amber steam'd."
                  (*Paradise Regained.*)

[2] A marked feature in the Flora, Professor Balfour states (*op. cit.*, p. 304), is the paucity of *Orchidaceæ*. Only four species have been determined; a fifth, a species of *Angræcum*, was found, but in too imperfect a state for identification. Professor Balfour knows of no plant on the island answering to Leguat's description, and can only suppose it to refer to some species of orchid, which has now passed away. A sweet-smelling orchid, *Angræcum fragrans*, is found in the Mascarene Islands.

are almost reduc'd to the Substance of Mould. The Odour of this Flower, strikes one agreeably at a hundred Paces distance.

The Air of this Isle will not suffer Lice or Fleas, as one may be assur'd by Experience after such a Voyage as ours. Neither were we troubled by any stinging Flies, nor other Insects that are so troublesom in the Night, or rather so intolerable, in other Places.

In those little Islands[1] before-mention'd where the Pigeons build, there are an infinite number of Sea-Fowl; their Flesh (is) not pleasant to the Taste, nor very wholesom, but their Eggs are very good. There's such abundance of these Birds,[2] that when they rise, the Sky is even darken'd by them.

They hatch on the Sand, and so near one another that they touch, tho' of different Kinds. These poor Creatures are so Tame, and so little Diffident, that they will not rise tho' you are almost upon them. They lay three times a year, and but one Egg at a time, like the *Solitaries;* which is the more Remarkable, for that if I am not Mistaken, we have no Example of any thing like it among our *European* Birds. I shall add one very particular thing which I observ'd in some of these Birds in *Maurice* Island, when I come to treat of that Isle.

Thus have I related the most considerable Observations we made in and about the Island of *Rodrigo.* I must now,

---

[1] These little islets are noticeable both in Leguat's sketch map and the Admiralty charts, facsimiles of which have been given for comparison. It will be seen that these islets extend from Booby Island (55 feet) on the north, round the west side of the island within the reefs to Port South-East, Crab Island being the highest of them (150 feet). Their names, Booby, Pierrot, and Frigate, etc., indicate their being the homes of land-birds and sea-fowl. It is not easy to identify any particular islet in Leguat's map.

[2] Probably terns, several species of which breed on the islets round Rodriguez. (Cf. *Phil. Trans., l. c.,* pp. 463 *et seq.*)

to give the Reader a true *Idæa* of the Place, take notice of
the disagreeable and inconvenient things in it : I shall
begin with what we first saw. As soon as we Landed, we
were surrounded by a prodigious Number of certain little
Flies which cover'd us. 'Twas in vain to kill them, for after
you had bruis'd ten Thousand of them to pieces, they wou'd
be no more mist, than ten drops of Water in the Sea. 'Tis
true, these little Creatures did not sting ; all the Inconvenience they put us to was a little tickling when they touch'd
our Faces. They retire to the Trees as soon as the Sun is
down, and leave them when it Rises. They always seek
shelter, and the mild cooling Breeze ; and after we had
fell'd the Trees about the Place where we built our Cabins,
it expos'd them so much to the Wind, that it drove 'em to
the Woods, and deliver'd all the extent of our Habitations
entirely from them. But we met with them every where
when we walkt out into the Island.

There's also a kind of great Flies which do not fear the
Wind as the others do, and are very Troublesom. Their
Bellies are full of Worms, which they lay on our Meat, and
sometimes let 'em fall as they fly along, so that those Provisions quickly tainted, when, instead of leaving them open
to the Air, we wrapt them up in Linen. The only means
we found out to cure this Evil, was to dip them in Sea-
Water from time to time. The Nerves or Fibres of the
Stalks of our Plantane-Leaves wou'd have made an excellent
fine Trellis which those Flies cou'd not Penetrate, and with
which we might have made a *Safe* to secure our Meat, but
we did not think of that Machine.

The Rats were our second Plague, they are like those in
Europe, are very Numerous, and very Troublesome.

They did not only eat the Seed we sow'd, but came into our
Cabbins, and nibbled everything they found there. I am
apt to doubt whether Mr. *de Rochefort* was well inform'd
when he wrote there were no Rats in the *American* Islands

before our Discoveries there[1]; for I have often found in the
Relation of Voyagers that they met with prodigious quantities in Desert and unknown Islands. It's not impossible
that some Ship might have touch'd, or been cast away there ;
but let our Modern Philosophers say what they will, I have
very good reason to believe, that Rats as well as other kind
of Vermin are engender'd sometimes by Corruption, tho' they
are also brought forth by the common way of Generation.
If 'tis the good pleasure of God, the Great Master of the
Universe, that it shou'd be so, what shou'd hinder Rats being
found in those Islands where never any vessel was ?[2]

Whereas the *Americans* have Adders which are naturally
bent to exterminate this Villanous Race, as also Cats and
Dogs that are taught to make War upon them, we had
nothing to assist us but Owls[3] and Traps. We soon banish'd
them from our Quarters, by the help of the latter; however
we must own, that a new Multitude sometimes return'd,
and found us new Work to clear them. The most ready and
sure way of getting rid of great Numbers of them, wou'd be
to lay poyson'd Meat for them; the Island not being very
big, this wou'd soon have a very good Effect ; and nothing
could come of it that we needed apprehend, if it happen'd
before the Isle was well setled.

[1] De Rochfort, in speaking of the various inconveniences to be met
with in the Antilles, says that it was only after ships began frequenting
these islands that rats multiplied to such an extent as to injure the
crops and vegetables; previously they were unknown to the Caraib
Indians. (*Histoire Naturelle des Iles Antilles*, L. de Poincy et C. de
Rochfort, 2nd edit., 1865, p. 277.)

[2] The rats were probably of recent introduction. Vessels had
touched at the island before Leguat's time on their way to India.

[3] The owls of Rodriguez are now extinct, but some bones found in
one of its caves by Sir E. Newton in 1874 attest Leguat's veracity.
These bones belong to two species, for one of which M. Alph. Milne
Edwards proposes the name of *Strix (Athene) murivora;* of the other
only one bone, a tibia, having been produced for examination, no
specific name could be given. (*Ann. des Sc. nat. Zool.* (5), xix, art. 3.)

The several Inconveniences occasion'd by these Animals when they come thus by Armies, render Credible what is said of that young *English* Adventurer (Richard Whittington, in the year 1397) who made his Fortune by a Cat which he carry'd out of his Country by chance, and which he presented to a Lord in some Island in the *Indies*. This little Prince charm'd with the Cat's admirable Hunting, liberally Rewarded him who brought it; and who having set a high Price upon it, return'd Rich to *London*, and became Lord Mayor. He is often to be seen painted with his Cat in his Mayors Habit, and serves for one of the *Signs* in that City.

The Land-Crabs[1] were our next Enemies. 'Tis impossible to destroy them, there's such a prodigious quantity of them in the low Grounds, and 'tis very difficult to get them out of their Holes.[2] Their Burroughs are very broad, and have several Entrances; they never go far from them, standing always upon their Guard.

They tore up our Plants in our Gardens day and Night, and if we shut up the Plants in a sort of a Cage in hopes of saving them, if they were not far off, they wou'd dig under Ground from their Burroughs to the Plants, and tear them up under the Cage. The back Scale or Shell of this Crab is of a dirty Russet Colour, is almost round, and about four Inches Diameter. They march directly with eight Claws or Paws, about four Inches from the Ground, and have two that are indented of an unequal Bigness, as we know all sorts of Crabs have, the Right Claw or Paw being bigger and

---

[1] The land-crabs described in our text appear to be allied or identical with *Birgus latro*, which Darwin observed in the Keeling Islands. He speaks of their burrowing habits and of their being provided with "very strong and heavy pincers", with which they crack the cocoa-nuts (*Voyage of the Beagle*, iii, p. 551). Messrs. Gulliver and Slater collected 189 specimens of crustaceæ at Rodriguez, representing thirty-five species. (*Phil. Trans.*, *l. c.*, p. 485.)

[2] "Elles se logent en terre, & creusent, jusqu'à ce qu'elles ayent trouvé de l'eau," omitted by translator.

stronger than the rest. You cannot see the Mouth of one
of them when it goes along, because it is downwards, but its
Eyes are much like those of the Crabs in *France* and *England,* are a good Inch one above another on the Brink, and
without the Shell.

When one approaches it, it presently retires; but when
we throw Stones after it, 'twill always run after the Stones,
by which it is easily struck; 'tis dangerous venturing to be
pinch'd by it. This Animal often cleans its Hole, and after
having made a little heap of the Ordures it finds there, it
carries them out by Pressing them against its Belly with its
Claws. This it do's often, and with so much nimbleness,
that it soon removes what is Troublesom to it. Its Flesh is
pretty good, and tasts something like River-Crabs.

A little before and after the Full-Moons in *July* and
August, these Crabs march by Millions, from all parts of the
Island to the Sea. We never met with one but what was
laden with Eggs. We might then have destroy'd great
quantities of them with ease, for they go in prodigious
Troops, and being far from their Burroughs, have no place
of Retreat. We have sometimes kill'd above three Thousand
in an Evening with Sticks, yet we cou'd not perceive the
next Day, that their Number was at all Diminish'd. The
Second year of our abode in this Isle, we thought of a way
to rid our selves of them, in some measure; which was, by
Sowing abundance of Seed in the places where they most
Inhabited; that finding Occupation enough at Home, they
might save our Plants, which if they had time to grow to
any bigness, were out of danger. This helpt us a little, and
we were so cautious as to Sow those Plants which we were
willing to Cultivate, in Places they did not frequent, as well
in our Gardens, as in Hills far from the Rivers where the
bottom was Rock.

One of our Companions who at all ventures had brought
two great Chests of Merchandise with him, which were in

demand in *India*, and also a good quantity of *louis d'ors*, but
was at least as Diffident as Rich, was pleasantly caught by
one of these little Beasts. His Pistoles were in several
Purses; and we observ'd, if he went at any time a little way
from his Cabbin, he took them along with him. He never
fail'd to hide them every Night before he went to Bed, in
the safest place he cou'd think of; but as cunning as he was
he found one that was as cunning as he, and was bubbled[1]
by a Thief, he did not think of, I mean, some Crab or Rat
that took away one of his Purses from him; which being of
Leather,[2] was no doubt very agreeable to the Robbers Tast.
The next day we perceiv'd he was Chagrin, and search'd for
something with great Application; we prest him to tell
what he had lost, and at last through Importunity, or
hoping we wou'd help him in finding it, he told us the whole
truth of the Matter. Tho' we cou'd not forbear Laughing a
little, we however went about with him to seek it, but all
our seeking signify'd nothing, and the Person Rob'd was
forc'd to comfort himself for the Robbery. 'Tis true, he ever
after made War[3] upon the whole Nation of Crabs, and we
assisted him in it. He never kill'd one without giving him
some blows after he was dead.

The Sea-Crabs are much better[4] than the Land, and the
Flesh easier to Digest.

There's also another sort which I am inform'd goes by the

---

1 To bubble, *i.e.*, to cheat, from It. *bubbola*, a hoopoe; in orig.
"fut la dupe", from the French for the same bird, from some tra-
dition of the habits of that bird of which we are ignorant. A familiar
instance of the use of the noun is the "South Sea bubble." Cf. Wedgwood's *Dict. of Eng. Etymology*; Nares' *Glossary*.

2 In orig.: "dont le cuir étant un peu gras," etc.

3 In orig.: "Il est vrai qu'il eut une permanente rancune contre
toute la nation des crabes, et que dans la guerre que nous leur faisons
souvent, il n'en tua jamais aucune," etc.

4 "Et beaucoup plus grosses, . . . et la chair en est aisée à digerer."

Name of *Tourlouroux*[1] in the *Antilles*, and are very like the
first Crabs I spoke of, but somewhat less.   They dwell
between the Sea and the Land like true Amphibious Creatures,
as they are; insomuch that the Sea twice a Day fills their
Holes with Water, and they are continually at work to keep
'em clean.

The Hurricanes[2] which we were terrify'd with every year,
in the Month of *January* or *February*, as I have already
noted, is also a dreadful Enemy.   We felt its rude Attacks
twice.   This furious Wind rises commonly after fair Weather,
and even after a great Calm; and its greatest Violence lasts
at least an Hour.   We then saw several huge Trees torn up
by the Roots in a Moment, and our Cabbins utterly overwhelm'd.   The Sea Raging and Foaming roar'd so, that it
frighted us; and lifting up its foaming Waves like Mountains,
dashed 'em against the Coasts with so much Impetuosity,
that it seem'd as if Nature was in such Convulsions, as wou'd
soon reduce her to her Original Chaos.   Heaven and Earth
mingled, a thick Darkness involv'd the Sky, and the Clouds
breaking discharg'd a Deluge of Rain, like that which
immerg'd the first World.   Our fair and fruitful Valleys
were immediately drown'd, and look'd like a new Ocean.
The Torrent overwhelm'd every thing that lay in its way;
and I believe if this Violence had lasted three Hours,

---

[1] De Rochfort, in his work on the Antilles (p. 253), mentions three
kinds of crabs under this name, applying it in particular to the smallest
of the three.   These crabs have a red shell with a black spot on it, are
agreeable to the taste, but, being small and producing dysentery, are
not in much request.

[2] In original: " ouragan ' (cf. p. 36, *supra*).   Rodriguez lies right in
the paths of the cyclones which traverse the southern Indian Ocean.
There is no positive law for their tracks, but, from the averages
observed, it seems that they nearly all pass from E.N.E. to W.S.W.,
but, from longitude 80° E. westward and when approaching the Mascarene group, they have a tendency to curve southward, frequently backing
to E.S.E. when they reach the southern tropic.

Dr. Meldrum has noticed that when the Mascarene Islands suffer from
drought the Indian Ocean is almost free from hurricanes.

there was not a Tree in the Island that could have resisted it. The Beasts by a natural Instinct of Gracious and wise Providence, foresaw these Storms before they happen'd, and sav'd themselves in the Cavities of the Mountains; but the next Day they appear'd abroad as before, for the Weather return'd to be as fair and clear as ever. The last Hurricane we felt at *Rodrigo*, was much more terrible than the first. In the midst of its greatest Fury, there was a sudden and profound Calm, not the least Noise was heard, and we believ'd all was over, when immediately the Storm return'd with more Violence than ever. It entirely destroy'd all our Gardens; for the force of the Wind rais'd up the Waters of the Sea, and blew about ev'ry where a deluge of Salt Water that burnt up or kill'd all our plants. But it doing no hurt to the Soil at bottom, as soon as we got out of the Holes of the Rocks to which we fled we sow'd more Plants, and they came up as before.

In fine, The fourth and last Enemy we had to Combat with, were little green Caterpillars, which always come after a Hurricane, and are certainly one of its secret Productions. These Insects troubled us very much, from the Month of *February*, to that of *April*; for they eat up our Melons, not leaving a Leaf on the Trees. Experience taught us the way to prevent it, which was by covering 'em all Night, and uncovering them in the Morning; Glass Bells wou'd have been a good Buckler for them. These Vermin did not touch our Succory, nor our Purslain; and we may therefore reasonably conclude, that there are several sorts of other Herbs and Plants which they will not meddle with, as not being to their Gust.[1]

In some Places we met with little Scorpions, especially on the Plantanes; but we did not find that they were any way dangerous, because we were several times stung by them,

[1] "Gust", Lat. *gustus*, relish, taste; cf. Shakespeare, "Allay the *gust* he hath in . . ." *Twelfth Night*, ii, 3.

without any Inconvenience afterwards. It only caus'd a little Pain for a Moment or two, like the prick of a Pin.

When we bath'd our selves in the Sea, or when we were oblig'd to walk in our Fishing, we were often surrounded with a great Troop of Sharks, among which some were very great, yet we were never attack'd by them. And when we were on that fatal Rock of the Isle *Maurice*, which I shall say more of hereafter, I have a hundred times seen a great Pack of Dogs follow a Stag into the Sea, and Swim after him in places where were abundance of Sharks; yet they never did them any hurt, any more than they did us when we were Bathing. Let the Reader therefore judge, whether this is such a Voracious Animal as 'tis represented to be, or whether the Sharks in these Seas are different from those in others. The Relations of such as have made Voyages to *America*, and several other parts of the World, tell us unanimously, that the Sharks in those Seas are extreamly dangerous and ravenous, and several Persons speak as if they had been Eye-Witnesses of it; wherefore 'tis most reasonable to conclude, that all the Sharks are not of the same kind.[1] This Fish is commonly fifteen or sixteen Foot long; its Mouth is so made, that it must necessarily turn upon its Back to swallow its Prey, or must thrust half its Head out of Water; it has several rows of Teeth, which are extreamly sharp, and like those of a Saw. I was told at *Batavia*, and elsewhere, that the Brain of a Shark had a Virtue in it, which made Womens Pains in Child-Bed not so racking to them, as they generally are; but we cou'd not try the Experiment in our Island. Some say, the little Fish which we call Succet,[2] or the Shark's Pilot, is his Guide, but that's

---

[1] All the known species (140) of sharks except four are carnivorous. Those observed by Leguat had doubtless ceased to be dangerous to man, owing to the abundance of animal food round the island. Forty years later we read a very different account of them; far from being harmless, they were then extremely aggressive and of great size. (*Gunther, l. c.*, p. 315; *Ann. Sc. nat. Zool.* (6), ii, art. 4.)

[2] Sucking-fish, *Echeneis remora*.

a Chimera, which Father *Tachard*[1] has very well Confuted. This Succet which is reasonably enough thought to be the Rhemora, those good Men of old (who are venerably call'd Antients,[2] and who often did not know very well what they said) have render'd so famous and formidable. This Succet, I say, has on its Head, and on the forepart of its Neck a grisly Membrane flat, & in Folds by which it sticks fast to the Back of the Sharks and Sea-Dogs, and sometimes to inanimate things as Wood; for we have seen it stick to the Deck of the Ship with its Belly upwards.[3] There are at least two sorts of them, different in Bigness and Colour, but shap'd alike; they have no Scales, and their Skin is as slick and slippery as an Eel's. Those of the biggest sort are two or three Foot long; the colour of their Backs is a greenish Brown, which towards the Belly turns whitish. The others are not longer than Herrings, hardly so long. Their Snouts are shorter, and not so dark Colour'd. The Flesh of both the one and the other is not firm, but 'tis not ill tasted. They are very well provided with Fins, and are thin and long; so that they dart into the Sea like an Arrow out of a Bow. Their Teeth are a little round at the end, and so short, they are scarce perceptible. 'Tis most certain that these Fish often stick to the Ships in the Water, and

[1] Père Guy Tachard. See *Voyage de Siam des Pères Jésuites*, Amsterdam, 1687-9, liv. i, p. 41.

[2] Our author is probably referring to Aristotle and Pliny, who described the Echeneis and attributed to this little fish the power of fastening itself to vessels, and so arresting their course. Thus, it was alleged, Antony's ship was delayed getting into action at the battle of Actium (cf. Rondelet, *Livre des Poissons*, p. 313). Ten different kinds of sucking-fish are known, of which *Echineis remora* and *E. naucrates* are the most common. (See Günther's *Study of Fishes*, p. 460.) An excellent specimen of this remarkable fish may be seen at the South Kensington Natural History Museum. Our author confuses the sucking-fish with *Naucrates ductor*, the pilot fish, which is said to follow large sharks.

[3] In orig.: "quand il est tout sortant de l'eau," omitted by translator.

when they do it in a great Number, they doubtless hinder her Course, because she cannot run so lightly over the Waves. I was the more willing to speak of this Animal at large, for that others have not done it; and I cannot help saying, *en passant,* that I sometimes wonder at the mighty Reputation the Famous *Rondelet* acquir'd; for I never consulted him concerning any thing within my Knowledge, but I found him very false and very dry.[1]

All our Employment as long as we staid in this Island was very Insignificant, as may be easily imagined; however, we cou'd not live without doing something. The looking after our Cabins, and Cultivating our Gardens, took up one part of our Time, Walking, another. We frequently went to the South of the Island, either in crossing it, or going about it; there's no Place upon it but we Visited very nicely; none of the Mountains or Hills are without Verdure, tho' they are very full of Rocks. The bottom which is Rock, is spread with two, three or four foot Earth, and amongst the Stones where there's no appearance of Earth, great Trees tall and straight grow, which at a distance gives one a better *Idæa* of the Island than it deserves, because one wou'd think it was compos'd of a Soil universally Excellent.

One may go every where all over it with ease, there being

[1] Our author is rather too severe in his criticism. Rondelet was Doctor Regent in Medicine at the University of Montpellier, and published several important works on natural history. He was a good observer, a diligent student, and a skilful anatomist. The work by which he is best known is that on fishes, entitled *De Piscibus marinis libri* xviii, *in quibus vivæ piscium imagines expositæ sunt.* Lyon, 1554. It was translated into French and published in 1558. This edition is illustrated by numerous woodcuts, evidently executed by a skilful artist, and drawn with great fidelity to nature. With the exception of a few that Rondelet could only have known by hearsay, they may be recognized at the present day. The original work is dedicated to Cardinal Tournon, whom the author accompanied on his travels in the capacity of physician. Rondelet died in 1566 at the age of 59. (*Biographie Universelle.*)

few or no parts of it, which are not very Accessible, and no
Place but affords abundantly Meat and Drink. Go where
you will, and if you see no Game, you need only strike
against a Tree, or cry out as hard as you can, and Game will
immediately offer it self of all sorts, which you may knock
down with a Stick or Stone. 'Twas Chance made us experience this, because when we walkt out together and wander'd
in the Woods, if any one of us lost Company with the rest,
we were forc'd to cry aloud to let him know where we were,
that he might come to us. We were then amaz'd to see
what quantities of Birds flew out, and ran up and down from
all parts about us ; Providence as it were bid us *Kill* and
Eat,[1] and we had nothing to do but to fire a Fuzee, and roast
what we kill'd to provide a Feast ; Turtles are to be met with
every where. The Air is so sweet and so temperate, that
one might lye down boldly under the Canopy of the Sky ;
but if we pleas'd, might at any time make a sort of Hutt
immediately with five or six Plantane-Leaves which we have
spoken of.

To return to our Employments, and the manner of spending our tedious Hours, I shall add without Boasting, that we
had every day our exercises of Devotion. On Sundays we
did as far as we cou'd what is practis'd in our *French*
Churches, for we had the Bible entire with us ; some Hymns,
a large Commentary on the Testament, and several Sermons
upon the *Old Rock*, which were sensible Discourses. If we
had believ'd we shou'd spend the rest of our Days there, or
at least stay some longer time than we did, or intended, what
shou'd have hinder'd the Wisest among us from taking upon
him the Ministerial Office ; and that these two or three
meeting together, and in the Name of God, shou'd not have
form'd a true Church, and have receiv'd those particular Con-
solations which are participated in the Holy Communions.

---

[1] The Acts x, 13 : " And there came a voice to him, Rise, Peter ; kill,
and eat."

H 2

I often thought of proposing it to my Companions; but on
one hand, I saw they were all dispos'd to endeavour suddenly,
at the hazard of their Lives, to return into the inhabited
World. On the other I had reason to fear there wou'd be
thought some kind of Affectation in that Design, which
they wou'd not have been pleas'd with. For in the Reflections we sometimes made upon Religion, we were always on
our Guard in an extraordinary manner, least we shou'd fall
into any Practice, or have any Idæa *which* tended in the
least to Superstition, the most dangerous and most fatal Pest
of Christianity. We were so happy, as to be united all in
the same Spirit, without the false Wisdom of the *Sages*, and
that Pernicious knowledge of the Learned, the Disputers
and Innovators of this Age, which have caus'd so many
wicked Sects, and other Disorders in the Christian World.
The Errors of the *Roman Catholicks* and some others in the
matter of the necessity of Baptism, ought to be a Lesson to
us, not to fall into the like Mistake, in the use of the other
Sacrament, the Practice of which by the common consent of
all the Christians this day alive is not in it self necessary.
We found a great Comfort in our selves, in keeping closely
to that Pure and Primitive Evangelical Doctrine, which all
Divines without exception say, contains the Soul and Essence
of saving Faith, without entring into any Inquiries, which had
the least appearance of Unprofitableness or Curiosity. We
delighted in, and often Repeated Passages out of the Scrip-
ture, and these offer'd themselves to our Remembrance. *All
that I propose to you is to know Jesus Christ, and him Cruci-
fy'd. This is eternal Life to know thee, the only true God, and
Jesus Christ whom thou hast sent. If thou confessest the Lord
Jesus with thy Mouth, and believe in thy Heart that God has
rais'd him from the Dead, thou shalt be Sav'd. Whoever believes
in me, has eternal Life. Whoever calls upon the Name of the
Lord shall be sav'd. I have declar'd unto you all the Counsel
of God, to wit, Repentance towards God, and Faith in Jesus*

Christ. The Religion that is Pure and without Spot towards our God and Father, is to visit the Orphans and Widows in their Tribulations, and to avoid the Defilements of the World, &c.[1] We were free from the accidental Theology of Controversies, from Chimerical and Heretical *Idæas,* which we look'd upon, as if they had never been ; from all Superstitious Fooleries, from all vain, impertinent rash Thoughts, which are as Pernicious to the Soul, as they are unreasonable ; and had a delicious Taste of the excellency of simple and pure Religion. We abhorr'd as the sacred Writers did, those Makers or Botchers[2] of Religion, who accommodate the Doctrine and Worship of Christianity to their own fancies, pretending to be more wise than Wisdom it self. We ador'd God the Creator in purity and simplicity of Heart. We worship'd Father, Son, and Holy Ghost, according to the Terms and Rules of Revelation, without valuing our selves on foolish Explanations, or endeavouring to unfold the sacred Mysteries, which by the confession of all Men are necessarily, and will always be hidden from mortal Men, and impenitrable to Human Eye ; or they wou'd cease to be *Mysteries.* We thus invok'd the Almighty with Joy and Confidence, (doing good as far as we cou'd) by the Meditation[3] of our Redeemer and Saviour Jesus Christ, the way, the Truth and the Life. In these happy Dispositions we look'd on Death, not as a Terror, but as the Messenger of glad Tidings.

Besides those great Walks, or rather those little Journeys we us'd to take, we never mist walking out in the Evening, in the Neighbourhood of our Habitations. We had one Walk among others on the Sea-shoar to the left of our Rivulet,

---

[1] 1 Cor. ii, 2 ; St. John xvii, 3 ; Rom. x, 9 ; St. John vi, 47 ; Acts ii, 21 ; Rom. x, 13 ; Acts xx, 27 and 21 ; St. James i, 27.

[2] In orig. : "accomodeurs". Botchers, *i.e.,* bunglers, probably derived from the Mantuan *puccia,* a slop, mess, or puddle. Hence It. *pozza,* a bungling piece of work.

[3] In orig. : "la Médiation."

and 'twas a very lovely one. 'Twas an avenue to it form'd
by Nature, as straight as if it had been planted by a Line at
a parallel Distance, from the Sea; and about twelve hundred Paces long, which is exactly the length of the Mall at
London, in the fine Park at *St. James's*.[1] We might have
lengthen'd it to seven or eight Miles if we wou'd, and upon
firm Ground, which was a perfect Level. We had on one
side of this delicious Walk a View of the vast extended
Ocean, and heard the confus'd murmur[2] of the Waves breaking against the Rocks, about a League off, so that 'twas not
loud enough to disturb our Conversation; it only threw us
often into Contemplations, to which we gave our selves up
with the greater Pleasure, because we had not much to say
to one another. On the other side (inland) our Prospect was
agreeably bounded by charming Hills, and the Valleys which
reach'd to it were like a fine Orchard in the sweet and rich
Seasons of Autumn.

Among the great number and variety of Trees in this
Island planted by Nature, there is one which is wonderful
and worthy our particular Observation, for its Beauty, Bigness, Roundness, and the rare Symmetry of its exact Branches;
the ends of which are every where very much tufted, and
its Leaves so great and thick, that they fall down almost to
the Ground all about it; so that come which way you will
at this Tree, you can perceive but a small part of its
Trunk, and that at the bottom of it; and sometimes you
can see nothing at all of it.[3]

---

[1] This paragraph seems to indicate an interpolation by Max. Misson.
The site of Leguat's settlement was on the north-north-west shore
(*vide ante*, p. 50), and was well known in 1760 as "*l'enfoncement de
François Leguat*". It is now occupied by the small town known as Port
Mathurin.

[2] In orig. : "le flux, ou reflux perpetuel venant à se rompre contre
les Brizans qui étoient à une lieüe de là, fasoit un murmure confus."

[3] At p. 130 of vol. i of the French edition of Leguat's voyage, this
wonderful tree is figured in a way to puzzle botanists were it not for

It being as one may imagine, all shady in the middle, the Branches are within-side like dry Poles, which seem to be

the accompanying descriptive text. The title on the plate is as follows : " Pavillon Arbre, nouvellement découvert." Leguat's Pavilion has been identified with the screw-pine, growing in abundance everywhere on this island from the sea-shore to the highest points. Prof. Balfour writes (*Phil. Trans.*, vol. cxlviii, p. 312) : " Every visitor to Rodriguez will be struck at once by the peculiar features impressed on the landscape by the prevalence of screw-pines. They are indeed the physiognomic plants, and far outstrip in numbers any other species ; but it is remarkable that, though individually so numerous, specifically the family is not rich, there being only two species of Pandanus on the island—*P. heterocarpus* and *P. tenuifolius*, both peculiar and very distinct from any other of the indigenous Mascarene forms. Three other specimens have been registered by various authorities ; they are *P. odoratissimus*, *P. utilis*, and *P. muricatus*."

P. Heterocarpus, the species to which Leguat's tree may be referred, is very variable, and the popular names indicate this—Vacoa calé rouge, V. calé blanc, V. sac, V. poteau, V. parasol, and V. mâle, are all applied to it according to its habit of growth, and the various uses to which its leaves and branches are put by the creoles. When on sites exposed to the wind it has a stunted habit, the branches are few, thick, and short, and the leaves also are short and erect. In such situations it is known as the *Vacoa calé*, and the inhabitants make a distinction between two varieties according as the head, peduncle, and united parts are red or are greenish yellow or yellow. The former they style *rouge*, the latter *blanc*. If the tree grows in suitable soil or in a sheltered position where it has room to develop its branches properly, then it forms a dense and compact dome, and the branches droop downwards so far as almost to conceal the stem, and it is then known as *Vacoa parasol*. When in any situation the tree develops a trunk of a good size, and is allowed to grow until the wood is hard and firm to the centre, and is capable of being used as a post for a house, then the tree is called *V. poteau*. The name *V. sac* is given to the young plants when the leaves are long and broad, and may be made into bags such as are used in Mauritius for sugar. *V. mâle* is of course the male tree, known by the inhabitants as not bearing fruit.

V. tenuifolius (Vacoa chevron) is a much smaller plant, with narrow delicate leaves and a few large druped fruits. It is easily distinguished from the foregoing, and is confined to the higher parts of the island and the upper parts of the valleys. (Balfour, *op. cit.*, p. 379.)

In the large palm-house in the Kew Gardens there is a fine specimen

the work of a Carpenter, and set there to bear up the Plumes or Branches which are quite about it, and thus make a sort of Cage or Tent of the Tree. 'Tis true, the greatest beauty of this Tent, is in its charming Outside, though the coolness and shelter of the inside have also their Charms; 'twas unhappy that its Fruit was not good to eat. Those of us who had the Curiosity to eat it, found it Sour, and knew by Experience, that was all the hurt that was in it. It has the smell of a very fine Quince; 'tis a sort of a Grape, the Seeds of which are close and all together. It lookt at a distance like the Fruit of the *Ananas*. For which reason we us'd to call these Trees *Ananas;* tho' there's a great difference between the two Plants. As for me, I was for calling it the *Pavilion* or Tent. The Leaves are of an admirable Green, and the Stalks of them are so short, that one wou'd think they grew immediately to the Wood. The greatest are four or five Inches broad, sharp at the end and about fifteen inches long. They form a great Bunch, and here and there one may see the Grapes, which are of divers Colours, according as they are more or less Ripe. I have often taken Pleasure to Survey these natural Palaces, and was equally ravish'd with its largeness and singular beauty. We sometimes play'd at Chess, at Trictrac,[1] at Drafts, at Bowls and at Scales.[2] Hunting and Fishing were so easie to

of *P. odoratissimus*, which has flowered and fruited this year (1890). The fruits, two in number, hang from the topmost branches, and bear a close resemblance to pine-apples, while the peculiar development of the long, straggling branches, stout enough for posts or rafters, surmounted by a tuft of leaves growing directly from the wood, and the pendulous roots from the main trunk, present a remarkable appearance, and are worth comparing with the description in our text.

[1] *Tric-trac*, a game somewhat like backgammon.

[2] In orig.: "Quilles", *i.e.*, ninepins. A variation of this game, called "quilles au bâton", is played with seven bits of wood set up on end, and a stick; the player tries to knock over as many as he can each throw. This latter may probably have been the game played by Leguat and his companions.

us, that it took away from the Pleasure. We often delighted our selves in teaching the Parrots[1] to speak, there being a vast number of them. We carry'd one to *Maurice* Isle, which talk'd *French* and *Dutch.*

We shall soon see that all the last year of our abode here, we were employ'd in building the fine Bark, of which we must speak in the Sequel of these Memoirs. If any one desires to know how we lighted our Cabbins when 'twas dark, or the Places we were then in, I must acquaint him that we brought Lamps with us ; and instead of Oil, made use of Turtles fat, which as I said before, never Congeal'd. We lighted our Fires with Burning-Glasses.

The Reader finding we had Abundance of Variety of Flesh and Fish, Roasted and Boil'd, Soops, Ragouts, Herbs, Roots, excellent Melons, other Fruits, Palm-Wine, clear and fresh Water, do's not apprehend the poor Adventurers in *Rodrigo* were in any danger of Starving.

But since he's so kind as to consern himself a little in their extraordinary manner of Living, I assure him they made very good Cheer without Surfeits, Indigestion, Diseases, and thanks be to God without Bread. The Captain had left them two great Barrels of Bisket,[2] but they seldom made use of it, except 'twas in Soops or Broth, and often they quite forgot it. When we had stay'd above a year in our new Island, we began to wonder we saw no Ship come ; for to say truth, some of us were not a little tir'd. They regretted the loss of their Youth, and were troubled to think they shou'd perhaps be oblig'd to pass the best part of their Lives in a strange Solitude, and intolerable Idleness. After several Deliberations, 'twas at last almost unanimously agreed, that when we had stay'd two whole years in expectation of *News from Mr. Du Quesne,* which we at first resolv'd to do, then if none came, we wou'd do our utmost to get to *Maurice* Island,

[1] *Vide ante,* p. 83 ; *Phil. Tr., loc. cit.,* p. 429.
[2] *Vide ante,* p. 55.

which belong'd to the *Dutch*, where we might embark to go
where we pleas'd, there being a Governor, and Ships coming
every year from the Cape of *Good Hope*. This Isle is above
one hundred and sixty Leagues from *Rodrigo*, a great way for
us to make; but we consider'd the Wind[1] blew generally one
way, and that fair for that Island; wherefore we put all
hands to Work to build a Bark as well as we cou'd, and if
there was any liklihood we might make use of it, we wou'd
convey our selves thither in it,[2] after having implor'd the
assistance of him, who Commands the Winds and the
Seas.

This Enterprize appear'd very difficult, even to those that
Projected it; but however, it did not seem to be wholly
impossible. We were to build a pretty big Boat, but we had
no Skilful Workmen, and few Tools; we had neither Pitch
nor Tar, nor Cordage, nor Anchor, nor Compass, nor a
hundred other Necessaries, and near two hundred Leagues[3] by
Sea was a great Voyage. The Wisest of us saw a thousand
other Difficulties, and were afraid our Design cou'd never
succeed. But those that projected it, were fix'd in it; and
'twas agreed upon, that we shou'd prepare to put it in
Execution, and by way of Diversion, to undertake the building of a Bark, tho' we lost our Labour. No sooner said than
done. And all eight of us without serving any Apprentice-
ship, became Carpenters, Smiths, Rope-makers, Mariners,
and generally every thing that was necessary for us to be.
In this Undertaking necessity was a Law to us, it supply'd
all our Defects. Every one propos'd what he thought wou'd
be most proper and advantageous, and we went all chear-
fully to Work, having a good Understanding one with another, as 'twas our Common Interest.

---

[1] The trade wind; *vide infra.*

[2] In orig.: "dans cette petite arche."

[3] Rodriguez lies 350 miles to the eastward of Mauritius. (*Vide*
Findlay, *op. cit.*, p. 512.)

Among other Instruments we had a great Saw and a little one, with which we began to saw Boards, and very happily made use of a Beam of Oak[1] which the Sea had sometime before thrown on our Coasts. If the Curious Reader demands by way of Parenthesis, from whence that Beam came, I must answer, that truly I cannot tell.[2] Let it come from whence it will, we had it, the Sea brought it to us, and we us'd it for the Purpose I tell him. We saw'd out some good Boards, but the great Saw breaking thrice, and being handled by unskilful Persons, the greater part of those Boards were of an unequal thickness, and Consequently not very good to the Eye, nor indeed fit for Use.

Our Bark was twenty Foot long at the Keel, six broad, and four deep, we rounded it at both ends. We had some Nails, but *John de la Haye* who was a Silver-Smith, had some Forge-Tools and other Instruments, helpt us to more; he mended our Saw for us several times. For Calking we made use of old Linen; and instead of Pitch and Tar, mingled Jet[3] with Gumms which we found on the Trees in Plenty, and temper'd it with Oil of Turtle. We work'd up several sorts of Ropes with the Threads or Fibres of the Stalks of the Plantane-Leaves; which Ropes were strong enough, but not very Supple, and were proper only for fix'd work, but were always frizing[4] out and untwisting when we employ'd 'em about running Work. Instead of an Anchor, we provided our selves with a piece of Rock, which weigh'd

---

[1] "Taillée en quarré & longue de soixante pieds," omitted by translator.

[2] It subsequently transpired that an English ship had been wrecked in this vicinity previous to the arrival of Leguat. Captain Valleau heard of this on his reaching Mauritius after leaving Leguat, and he returned to search for this wreck, from which, evidently, this oak timber had drifted. (*Vide infra*, Part II.)

[3] "Dont j'ai parlé," omitted by translator. Leguat is referring to bitumen, which he has mentioned above. Cf. *supra*, p. 87.

[4] From the Fr. *friser*, to curl. In the orig. the word used is *s'érailler*, to fray.

one hundred and fifty pound Weight, and we made a Sail as well as we could.

Every Man was Industrious as it lay in his Power to be, to carry on this Work, and the two years being almost expir'd, we were so forward in it, that the Bark was Lanch'd, no one of us sparing his Labour[1] on this Occasion.

As for Provisions we dry'd[2] Lamentins Flesh, we fill'd the Barrels we had for that use with Fresh Water; the little Biskit that was left us we put aboard, and supply'd our selves with Land and Water Melons. The latter wou'd keep a long time; What I have said is true, we began the building our Boat knowing we had no Compass,[3] and so we finish'd it; but every Body seeking for something Useful towards supplying its Place, one of us found a little Solar Quadrant of Loadstone[4] which cost him three Pence at *Amsterdam*;

---

[1] In orig.: " à force de bras et d'epaules."

[2] In orig.: "nous fimes *boucaner*." From this word comes our word "buccaneer".

[3] Maximilian Misson, supposed by some to have written Leguat's preface, and to have translated his Voyage, in his *New Voyage to Italy*, 1637, observes, vol. i, p. 640, that " the city of Amalphis boasts of having given birth to Flavio Gioia, as being the Inventor of the Compass (in the year 1300), upon which M[r] Magnati cites the following Verse of Panormita : ' Prima dedit Nautis usum Magnetis Amalphis'." But Father Fournier, the author of a learned work on navigation entitled *Hydrographia*, shews (p. 399), by the verses which he takes out of the Poet Guyot ("Auteur du Roman qu'il intitula *la Bible de Guyot*"), who lived one hundred years before Gioia was born (at the end of the twelfth century), that the use of the *Boussole*, then called *Marinette*, was known in France at that time :—

> " Icelle Estoille ne se muet
> Un Art font qui mentir ne puet
> Par vertu de la Marinette,
> Une pierre laide & noirette
> Où le fer volontiers se ioint," &c.

[4] In orig.: " un petit quadran solaire aimanté," a sun-dial with a compass to allow of adjustment. The one mentioned by Leguat appears to have been a toy pocket-dial. Such instruments were much in use in the latter part of the 17th and beginning of the 18th century, before

and tho' 'twas not good we were glad he had found it, hoping
to reap some Benefit by it.

When the Bark was in the Water, we were all surpris'd to
find she did not obey the Rudder, and that to turn it we
must make use of an Oar.

The day of our Departure, was fix'd to be *Saturday* the
19th of *April* 1693.   The Moon being then near at the Full,
the Sea wou'd be high, and consequently the easier to pass
above the Shelves.   The Reason why we did not choose the
time when the Moon wou'd be quite at the Full was, because
we wou'd have as much as we cou'd of her Light.

These Shelves of which I have often spoken,[1] are (to inform,
en passant, those who do not understand the Term) Rocks
rising up in the Sea like a sort of Wall,[2] with which the

clocks and watches took their place. In the collection at the S. Kensington Museum there are several of that period; one in particular, of
French make, with the hours and names of cities engraved on it, might
serve to illustrate our text.

[1] Cf. *supra*, p. 47, and note, *ib.*

[2] The island of Rodriguez is bound to the north, the south, and the
west with chains or reefs of rocks, nearly even with the water's edge,
on which are scattered the rocky islets mentioned above at page 88.
This bank or wall, as the text says, extends a league and a half from
the coast, and the north-east side is the least dangerous, as the reef
recedes sufficiently here to admit of ranging along the isle on that side.
(Grant's *History of Mauritius*, p. 310.)

Mr. J. Murray, of the *Challenger* expedition, has shown that it is not
necessary to call in the subsidences required by Darwin's theory (*A
Naturalist's Voyage*, pp. 557 *seqq.*) to explain the characteristics of
these barrier reefs. He shows that the foundations for barrier reefs, such
as those at Rodriguez, have been prepared by the disintegration of
volcanic islands and by the building up of submarine volcanoes by the
deposition on their summits of organic sediments ; that barrier reefs have
been built up by coral plantations from the shore on a foundation of
volcanic *débris*, or on a talus of coral blocks, coral sediments, and pelagic
shells and the lagoon channel formed by the solvent action of the sea-
water thrown over the reefs at each tide and by currents, etc. (See
Structure and Origin of Coral Reefs and Islands, by Mr. John Murray,
1880 ; *Nature*, vol. xxii, p. 351.)

The coral animals by which the stony, cellular scaffoldings which com-

Island is encompast at an unequal Distance; except in two Places, where there's a Breach about 10 or 12 Foot broad, that gives access to the Isle. This is not to be seen in the Map.[1]

When we arriv'd on the Island, we perceiv'd the Names of some *Dutchmen*, who had Landed there before, Written on the Bark of some Trees,[2] with the date of the Time; and this put us in mind of doing the same when we left it. We therefore wrote an Abridgment of our History in *French* and *Dutch*,[3] with the date of our Arrival, the time of our Abode, and our Departure. We put it into a Viol, with a Note to Passengers to look into. We plac'd it in a sort of a Niche Dug in the Trunk of the great Tree,[4] under which we us'd

pose coral reefs (or, as Dioscorides designates them, a forest of stony trees, *lithodendra*) surrounding the island of Rodriguez, have been built up in thick, wall-like masses, are closely related to those of Mauritius, Madagascar, and the Seychelles. Dr. Brüggemann has examined and identified 102 specimens collected at Rodriguez by MM. Slater and Gulliver, which belong to 49 species: including Alcyoniidæ, Milleporidæ, Astræidæ, Actiniidæ, Madraporidæ, Fungidæ, etc. (See *Philosophical Transactions, op. cit.*, p. 569.)

[1] In orig.: "on peut voir cela dans la carte." The two entrances *are* shown on the map. That to the north opposite the settlements is the most convenient for landing, while that on the south side is so winding that it requires considerable practice to navigate it with safety. (Grant, *op. et loc. cit.*)

[2] Adanson found trunks of the Baobab on the Magdalena Is. in 1748, with a diameter of five and six feet, all bearing the names of Europeans deeply carved on their bark. One inscription was of the 15th, another of the 16th century, and the characters were about six inches long. (*Voyage au Sénégal*, p. 66.)

"Le vingt cinquiesme Juin (1638) nous abordasmes l'isle de Diego Rois, . . . Nous y descendismes, et y arborames les armes de France contre un tronc d'arbre par les mains de Salomon Gobert. Nostre navire fut tousiours en mer, n'ayant pû anchre, le fond estant trop bas; aussi·tost que les armes du Roy y furent posées, ceux qui auoient eu charge de ce faire, retournerent à nous dans la chaloupe qui les y auoit portez." (*Relation du Voyage de François Cauche*, 1651, p. 7.)

[3] In orig.: "Flamand."

[4] Probably a *bois d'olive*. *Vide ante*, p. 52.

to eat, and which we had experienc'd to be proof against Hurricanes.

At last the appointed Day for which my young Companions heartily long'd, arrived, and having put up our Prayers to Heaven for the Divine Assistance, we embark'd about Noon with our Provisions and Goods. The Weather was extremely fair, and the Wind the same ; so that tho' we wanted a Rudder,[1] Cordage, Anchors, and almost everything necessary for our Boat, weak and ill-built as it was, we were full of Hope, that we shoul'd do very well in her. We reckoned the fair Weather wou'd continue, and if so, we might depend upon the Trade-Wind,[2] of which I have spoken ; and which according to our Calculation, founded upon what we had heard the Captain and Seamen say, always blow'd at that time of the year, and as long as the Weather was fair. In such case we might expect to make *St. Maurice* Island in[3] two Days and two Nights.

We therefore departed with Joy, and earnestly desiring to arrive in some Place where we might see the Inhabitants of the World, we past swiftly enough to the Shelves. But

---

[1] " Boussole" omitted by translator.

[2] In orig. : "cette espèce de Vent Alizé." The general system of winds in the Indian Ocean, writes Findlay, may be said to be divided into :—1, The region of the N.W. anti-trades or passage winds, south of 25° or 30° S. ; 2, The region of the S.E. trade winds, between lats. 10° and 25° or 30° S. ; 3, The belt of calms to the N. and N.W. of the trades ; 4, The area of the south-*east* and north-*west* monsoons, between the equator and 10° S. ; and 5, The part N. of the equator, where the monsoons alternately blow in opposite seasons from northward or southward. Rodriguez, in 19° 42′ S., is therefore in the very heart of the S.E. trade winds, the "*espèce de Vent Alizé*" noticed by Leguat.

The regularity of this wind is only affected in some seasons W. of 70° E. (*i.e.*, 7° W. of Rodriguez), and the northern and southern limits of this aerial current are extended or contracted according to the season of the year. The occasional disturbances caused in the atmosphere by cyclones will be noticed hereafter, when they are more particularly noticed by Leguat. (See Findlay's *Indian Ocean Directory*, p. 17 *et seq.*)

[3] In orig. : " en moins de deux jours & deux nuits."

instead of seeking for one of the two Breaches before mention'd, and to Hale[1] the Ship by Land or by Sea, to a Place
where 'tis easy to pass, we depended too much on our good
Fortune, and thinking to go thro' directly, we happen'd to
strike. We went so swiftly along,[2] that we cou'd hardly perceive when we struck, and thought we only brusht by the
Rock. Wherefore we proceeded, and were got about fifty
Paces beyond the Shelves, flattering ourselves we were past
the greatest Danger, when on a sudden we were sadly convinced of our Mistake[3] ; for the Water came pouring in, and
we saw 'twas time for us to return as fast as we cou'd to
Land. In the meantime the poor Boat fill'd apace, the
Rudder cou'd not guide us. The Wind in spite of us, drove
us farther off Shoar. Fear depriv'd us of the little Skill we
had, and as for myself in particular, I believ'd our time was
come ; one may easily imagine the Condition we were in, our
Peril was so terrible and apparent. The Desire of Living
made us set to work to save ourselves ; but the truth is,
'twas to no purpose[4]; one endeavour'd to lave[5] the Water out
of the Bark[6] with his Hat, another employ'd himself with
Labour every whit as unprofitable, and all cry'd out or Pray'd
like lost Men. However at last one of us handled an Oar so

---

[1] *I.e.*, to haul or drag along. Cf. Dampier's *Voyages* (1681).

[2] In orig.: " comme nous voguions avec beaucoup de légèreté." The
idea of lightness or buoyancy is hardly expressed by the word " swiftly"
in our text.

[3] In orig. : " car l'eau paroissant' tout incontinent, & croissant à vuë
d'œil on s'écria qu'il falloit promptement retourner en arrière, & rega-
gner terre."

[4] In orig.: " ma^is la vérité est que nous perdimes tous la tramontane." *Vide ante*, p. 38, and note, *ib.*

[5] " Some stow their oars, or stop the leaky sides,
    Another bolder yet the yard bestrides,
    And folds the sails ; a fourth, with labour, *laves*
    Th' intruding seas, and waves ejects on waves."
                    Dryden, *Ovid. Metam.*, " Ceyx and Alcyone".

[6] In orig. : " qui étoit presque pleine," omitted by translator.

effectually, that the Bark tack'd about, and the Wind being
brisk, it drove us (back) in four Minutes time on the other
side of the Shelves ; but thirty Paces from thence[1] nearer the
Island the Boat sank down to the Bottom. If that Misfortune had happened to us half an Hour before,[2] we had
been drown'd every Man of us ; but there being not above
six[3] foot Water, and the Bark not Over-setting, we stood all
of us upright on the Deck, with the Water up to our Middles.
'Twas a Happiness in our Trouble, that the Rock on which
we struck made such a hole in the Boat, that we saw the
Water enter immediately ; for if we had not so visibly and
readily seen it, we should have kept on our way, and then
had infallibly Perish'd.   However, as it was, we were very
unpleasantly Posted in the Water on one end of the Deck.
Tho' it began to Ebb, and we were but half a League from
the Shoar, we cou'd not tell what to resolve on.   'Twas concluded after we had thought of it a little, we wou'd stay till
the Water was so low that we might get to Shoar, haling our
Chests and Barrels after us as they floated in the Water ty'd
to one another.

This was accordingly done, but not without putting us to
terrible Fatigues ; for we had several Voyages to make,
sometimes up to the Neck in Water, the Bottom being
uneven, and sometimes we were oblig'd to Swim, it being
out of our Depths, and draw our Chests after us with Ropes
ty'd about our Wasts.   We all of us stript, that we might
have the more liberty in Swimming, and the sharp and keen

[1] In orig. : " au dela de ce même brisant," omitted by translator.
[2] In orig. : " un demi-quart d'heure plutôt."
[3] It is high water, full, and change at Port Mathurin at 0hr. 30m. ;
spring tides, such as those chosen by Leguat's comrades for passing the
reefs, rise, according to Findlay, $4\frac{1}{2}$ feet, the neaps to $1\frac{1}{2}$ foot only.
The tidal streams are not appreciable except in the channels or passes.
Occasionally rollers set in (ras-de-marées), causing heavy breakers on
all the dangerous reefs and rocks, and a nasty swell in Mathurin
Bay. (Findlay.)

Stones[1] made our Feet all bloody. To add to our Misfortunes, the Current ev'ry now and then carry'd away part of our Baggage, nevertheless we sav'd most of our things the same day, and put the heavy part of our Luggage out of the Bark on the Land; the Sea cou'd not sweep that away, and when the Tide was quite out, we might at our Leasure recover it, which we intended to do next Day, and see if we cou'd hale our poor Boat after us. We now ty'd it to a Rock, and at last got to Land with much joy, and much Sorrow, having made proof by a woful and happy Experience, that evil and good things are often mix'd together by Fortune.

The next Morning as soon as 'twas Light we went to the Bark, which now lay a-shoar, to Refit her as well as we cou'd. We Launch'd her when the Tide came in, put our heavy Goods aboard, and got safe to a Place where we cou'd conveniently Land them.[2] Each of us lost something in this Shipwreck, and what we had left was generally damag'd; but we had sav'd our Lives almost by a Miracle. We return'd our most humble thanks to God, the Gracious and Mighty Protector, who had assisted us in our extreme Peril.

In the mean time one of us who seem'd to be the most Strong and Vigorous Man in the Company, found himself very much out of Order after so great a fatigue. As soon as he got a-shoar naked and frozen,[3] as he was, he laid himself all along upon the Sand, which the Sun had heated extraordinarily. He thought at first he wanted only a little Rest, but a while after his Face turn'd as red as Scarlet; his Head grew very heavy, and his Distemper increas'd

---

[1] The upper surface of coral reefs always presents a series of sharp and jagged edges most dangerous to tread on without protection to the feet.

[2] "Boats land now at the upper end of the creek in Mathurin Bay, at a small pier extending from the village, during high tide, but they cannot get within 400 yards at low tide, and wading must be resorted to." (Findlay, *op. cit.*, p. 516.)

[3] In orig.: "transi," *i.e.*, chilled.

ev'ry Minute. We carry'd him to his Cabbin with much
adoe, and being of a very Vigorous Complexion, 'twas three
or four days before he would confine himself to his Bed, but
at last he yielded. His Head swell'd, and so many Impos-
thumes appear'd in it, that we cou'd scarce open all to let out
the Corruption. We were at first sorry that our Rogue of a
Captain had left us no Ungents or Drugs, as I have said before.[1]
However we consider'd none of us understood very well
how to Administer them, if we had had them; and indeed,
that take it all together what we call Physick or Pharmacy
is commonly nothing but a Cheat more Pernicious than
Useful to Mankind; so we did not trouble our selves much
for the want of it till now. We had a Consultation, whether
the Patient ought not to be Blooded.[2] Some cry'd he wou'd
die in the Operation, if he lost one drop of Blood only,
others cry'd out louder, then he wou'd give up the Ghost in
three Minutes, if he was not Blooded; and we were all so
warm in the Vindication of our several Opinions, that whoever had seen us, wou'd have taken us for true Physicians.[3]
Nevertheless we did not come to Blows, and there being four
out of seven Voices for Bleeding, 'twas not necessary that
we should stay for any other way of deciding the Question,
tho' the Sacred Ministers of *Æsculapius*, have recourse sometimes to others in such Cases.[4] The Boldest of the four
Phlebotomists[5] sharpen'd as well as he cou'd the point of his
Pen-knife, and made Incisions in several parts of the poor
dying Man's Arm, but 'twas all to no Purpose; the Fever

---

[1] *Vide ante*, p. 55.

[2] " *To blood*," i.e., *to let blood*, a term formerly used in surgery, was
superseded by *bleed*. See a few lines below, in the text.

[3] Evidently, says M. Muller, an allusion to the famous scene from
L'Amour Médecin, of Molière.

[4] In orig.: " ce qui est l'unique moyen de décision quand il y a
contrariété d'opinion entre les sacrez Ministres d'Esculape."

[5] Phlebotomists, lit. vein cutters, from φλέψ, φλεβός a vein, and τέμνειν,
to cut.

Augmented,[1] he grew Delirious, and remain'd so some Days. We cou'd then do nothing for him, but apply to the Great Physician of Body and Soul, which we had done all along. Before this Struggle was over, we had the Satisfaction to see our Dear Brother recover his Understanding, and give us the most certain and most edifying Tokens of a sincere Repentance, and holy hope of his Salvation. Thus it continu'd with him[2] till the eighth of *May* 1693, when he expir'd in the 29th year of his Age, after three Weeks Sickness. Such was the end of honest *Isaac Boyer*, the eighth part of the Kings and the Inhabitants of *Rodrigo*. And that you may not, kind Reader, go so far as this New World without seeing some Monument, Read if you think fit, the Epitaph that I add here.[3]

"Beneath these Immortal Palms,
In the faithful Bosom of a Virgin Earth,
Are piously deposited
The Bones
Of ISAAC BOYER,
An honest and faithful *Gascon*, descended from *Adam*,
Of as Noble Blood as any of the Mortals his Brethren,

---

[1] In orig. : " & le transport s'étant fait au cerveau," omitted by translator.

[2] In orig. : " Enfin il rendit son Ame à Dieu."

[3] This epitaph is printed in the original on a quarto sheet, in two columns, surmounted by a strange device, in imitation or mockery, as we may suppose, of the heraldic ornaments which decorated the pompous epitaphs on contemporary monuments of the 17th century. The centre is a coat of arms, with the name " Boyer" under a fleur-de-lys and a star *or*, on a field *azure*, between two cherubims proper on a field *or*; surmounted by the name of Jehovah in Hebrew characters. On either side are two medallions ; on one of which is represented the adventurer's boat at sea, with the legend, " *Nous n'avons point icy de cité permanente*," circumscribed. On the other side is the conventional phœnix on its burning nest, with its circumscription, " *Dans la mort l'immortalité.*" Above all is a scroll bearing the Latin words : "*Nascimur pares ; pares morimur.*" The whole appearance of these fanciful designs is in keeping with the fashion then in vogue, as displayed in the emblems of Jacob Cats, of a few years' earlier date.

Who all Reckon, among their Ancestors
Bishops and Millers.
*   *   *   *   *
If all Men would live as He liv'd,
Dancing, Laces, Bayliffs, Locks and Keys,
Cannon, Prisons, Tax-Gatherers, Monarchs,
Would be useless things in the World.
*   *   *   *   *
He was Wise, and more a Philosopher than the Philosophers.
He was a Christian, and more a Divine than the Divines.
He knew his Ignorance, and was more a Doctor than the Doctors.
He was more Independant than Sovereigns,
Being neither plagu'd with Flatterers, nor drunk with Ambition.
He was richer than Kings, for he wanted but one Thing,

A WIFE.
*   *   *   *   *
In that Execrable Time
Which makes my Pen tremble with Horror,
He was forc'd to abandon his Dear Country
And every thing with it,
To fly from the
Furious Ministers of the great Tribulation.
*   *   *   *   *
He cross'd Mountains and Seas,
And coming to this Island,
Found here the true Port of Safety.
*   *   *   *   *
Himself and seven Companions of the same Fortune,
Stay'd here two whole years,
The people and the Rulers of the Place.
He had longer enjoy'd
The Delights of this new World,
If his Heart had not been touch'd
With a secret Desire for
The Too lovely Sex,
Which engag'd him in an Enterprize
That caus'd his Death.
*   *   *   *   *
He wrestled boldly with that terrible Enemy,
And came off Conqueror ;
Since at the same time that he yielded Dust to Dust,
He procur'd the Honour for the Isle of Rodrigo,
To
Render to the Lord one of the Blessed at the Resurrection.

His Soul
Is gone Triumphantly
Into the Palace of Immortality.

*   *   *   *   *

His few and evil Days
Were not at most above
Ten Thousand Six Hundred ;
And
That in which he took his leave of the World,
Was the Eighth of May, in the Year of our Redemption,
MDCXCIII.
Whosoever thou art, Passenger, that reads this,
Remember
Thou must die in a little while,
And
Improve thy Time."

A * Ω.

Neither our Sorrow for the loss of a dear and useful Friend, nor the bad Success of our first Enterprize hinder'd us from thinking of leaving the Island. These young Men had, as *Horace* says, Hearts of Oak and Brass,[1] which made them freely expose their Lives in the weakest of all Boats, and rashly to defie the fury of the Winds. They persisted therefore obstinately in their first Resolution, and added to the Fundamental Reasons alledg'd in the beginning, that they wou'd benefit themselves by the Misfortune that had happened to them, and take better measure for the future. They said they wou'd strengthen the Bark in Repairing it, that they wou'd lay some Buoys, or some other Tokens in their way to direct them in this Case, and wou'd depart when the Tides were highest, that they might not run the Risk of touching the Shelves, without spending time in seeking after

[1] " Illi robur et æs triplex
    Circa pectus erat, qui fragilem truci
  Commisit pelago ratem
    Primus, nec timuit præcipitem Africum
  Decertantem Aquilonibus,
    Nec tristes Hyades, nec rabiem Noti."
              (Horace, *Carminum*, lib. I, iii, *ad Virgilium*.)

other Breaches, if they cou'd not follow exactly the way
mark'd them out by the Buoys.[1]

I was, as well as they, a little weary of Confinement, and
cou'd not with Pleasure think of living all the rest of my
Days in one of the Islands of the *Antipodes;* but I did not
imagine such a sorry Gondola[2] as our Boat, was capable of
carrying us such a vast way, especially having no necessaries
for the Voyage : Wherefore I oppos'd the execution of the
first Design with all my Might. As Resolute as they seem'd
to be, to be gone, I beg'd them in the most perswasive Terms
I cou'd use, to reflect a little more upon what they were going
about; and not to shock them too much at first, I highly
commended their Courage, and gave way to their most
plausible Reasons. But I conjur'd them also to consider, that
this was an Affair of the last Importance, both for the Body
and the Soul ; that without a second Miracle, we must be a
second time Ship-wreck'd, and that then they wou'd never
be able to avoid Reproaches very like Despair, for having
tempted God. I added, Experience ought to make us wiser
than we were before ; that it had already cost us one of our
Companions Lives, and we shou'd look upon that sad Accident as the Warning of Providence, and the Manifestation
of God's Will, of whom we had demanded with Fasting and
Resignation, that he wou'd be pleased to inspire us what we
shou'd do. I told them farther, that since those that were

---

[1] The channel buoyed by Leguat's companions was probably the
western point into Mathurin Bay, the sole practicable harbour at
Rodriguez. "The most convenient anchorage in Mathurin Bay is in
10 fathoms, bottom of sand and mud, off a small buoy marking the
entrance to the creek. The creek is narrow but deep, running into the
coral reef towards the settlement, and makes a good berth for the small
schooners (*chasse-marées*, in Creole) which carry on the trade of the
island. These place their anchors on the coral at the end of the creek
about a quarter of a mile from the small town or village, mooring head
and stern." (Findlay, *op. cit.*, p. 516.)

[2] Another of Misson's Italian references (?). See his *Voyage to Italy*,
letter xvii.

to follow us, had not promis'd to come till after two years, 'twas convenient to outstay that time a little; perhaps Succour was now upon Sea for us, and might arrive ev'n when we were the deplorable sport of the Waves, if we were not before that Food for the Monsters of the Sea. Besides, since we were in a good Place, we ought to have a little Patience; and in the mean time have Recourse to a reasonable Means, which no Body had yet thought of; and that was, to light great Fires on the top of our high Mountain,[1] and set Lanthorns[2] all about the Island, to invite Ships that past by us, to come to our Assistance. The Cotton[3] of our Plantanes, and our Turtles Oil, made the execution of this Design easy; and we had stuff enough to cover it with, and make a kind of Lanthorns if it had been necessary.

I had a thousand things more to say, if I had had to do with Men of ripe Understanding, and well reclaim'd from the follies of the World. For to cast up all things, what cou'd be comparable to the Sweetness, the Innocence, the Advantages, and Delight in a Solitude so much resembling an Earthly Paradise as ours? What can be imagin'd more happy, after having groan'd and suffer'd under the Yoak of Tyranny, than to live in Independence and Ease, without danger of Worldly Temptations: But when a Man is young, he is not capable of making such Reflections. I therefore finish'd my Speech, in representing further to them the length of the Voyage, the weakness of our Vessel, the wretched Tackling we had, and their Unskilfulness. They heard me patiently; several of them seem'd not to digest it, and one of them whom I had touch'd in a sore Place, of

---

[1] In orig.; "sur quelques hauteurs." The highest point is Mount Limon, 1,300 feet.

[2] The spelling of *lanthorn* which so long prevailed was doubtless influenced by the use of transparent sheets of horn for the sides of the lantern. (Wedgwood's *Dict. of Eng. Etymology.*)

[3] The *capoc* of the Latanier palm, mentioned before. (*Vide supra*, p. 65.)

which I was not aware, alledg'd briskly, a new Reason for our
Departure : which was so agreeable to the relish of the rest,
that it occasion'd a new Discourse, and all my Arguments
were forgotten. *Do you imagine,* said this young Man,[1]
*That we will condemn ourselves to spend all our Lives here
without Wives. Do you think your Earthly Paradise more
excellent, than that which God prepar'd for Adam ; where he
declared with his Mouth, it is not good that Man shou'd be alone:*
I reply'd,[2] *My dear Friend,* Adam's *Wife proved such a Curse
to him, and all his Posterity, that certainly our Paradise
wou'd not be much improv'd by the Company of such an Eve
among us.* They all Laugh'd, and what I little thought of,
all the Discourse was afterwards on the Subject of the
Ladies, which was, as is said, the Gospel of the Day.[3] I soon
saw where the Shooe pinch'd,[4] and in the reign of *Quolibets*
some fine Wit wou'd certainly have said on this occasion, there
was not one of my Adventurers who wou'd not have lov'd
a *Chimène*[4] much better than a *Rodrigo.* The most Moderate of us (and 'twas time to be moderate after Fifty and I
do not know how many more Winters) put on a serious Air ;
and the business of Marriage and Women not being a question that is entirely decided, for or against it, more than one of
our Company joyn'd with him, as to the Inconveniences that
attended them. 'Twas said that an eternal Slavery, and a
just and natural Love of Liberty were incompatible ; that
'twas a strange Resolution to subscribe one's self voluntarily,
to a Bondage that has no end. And if all Animals were

[1] Evidently Paul Bénelle.
[2] In orig. : " répondit quelcun."
[3] In orig. : " De l'abondance du cœur la bouche parla," which is
omitted by translator.
[4] " Il ne me fut pas difficile de voir où gissit le lieure (si je puis
ajoûter proverbe à proverbe)."
[5] La Belle Chimène, or Ximena, daughter of Count Lozano de
Gormaz, who married the Cid, Rodrigue Diaz de Bivar. (*Le Cid,*
written by *Le grand Corneille* in 1636.)

born with a desire of Conjunction, Nature had for all that,
loaden them with Irons. The Cares and Tribulations mentioned by *St. Paul*,[1] were also urg'd against them ; and 'twas
said, the Beauty of Women was no more durable, than that of
Flowers. That the Sweets which we fansie we may enjoy
with them, are no solid good ; and after all, this just devise
of Marry'd Men, will be eternally true ; *for one Pleasure, a
thousand Pains.* That notwithstanding all the Precautions
we endeavour to take, we shall often find our selves coupled
with Harpyes and Traiteresses; and the Rage of Jealousie,
together with all the Misfortunes that accompany Marriage,
are often the fruit of the greatest Love. The quarrelsome
Contentious Women, of whom *Solomon*[2] speaks, were not
omitted ; nor the famous Passages[3] in the xxv and xlii
Chapters of the excellent Book of *Ecclesiasticus*, where 'tis
said, *All Malice is little, and all Wickedness supportable, provided the Malice of a Woman is excepted ; and the Iniquity of
a Man is of more Worth, than the Woman that do's good*, or
than the goodness of a Woman, as some Authors Translate it.
Besides[4] we consider'd, that if such a thing has been heard
of, that the Union between Man and Wife is very great, the
thoughts of an unavoidable Separation, and the grief of Part-
ing, must be most Cruel and most Bitter.

The Subject being Fertile, it gave occasion to other Reflec-
tions against the Sex, with which I would not tire the
Ladies,[5] who shall vouchsafe to cast their fair Eyes on this
Relation.

One of the youngest[6] said with a modest and pleasant Air,

[1] 1 Corinthians, vii, 28, 29.
[2] Proverbs, xix, 13.
[3] Cf. Ecclesiasticus, xxv, 13, 19 ; xlii, 14.
[4] In orig. : " On considéra encore qu'après tout, si l'union avoit
été grande entre deux Epoux, chose qui à la vérité n'étoit pas inouïe,
la douleur d'une inévitable séparation devoit être plus cuisante & plus
amère."
[5] In orig. : "les oreilles des dames."
[6] M. Bénelle again.

that he did not believe any one of the Company thought then
of Marriage or Debauchery; but that in truth 'twas very hard
to him, to think he must for ever be depriv'd of the Company of a Woman; and the more, because God had otherwise
order'd things from the Beginning.[1] That all that had been
said against them in General, seem'd to him to be very
unjust; and for his part he own'd he lookt upon them as the
most lovely half of the World.

*Reader, 'Tis at your own choice to look over, or pass by this[2]
Discourse; when once it was a foot,[3] our young Men who did
not want wit, said several pleasant things which I put here
together, and the more willingly because these sorts of Subjects
are rarely disagreeable.*

'Tis not enough, said he with a loud Voice who had demanded *Eve's* for the *Adam's* of our *Eden;* the Women are
not only the most lovely half of the World, they are also
the best half. (His Temper being a little quick, his expressions also were sometimes a little Vigorous.) 'Tis a shame,
added he, to talk of Women, as some among us have done,
and I cannot bear their Injurious Reflections. If there are
wicked Women, there are without Comparison, a much
greater Number of Rogues of our own Sex. If there are
Impudent Women, 'twas certainly the infamous Temptation
of Men that corrupted them. Whoever[4] have said or Thought,
that *the Wickedness of Men is Preferable to the Goodness of
Women,* have said so Impertinent and Extravagant a thing,

1 "Comme cela avoit été dit," omitted by translator.

2 "Il est à votre choix, Lecteur, de lire ou du doit, ou des yeux, les
suites de cet Entretien." "*Lire du doigt,*" a naïve expression for turning
over the pages without stopping. (*Muller.*)

3 In orig.: "quand une fois la matière eût été mise en mouvement."

4 *Vide supra.* Solomon's text in Ecclesiasticus is here criticised, but
it is quoted without the context of the English version. Bénelle says
(in orig.): "les méchancetez des Hommes sont préférables aux bonnes
actions des Femmes." The old French version is: "Mieux vaut la
malice de l'homme que la femme qui fait bien; & la femme desbauchée
est en opprobre." (See old French version of 1678.)

that 'tis not worth answering. No Body denies, but there are scolding,[1] Contentious Women ; and what Consequence can be drawn from thence to the Prejudice of those Wise and Virtuous Women of whom the same *Solomon* speaks. Those worthy wives, who, according to him, are the Happiness, the Joy and the Crown of their Husbands[2]; a Gift of God, and a Favour of Heaven. Those excellent Women whom *St. Paul* calls the Glory of a Man,[3] the first of whom was the Master-piece and Crowning-Work of the Creation.

We may with boldness affirm, that the positive Will, and the certain and manifest Destiny of the Master of the World, is, that all the Descendants of *Adam*, shou'd each have his Help-Mate, as he our Common Father had. Those Continent Persons *St. Paul*[4] speaks of, who, either by their Stripes, their Fastings or Mortifications, have vanquish'd or overwhelm'd Nature, as being born with a Constitution that rendered them Monstrous ; that is, Animals, whose Disposition was against the Order of Nature, these Persons I say, are of a particular Species, so rare, that the Laws were not made for them. *Encrease*[5] *and Multiply ; it is not good that Man should be alone*[6]: *a Man shall leave his Father and Mother, and cleave unto his Wife.*[7] These are Oracles pronounc'd when the World was made, the Primi-

---

[1] Scolding, in orig. : "rioteuses." Contentious, in orig. : "goutières."

[2] Proverbs, xviii, 22.

[3] 1 Corinthians, xi, 7 : "For a man indeed ought not to cover his head, forasmuch as he is the image and glory of God ; but the woman is the glory of the man."

[4] Max. Misson, writing from Rome, April 11, 1688, says, with regard to the liberty allowed to women in England, and the confinement of the *Italian* ladies : "That this Custom was introduc'd into *Italy* as a necessary Caution where three parts of the Men living under the constraint of Celibacy, would without this Precaution create most dreadful Disorders ; but Answer being made, That *St. Paul's* Advice might be a much better and more convenient Remedy against this Danger, we chang'd the Discourse."

[5] Genesis, i, 28.   [6] Genesis, ii, 18.   [7] Genesis, ii, 24.

tive Indispensable Laws that ought to be deeply engraven on Marble and Brass, and transmitted to Posterity in Letters of Gold in civiliz'd Governments. I call them Laws, and not a simple Permission, which leaves Man at his liberty to do what he pleases, according to his Fancy or Caprice. The first *Eve* was not made to live a Virgin, but to become a Mother and begin to People the World; and the *Eve's* of the following Ages are not given us, let 'em be what they will, but to perpetuate the Work of the Creation. If there are a sort of Men, who like those vile Insects, of which some speak, grow out of Mud and Corruption, let those Men live by themselves as long as they please, and wallow as much as they please in the Filth and Ordure of their Origin. But 'tis not thus, that the Noble Race of the Children of *Adam* are Immortaliz'd. A single Man, to a single Woman, are not each properly speaking, but a part of themselves. These two half's together, make one whole. How unjust and cruel is it, to keep these imperfect Portions always naturally desiring to be joyn'd and destin'd to Union by Eternal Wisdom[1] in a state of Separation. Let us therefore conclude thus, Dear Companion, that Women are entirely all that's Fine in the World, all that is Lovely, all that is Necessary; and that we ought to be unspeakably pleas'd in Loving them, and being belov'd by them, as also in seeing them bring forth, and breed up the Pledges they give of Mutual Love. Call them Yoaks or Fetters, or what you please; and give the Union of Marriage the odious Name of Chains, but let us remember we are never weary of enjoying what we Love, and should not think it a tiresom slavery, to keep our Treasure a long time. Our sorrowful and imperfect Society, can have no

---

1 Vide *La Manière de célébrer le Mariage*, in the old French Huguenot prayer-book. "Et ce saint Mariage institué de Dieu est de telle vertu, que par icelui le mari n'a point la puissance de son corps, mais la femme; aussi la femme n'a point la puissance de son corps mais le mari. C'est pourquoi étans conjoints de Dieu, ils ne peuvent être séparez," etc.

Relief, no Support here ; we shall die, and our Island
remain Desert. He who dies last, will have no Body to
Assist and Comfort him, his Corps have no other Burial but
the Belly of those filthy Batts,[1] that seem now ready to
devour us alive. A little Water wou'd perhaps Refresh him
in his Bed of Languishing Sickness, but his weakness not
permitting him to fetch it, he will see himself consum'd by
a heat without Remedy, and all his Distresses will be
extream. Let us therefore save our selves from this fate,
and for a more happy Society. We have Philosophers
among us, who they say, love their Liberty ; with all our
Hearts, let them enjoy it. The Isle is their own, and they
may be as free as they please in these Forests. They need
not fear that any Nymph will come and trouble the Pleasures
of their Contemplative Life. As for us, Let us go and submit
to the agreeable Yoak (if it must be a Yoak) the amiable
Yoak of those whose Victorious Charms ought in my Opinion
to be preferable to the most sweet Oil of our Turtles. But we
lose Time, we have said enough on this Subject ; follow me,
my Friends, and let us immediately think of what we ought
to do, in order to our Departure.

The truth is, we rose up all hastily, and as if the question
had been decided by an Oracle, not a Word was said, but of
refitting the Bark, and preparing things necessary for our
Voyage. However I made a new Proposition to gain Time,
but they wou'd not hearken to me, and 'twas resolv'd we
shou'd re-embark the next time the Moon was at the
Full.[2]

Since nothing cou'd happen worse to me, than to Live and
Die alone in an Island of the other World, I resolv'd, yet
not without some contrary Reflection, to go with them.
The day prefix'd arriving, we bad this Charming Island
adieu, and with the Island, what is worst of all, we bad adieu

---

[1] *Vide supra*, p. 83.   In orig. it is, however, " ces vilains *Rats*."
[2] At spring-tide.

to our true and noble titles of *Freemen,* to become e'er long
the Sport and Prey of a little Scoundrel Tyrant.[1]

I have already shewn, that the day before our first Departure, we left a little Monument behind us, to inform all
such as might one time or other happen to Land in this Isle
of our Adventures. But that being very short, and containing some General Things, I had a mind before our second
Departure, to add some Particulars in a little Writing, a Copy
of which I have here very freely inserted. If the Reader
is of Opinion that it breaks off the Thread of the History, it
is easie for him to turn over and pass it by, and he will soon
come at what he seeks after.

"Dear Adventurer:
Read, if thou wilt, this weak and slight Monument.

FRANCIS LEGUAT,

Who now writes these Lines with his own Hand,
Was born and honourably bred,
In the good and little Province of *Bresse*[2] ;
Which our Predecessors, call'd the Country of the
Sebusians[3] some thousands of years agoe.
'Tis a fruitful Peninsula,
Form'd by the *Rhosne* and the *Soane.*[4]
And blest with the most benign Aspects of the Father of Nature.
There I liv'd Innocently in Prosperity and Peace,
When an Irruption of wild Beasts,
Which rose out of the bottomless Pit,
Like a Vomit of Fire,
Impetuously falling from the horrible *Vesuvius,*[5]

---

[1] Diodati, Governor of Mauritius. (*Vide infra.*)

[2] Bresse was an old division of France, now comprised in the department Ain. It was obtained by exchange from Savoy in 1601.

[3] *Sebusians,* in orig., Sebusiens, probably a misprint for Segusiens, *i.e.,*
Segusiani, a people of Gallia Lugdunensis, on the banks of the Rhône
and Saone.

[4] In orig.: "le Rhône & la Saone."

[5] Max. Misson ascended to the summit of Mount Vesuvius in March
1688, and descended into the crater, which he describes as a vast sub-
terraneous abyss. He gives a careful account of the volcano in Letter
xxii.

Cruelly plunder'd my Habitation.
A little after a Hurricane quite over-whelm'd it,[1]
And Transported me and several of my Countrymen
Into the Republick, blest by Heaven,
Which is Famous all over the World,
By the Name of

H O L L A N D.

I was scarce recover'd of the Fright I was in,
Which seem'd to me to be the effects of a Dream,
When a Voice call'd me
From within a Ship then ready to Sail,
I ran,
And after a long and dangerous Voyage,
I was brought to this Island with my Companions,
Whose Names are not unknown to thee ;
And one of whom is departed a Moment since
For his true Country.
We have seen in this delicious Abode,
Two whole Revolutions of Years,
Which I thought was a little Golden Age ;
I, who in an Age of Reflection,
Desire nothing more than what is truly Necessary.
But my Companions who were but just
Coming into the World,
And knew not the little worth of it,
Cry'd, that they wou'd have Wives.
Wives ! said they, the only Joy
Of Man,
And the Masterpiece of the Creator.
The Latent Fire of their Imaginations Kindled,
They wou'd have Wives.
And such was the wretched Bridge[2] they made themselves,
To pass over it in quest of the Soveraign Good,
I must therefore stay here alone,
Or suffer my self to be torn away from my Repose,
By the Violence of the Torrent,
Which drove me into a thousand Dangers.
Pity my Destiny I pray thee,
Thou Dear Confident[3] of my Adventures ;

---

[1] In orig. : " Incontinent après, un Ouragan m'enleva tout d'un coup."
[2] In orig. : " Et voilà un chétif Pont-volant qu'ils ont fait."
[3] In orig. : " Confidant."

And let no more hurt ever happen to thee,
Than what I wou'd do thee!
Further,
I cou'd not leave thee this Memorial,
In a more Universal and more Noble[1] Tongue,
Than that of Glorious and Formidable *France*,
My Dear and Desolate Country.
Given in the Palace of the Eight Kings of *Rodrigo*,
The Twenty First of the Month we call *May*,
And the Year which the *Christians*, Successors to the
Israelites,
Compute to be One thousand six hundred ninety three
After the coming of the *Messias*:
The fourth Year of the Reign
Of the Most Wise and most Mighty Princes,

WILLIAM and MARY,

Defenders of the Faith,
Restorers of Religion,
And of Liberty when they were shaken in *Europe*.[2]
In that year of the World which no true Learned Man
Will ever be so bold as to pretend to Design,
Thou
Little and lovely Island,
I wou'd render thee famous above all the Isles of the East,
If my Power was answerable to my Will ;
My Mouth confesses from the abundance of my Heart,
That my Soul is touch'd with Sorrow,[3]
Now I am about to leave thy wholesom Air,
Thy good Palm-Wine, thy excellent Melons ;
Thy Solitaries ; thy Lamentines ;
Thy Hills always Verdant ;
The clear Water of thy Rivers ;
Thy fruitful and smiling Sun ;
And all thy Innocent and Rare Delights.
Can I forget the precious Treasure of Liberty ?
Thou shalt never be call'd Barren,
Since thou broughtest us forth Plenty of exquisite Meats ;
And at the Day of Eternal Doom,[4]
A new ISAAC who has been sown in Corruption

---

[1] Plus honorée.
[2] In orig. : " que l'Europe voyoit ébranlée."
[3] In orig. : " triste regret."
[4] In orig. : " Rétablissement éternel."

K

In thy Earth,
Shall rise to Immortality and Glory.
O Isle, most desirable among the
Daughters of the Ocean !
How many good and laudable Things may be said of thee !
May a wiser and happier People than We,
One day Cultivate with joy thy fertile Soil ;
And without Interruption, enjoy all thy Natural Riches.
May that People Multiply !
May they Prosper without Trouble and Alarms,
And no Successor in the Government,
Ever call thy Inhabitants his Inheritance,
And never become their Enemy and Destroyer.
May never King nor Viceroy suck thy Blood,
Nor break thy Bones.
May Heaven preserve thee from all wicked Judges,
From all pretended Distributors of Justice,
Who sit in the Seat of Discord, Rapine and Iniquity.
May Heaven preserve thee from the Pride of the Great,
And the Wantonness of the Rich.
May Heaven for ever preserve thee
From that pernicious Race of Animals,[1]
Who without Wisdom, Virtue, Courage or Honour,
Assume the fair Name of Noble.
May the Cry of the Poor in Distress
Never be heard on thy Coasts.
May never Begging Ambassador,
Carrying on his Shoulders
The Miserable Dirty train that seem to follow him,
Raise Pity in thy People.
May never any wicked Heretick,nor Orthodox Fool,
Nor rascally Monk,[2]
Trouble thy Peace.
May thy holy Religion never depend
On the Sword, or on Custom.
May no Sellers and Buyers of Holy Things,[3]
Ever set foot on thy Land.

---

[1] In orig. : " engeance de tout Animal."

[2] In orig. : " Religieux Scélerat."

[3] Max. Misson, writing from Rome, April 24, 1688, says : " I can't for my life see why the Church of Rome should make such a bluster to hide this Disgrace, when *Baronius* bestows the Title of *Monsters* upon several other Popes, and not without reason, considering the

> May no Proud-youth and ignorant Declaimer
> Ever sound his poor Orations in thy Land,
> Nor his Antichristian Satyrs
> Under the Name of Preaching.
> May no unskilful Copyist, nor bold Parrot,
> Have the liberty to pretend to teach thy People.
> May thy sacred Sanctuaries.
> (The Palaces of the Holiness of the Almighty,)
> Never be miserably chang'd
> Into Theaters, Shops, and Retreats for Robbers.
> Let never Dispute upon a Word,[1] create Schism, Hatred or Cruelty
> Among thy Children.
> Let never any foolish or superstitious Bigot,
> Corrupt or dishonour the Divine Laws,
> By his Trifles or Fables.
> Never let any Man by his extravagant Devotion,[2]

Enormities the Popes have been guilty of, distributing scepters and treading crown'd Heads under their Feet, notwithstanding they retain'd the qualities of Priests ; and what is worse than all the rest, to set a certain rate of Absolution upon the most abominable Crimes that can be committed ; witness the Book intituled *The Rates of the Apostolical Chamber* (sold publickly to this day at Paris), which I bought some days ago. 'Tis true they have since endeavour'd to suppress the Book, by inserting it in the *Index Expurgatorius* of the *Council of Trent*, but continue nevertheless in selling their Dispensations.

> ' Venalia nobis
> Templa, Sacerdotes, Altaria, Sacra, Coronæ,
> Ignis thura preces, Cœlum est venale Deus.' "
>
> (*B. Mant.*)

[1] Allusion to the dispute on the word *filioque* in the Creed between the Oriental Greek and Roman Churches. Writing from Venice, January 20, 1688, Max. Misson mentions with regard to this : " They (the Greeks) use Confession, but not after the manner of the Romanists : concerning the Article of the *Proceeding of the Holy Ghost*, they say as little now as they did formerly dispute upon it, looking upon it as a point that has more of nicety than usefulness ; they also preserve Relicks, but never worship them." (*Letter xvi.*)

[2] In orig : " Que jamais extravagant Dévot."

Max. Misson, writing from Loretto, February 26, 1688, says : " But the greatest Curiosity is, the Processions of the Devotees, who crawl round the *Holy House* upon their Knees, some five times, others seven, and others twelve times, according to the different degrees of their

Expose Piety to Laughter,
Nor render the sacred Truths suspected, Scandalous and Ridiculous,
To such as want Knowledge and Discernment.
May Heaven to the end of the World preserve thee
From all these presumptuous Earthworms,
Who proudly boast they can explain Mysteries,
And pretend to Embellish[1] Faith and Worship,
According to their Folly or Rashness.
May no Astrologer ever be permitted in thy Common-Wealth.
No learner of passages out of Homer,
No Slave of musty Otho's,[2]
No Searcher after the Philosophers Stone.[3]
No Poetaster.
And may no Man be ever so Ridiculous,

Devotions; some of these creep along from one side whilst others meet
them coming from the other, but all furnished with Beads and mutter-
ing *Pater Nosters.*"

[1] In orig. : "qui s'érige en Embellisseur de Créance."

[2] In orig. : "Aucun Esclave d'Othons rouillez." This allusion is not
too easily to be comprehended.   Rusty Othons can hardly refer to the
German Othos, Emperors, of the tenth century : can it not more probably have reference to the manuscripts and books relating to their
deeds, as, for instance, Hroswitha, *de Gestis Oddonis?*   The formidable Otho the Great died on Christmas Day, 967.   The valuable
chronicle, recovered by the industry of Pertz, records the death of
Otho II ; and Otho III, the religious Otho, was poisoned by the
remorseless Stephania in 1002.   (See Milman's *History of Latin
Christianity,* vol. ii, pp. 389-418.)

[3] In orig. : "Aucun chercheur de Pierre Philosophale."   Archbishop
Gerbert, subsequently known as Pope Silvester II, who succeeded to
the Pontificate in 999, was celebrated for his Arabian skill in arithmetic,
geometry, and astrology, which he had studied under Caliph Hakim II,
in Cordova.   In remote Britain, according to William of Malmesbury,
the magical arts and enchantments of Gerbert were commonly believed,
and his funeral oration, in the *Vit. Pontif. Ravennat,* is "Homagium
diabolo fecit et male finivit."   Compare "Hist. Lit. de la France" and
Vincent of Beauvais in the *Encyclopædia of the Middle Ages.*   Gerbert,
in Spain, fell in love with the daughter of one of those accursed doctors ;
he stole his books.   The Magician, by the aid of the stars, pursued the
robber.   But Gerbert, too, had learned to read the stars.   By their
counsel he lay hid under a bridge, when the devil descended and bore
him away, designing him for the Pontifical chair.   (See Milman's *Latin
Christianity,* vol. ii, p. 419.)

As to hope to get Honour by vain Sciences,
Or other such like things which he has Learn'd,
And of which wise Men know only enough to despise them.
Mayst thou ever be defended
From the poor and wretched Set of Antiquaries,[1]
A Race of Monkeys, Parrots, and not of Reasonable Creatures.
May no mad Pedant
Ever dedicate, within the bounds of thy Coasts,[2]
The short course of his Life,
(Which ought to be imploy'd about Important Duties)
To such sort of Studies that bring Content to the Mind,
And that are made Famous only
By miserable Custom,
Founded upon popular Prejudice.
May never any Echo of the Multitude,
Be Taken by thee for anything else but an Echo.
May no Honourable Robber or Murderer
Set up the obliging Trade
To cheat thee of thy Money,
By shortning with Impunity the Days of thy
Inhabitants,
After[3] having a long time kept them on the
Rack in a Bed of Sickness.
May no unprofitable Visiters[4]
Ever come to disturb the good Employments
of thy Sages.
May never Dragoons,[5] nor Highnesses, nor Monks,
Nor Louvres, nor Dungeons,[6]
Nor Reprisals, nor Complements,
Nor Slavery, nor troublesome Fashion,
Nor Powder for the Cartridge or Dressing-Box,[7]

---

[1] " Secte des Anciennistes."　　　　　　　　[2] " Chez toi."

[3] In orig. : " Après les avoir martyrisez."

[4] In orig.: " Faiseur de Visites inutiles."

[5] " The Pope [Innocent XI], tho' really old and infirm, yet often makes the want of Health serve for a pretext to excuse his absence at those numerous ceremonies used at Rome.　I had it from very credible persons that he did in no wise approve of the French way of converting People by Dragooning, and shew'd a great deal of aversion to those who pretended to propose certain methods of accommodation to him with the Crown of France." (Max. Misson, Letter xxv.)

[6] In orig. : "ni Cachets."

[7] In orig. : " Ni Poudre à poudrer, ni Poudre à Canon."

> Ever be known
> Among thy Peaceable, Reasonable, and Happy Society ;
> Mayst thou ever be free
> From Fraud, Ambition, Avarice,
> Tyranny, and all Villany.
> May
> Virtue, Wisdom, Truth, Fidelity, Innocence,
> Justice, Safety, Abundance,
> Happiness, Peace and Joy,
> Make thy little Terrestrial Paradise the Desire or
> Envy of all Men,
> As a Tast or Semblance
> Of the Paradise which the Angels
> Inhabit."

As I had done writing these my Vows for this charming Isle, I remember'd I had read in the History of the *War with the Vandals*, written by *Procopius*, that when that Author was in *Africa* with *Belisarius*,[1] he found in a city of *Numidia* two Stone Pillars, on which was Ingrav'd this Inscription in the *Phœnician* Tongue ; *We are some of those that fled from Joshua the Great Robber*.[2]   I had neither Stone nor Marble to

---

[1] The greatest of Justinian's generals.   He was born in Illyria, and his Slavonic name signifies " White Prince", or Bieli Tsar, the title usually bestowed upon the Emperor of Russia by Asiatics.   The actual edition, probably, here quoted by Max. Misson was the following :—

" *Vide. Historia Gothorvm Vandalorvm & Langobardorvm : ab Hugone Grotio.*   Amstelodami, apud Ludovicum Elzevirium (1655).

"*Art.*   Vandalica et Gothica, Procopii emendata plurimis locis : accedentibus supplementis é Manuscriptis : & sic versa Latine ab Hugone Grotio.

"Procopii Cæsareensis Historiæ Vandalicæ Liber Secundus, p. 88.

" ' Etiam in Numidia castellum posuere quo loco nunc urbs est dicta Tingis.   Hic duæ stant é lapide candido columnæ propter magnum fontem, inscriptæ Phœnicias literas, quarum ex sermoue Phœuicio hæc est interpretatio.   Nos illi sumus qui prædonem effugimus Iesum Navæ filium.' "

[2] Procopius, *De Bello Vandalico*, lib. II, cap. vii.   The historian of Justinian's wars, speaking of the origin of the Moors in Africa, whom he identifies with the Gergesites and Jebusites and other nations overthrown by the Israelites when they entered Canaan, says these nations, seeing this new captain (Joshua) irresistible, removed from their own

make anything like a Pillar; but having a small piece of Vellom which may last as long as Brass, if 'twas kept in the Vial I have spoke of, I made a Draught of a Pillar after my Way; on the top I plac'd the Cross and Thorns of our Tribulations, wrote our Names[1] on one side, and these words on the other:

> " We are some of those
> Hundreds of Thousands
> To whom Wings have been given
> To
> Escape the furious Dragoons[2]

---

country into Egypt, and finding no room there, went on into Africa, where they built many cities and possessed it all unto the Pillars of Hercules, and to this day continue there, using the Phœnician language. " In Numidia they built a castle where now is the citie of Tigisis. In which stand two pillars near the great conduit, with these words engraven in the Phœnician language: *We are they who fled before Joshua the chief, the son of Nun.*" (Holcroft's translation of Procopius' history, 1653 ; *The Vandal Wars*, p. 36.)

[1] The names appear as follows :—Franciscus Leguat ; Paulus Be***le ; Jacobus de la Case ; Joannes Testard ; Isaacus Boyer : Joannes de la Haye ; Robertus Anselin ; Petrus Thomas ; Isaacus Boyer Mundo Valedicens Ad Celestem Patriam abiit Maj. D. 8 A. 1693.

[2] "The following inscription" (writes Max. Misson, dating from Strasburg, July 22, 1688) " was lately placed over the Gate of the *Manufactory Hall*, at Bern, the capital city of the most potent Canton among the Swiss :—

" ' Tempore quo crassa Clericorum ignorantia, cum gratia & privilegio Regis in verum Dei cultum fureret, atque DRACONUM opera nos quos Huguenotos vocant, ferro flamma, & omnis generis cruce e regno pelleret, supremus Magistratus cruderibus Cinobii, olim Prædicatorium has ædes exstruxit, ut pietatem simul & artem GALLIÆ exulantes hospitalibus tectis exciperat ; Fanit Deus T. O. M. ut charitatis hoc Opificium situri cremento patriæ.'

" This Inscription being, as I am informed, remov'd from thence in 1692" [this is a subsequent addition by Max. Misson in his translation of the original letters] " at the request of the *French* Ambassadour, I can't omit to give you a translation of it :

" ' When the blind Ignorance of the Clergy, supported by the King's Favour and Authority, did exert its Rage against the true Worship of God, and by the force of DRAGOONS with fire and sword and all manner

Of

The Great Loyola." [1]

But after I had a little reflected upon it, two things
oblig'd me to blot out this Inscription. First, I thought the
Comparison was not very Just; and Secondly I imagin'd it
might displease the *Jesuits,* a Venerable Society, somewhat
false and Dangerous, 'tis true; but my Companions and I
were very much oblig'd to them. I therefore took away this
Inscription, and put two verses of *Virgil*[2] in the place of it;

of Torments, drove those call'd *Huguenots* out of the Kingdom, this House
was erected by the supream Magistrates, upon the ruins of the old Monas-
tery belonging formerly to the Predicant Friers, that Piety and Industry,
banish'd at once out of *France,* might meet there with an hospitable
entertainment : May it please the most Great and Good God, that this
Charitable Act may tend to the advantage of our Native Country.'" (*A
New Voyage to Italy,* by Maxmilian Misson, Done into English, Letter
xxxv.)

[1] Ignatius de Loyola, the famous Spaniard who founded the order of
the Jesuits, and inspired the King of Spain, Philippe II, to become the
champion of Catholicism, under whom the dragoons of the cruel Duke
of Alva inundated with blood the Flemish and Dutch provinces, 1568-
1572.

[2] *Æneidos,* lib. viii, 333-336 :

> " Me pulsum* patriâ, pelagique extrema sequentem
> Fortuna omnipotens et ineluctabile fatum
> His posuere locis, matrisque egere tremenda
> Carmentis Nymphæ monita, et deus auctor Apollo."

(King Evander is speaking, and alludes to an accidental murder which
compelled him to leave Arcadia) :

> " Myself, an exile from my home,
> Went wandering far along the foam,
> Till mighty chance and destined doom
> Constrained my errant choice :
> So came I to these regions driven
> By warning from my mother given,
> And Phœbus' awful voice."

Professor Conington's *Translation.*

Only the first portion of the Virgilian lines given above is inscribed

* *Me pulsum Patriâ* is changed into *Nos patriâ pulsos* in the
inscription ; *vide* frontispiece.

which represent our condition plain enough, as the Reader
may see by looking upon the Pillar here presented to him.
I do not love *Latin* in *French* Books, and indeed I have
almost forgot all I knew of that Language, but 'tis difficult
to Translate these Verses, without taking away their Force
and Beauty.

on the simulated column as far as " locis"; afterwards is inserted :
" An. Dom. M. DC. XCI. xxx Aprilis. Biennio cum 21 diebus ibidem
peractis, Fragilem truci Pelago commissimus ratem. Die xx Maj. An.
Dom. M. DC. XCIII."

THE END OF THE FIRST PART.

[In the original French, Leguat's book is divided into two separate
volumes, the " premier tome" occupying 164 pages of print, whilst the
first part of the English version fills only 120 pages of larger size. The
frontispiece of the first volume is repeated in the second, which fills
180 pages of type in the French, and 123 in the English edition. The
Dutch version is in one small quarto volume, with 178 pages of text
and 14 pages of index. This version has the dates given, in years, at
the top of each page and marginal references, being also divided into
chapters, the headings of which are given above at page lxiii.]

LONDON : WHITING AND CO., 30 AND 32, SARDINIA STREET, W.C.

For EU product safety concerns, contact us at Calle de José Abascal, 56–1°, 28003 Madrid, Spain or eugpsr@cambridge.org.